I0750541

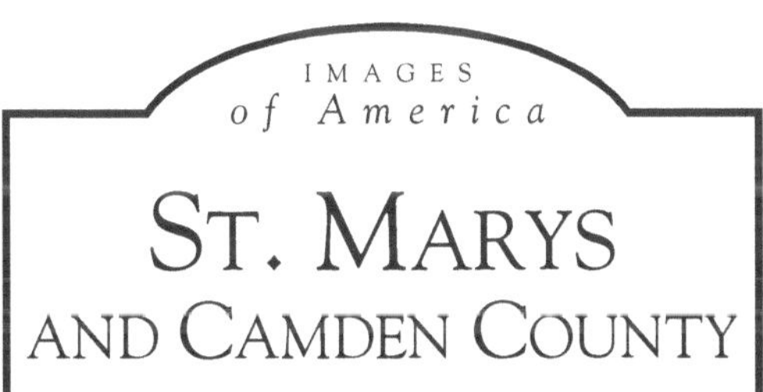
IMAGES
of America
ST. MARYS
AND CAMDEN COUNTY

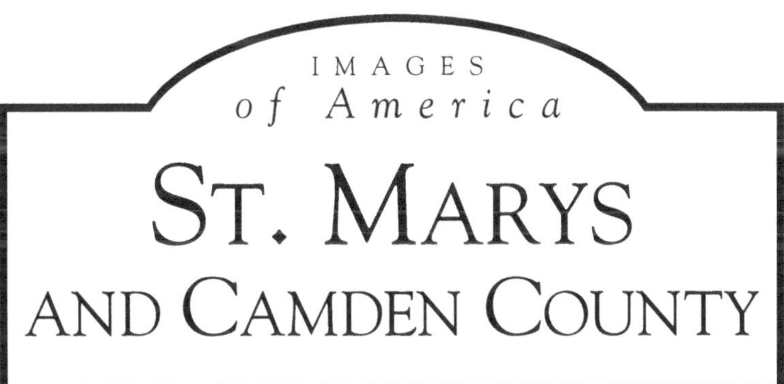

Patricia Barefoot

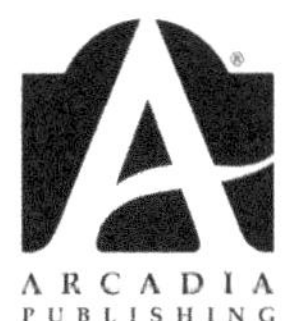

ISBN 978-0-7385-1385-0

Published by Arcadia Publishing
Charleston, South Carolina

Library of Congress Catalog Card Number: 2001092146

For all general information contact Arcadia Publishing at:
Telephone 843-853-2070
Fax 843-853-0044
E-mail sales@arcadiapublishing.com
For customer service and orders:
Toll-Free 1-888-313-2665

Visit us on the Internet at www.arcadiapublishing.com

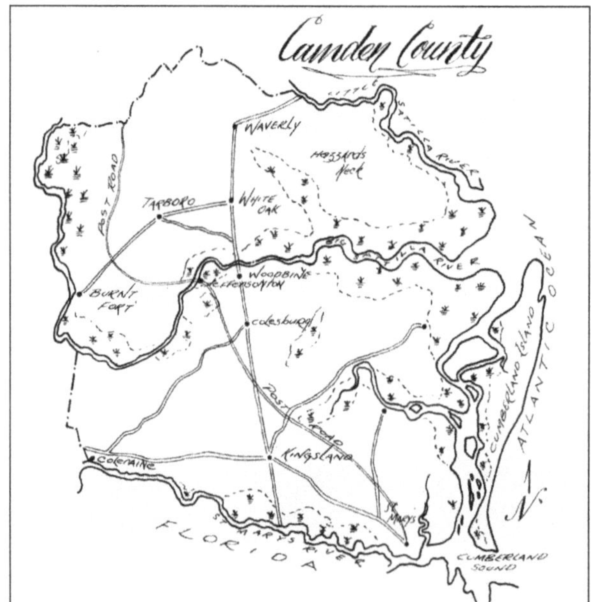

In Jim Talley's map glimpse key communities Waverly, Tarboro, and Burnt Fort; small cities such as Woodbine (the county seat), Kingsland, and St. Marys; and major roadways and boundaries. Bounded on the north by the Little Satilla River from neighboring Glynn County, Camden's southern boundary at the St. Marys River separates Georgia from Florida. An ancient Indian route represented by the Post Road connected with St. Marys and, from the old port of St. Marys, led west on the Coleraine Road, another old Indian trail. U.S. Highway 17 bisects Camden's 684 square miles, forming a major north/south route from Maine to Miami prior to the construction of Interstate 95. In the 1970s Naval Submarine Base, Kings Bay impact funds and burgeoning facilities arrived in the county. A sleepy Camden bustled with activity and, today, exhibits great diversity due to a huge population influx influenced by the Navy's presence. (Courtesy of Jim Talley.)

Contents

Acknowledgments		6
Introduction		7
1.	Early Camden Days	9
2.	Port of St. Marys, Villages, and Rail Transport	17
3.	Landmarks and Historic Structures	37
4.	People of Camden	65
5.	Gatherings and Special Events	89
6.	Education	105
7.	Social, Religious, and Cultural Affairs	115

ACKNOWLEDGMENTS

Discussions with my husband, Forrest "Frosty" Barefoot, showed me the way where I saw none while in pursuit of the richness of Camden's past and present. Together we searched the Georgia Historical Society records for Camden memorabilia, only to realize that, with little exception, Camden's past remained there, and this knowledge radically changed my strategy. While I focused on the people of Camden and what they wished to share, a short deadline for completion of this book loomed, and I have in no way exhausted the resources of so many kind and trusting people. You made this fun, and I am grateful for each and every one of you, especially those who showed such enthusiasm, encouraging my effort to contribute toward telling the Camden story. It is a complex and fascinating one filled with everyday people going about life's work, heroes and heroines, rogues and rascals who embellish the pages of history and spice the musty historic records that document Camden County's vast dimensions.

Readers will note a number of images that reflect the cultural history of Cumberland Island National Seashore, National Park Service. While the NPS staff was aware, at all times, of this book's progress, the photographs used were taken by the author, purchased through Georgia Archives, or loaned courtesy of Camden Countians.

Mrs. Eloise Bailey Thompson aided in my search, sharing with me her vast collection of Camden images, her valuable advice and time, and lovely, comfortable home on the Mush Bluff overlooking the beautiful Crooked River. I am grateful for "Miss Eloise's" exactness in suggesting and editing this manuscript and her encouragement in the completion of this visual history. Shirley Joiner Thompson of the Bartram Trail/Old Post Road made suggestions and shared family photographs as well as her wealth of knowledge and has helped me comprehend life in the sandhills. Staff at the Bryan-Lang Historical Library in Woodbine—library director Darren Harper and his able assistants Mrs. Winnie Wainwright, Mrs. Katie Cooler, and, in particular, Ms. Carolyn Rock, who went beyond the call of duty in locating images, tuning fine details, and answering questions—have been ever attentive and assisted with this endeavor. I am indebted to the following people for their interest, generous contributions, and support: B.A. Russell and Martha Couper Russell, Mary Alice Lord, Jasper N. Lang and Lynn Lang, Lillian Lang Meyers and Mary L. Morris, Sheila McNeill, Woodbine's city administrator Sandy Rayson, Dorothy and C.S. Tait Jr., Hazel McCarthy White, James B.F. Russell, Newt Boring Jr., Mr. and Mrs. Henry E. Williams Sr., Dr. Ann H. Stoddard, Phorestine Appling and Abra Lattany Reed, Mr. W. Curtis Tucker, Hana Ozaki, Victor Howard for valuable Civil War reminiscences, Beth Berrie Williams and Brian Berrie, Neil Buie McClurd, Miriam Cate Manning Davis and Adele Brown Folsom, Carson Odum, Bessie Dent and Hazel Dean Overstreet, Harlan Hambright, and Diane H. Jackson of the Three Rivers Regional Library in Brunswick for her diligent and expert help. Helen Rowell of Blackshear climbed in musty attics and searched along with Betty Hall of Waycross for a 1912 image of the Coleraine monument dedication. The search continues at this writing. Don Peeples; his mother, Helen R. Peeples; and Daniel Peeples have enriched my "sense of place" through their stories and images and their careful consideration of my requests. Any mistakes in this work should in no way reflect upon these contributors but are solely the author's responsibility. I owe a huge debt of gratitude and appreciation to my parents, Sam Cofer and Marie Joyner Cofer, who provided priceless memories when we spent time near the tannic waters of the great Satilla River at the old Ivanhoe Plantation, and my ingenious and ever-caring brother Donnie, who steadfastly supports my freelance writing. How can I ever sufficiently thank Linda and Rodney Sheffield for their sharing and caring and their awesome support of my needs? Patrick Shell of Vicksburg, Mississippi empowered me to make deadline for this book through his judicious support for which I owe him much gratitude. Finally, I dedicate this book to my wonderful, supportive husband, Forrest "Frosty" Barefoot.

INTRODUCTION

Today, Camden's "challenge" remains bound up with the affairs of government—a major north/sound I-95 corridor bringing with it the good and the bad, the mighty submarines of Naval Submarine Base, Kings Bay, and the future prospects for the development of the facility. Tourism use and the conservation/preservation issues associated with the beautiful island Wissoe (meaning "the island of sassafras") at Cumberland Island National Seashore pose ongoing hurdles, while the quaint town of St. Marys serves as a point of departure and charms the casual visitor. While traditionally Camden's economy was based in rural family farms, naval stores production, and timbering activities, by the early 1940s, the Gilman family's paper mill arrived bringing with its presence, employment opportunities; in a word—jobs. No longer did Camden men need to leave in search of livelihood. Closure of the mill at St. Marys in November 2002 presented new challenges for the 900 men whose livelihood ended, impacting their families and creating a ripple effect throughout the Camden community. In characteristic fashion, Camden Countians demonstrated a high level of resiliency, rising to the occasion and this challenging new bump in the road. Then, within the late 20th century, federal impact funds created, among others, greater educational opportunities for all Camden Countians, assuming that a lifetime of learning remains a priority.

Within the 30 or so years after the coming of such a strong military presence, much of old Camden's complexion has changed, especially in the south end of the county, altered as it has been by a huge population increase and the change in its landscape as entrepreneurs develop consumer corridors to provide goods and services. Right across the border provided by the St. Marys River, Florida promises sun and fun for vacationing tourists. They whisk down the interstate highway and through the county. No longer can ambling eccentrics ramble the roadways, such as Ches McCartney, "the Goatman," once did. River villages once thrived here, dependent upon vessels such as the *Hildegarde* for supplies and transport for people. But today, the beautiful river corridors offer not a lifeline for survival, but serve as primary recreation outlets for boating and fishing enthusiasts.

While in the past businesses along the old Highway 17 corridor dwindled, shriveled, and dried up when the I-95 project was completed and the federal roadway opened, now a move is underfoot to revitalize the scenic corridor. This promises a new day and can create opportunities for those willing to invest in gracious cityscapes and heritage tourism, capitalizing on a critical asset—a most valuable "sense of place" possessed by the people of Camden County. In unique ways, the three small cities—St. Marys, Kingsland, and Woodbine—can promote and perpetuate the ambience of a rural, Southern town characterized by friendliness, hospitality, and genuine, neighborly concern. When family get-togethers remain an essential element through which people identify and connect, should it be surprising that Woodbine can boast of a visionary's dream and the Bryan-Lang Historical Library, preserving the records of Camden's proud past? With these thoughts, I offer a glimpse of "old-timey" photographs, contemporary images, and the people of Camden.

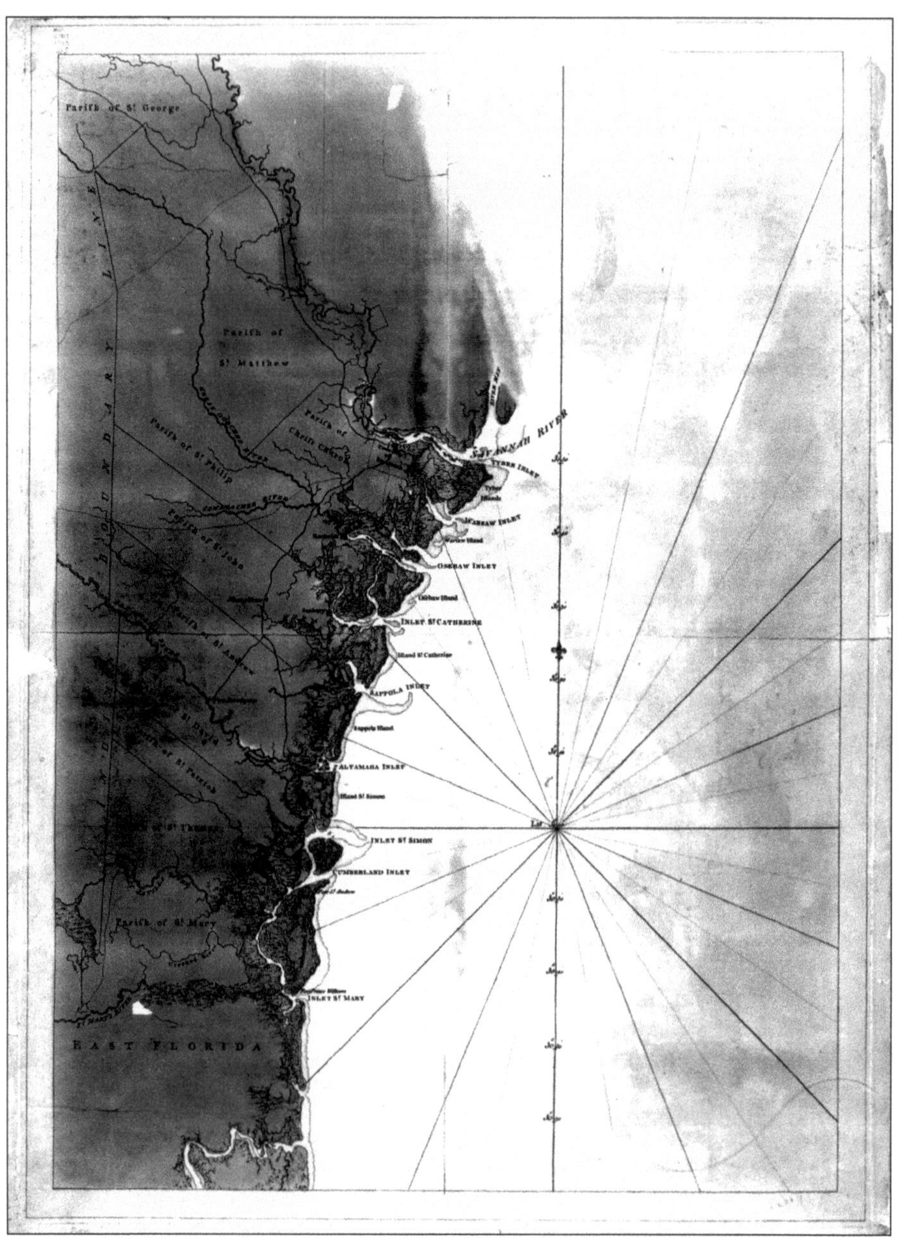

Meeting in Savannah on February 5, 1777, Georgia's Provincial Congress ratified the 1st Constitution for the State, creating eight "original" counties from the old parishes. Previously, Camden County had consisted of St. Thomas and St. Mary Parishes, but the fourth article of the new Constitution eliminated the parish designation; with one exception, the counties were named after English apologists for America. Seen in a 1780 image, St. Thomas Parish followed the Little Satilla River corridor and encompassed lands south to the Big Satilla River where it joined St. Mary Parish with territory extending south and dividing East Florida from Georgia lands. The new county was named after the distinguished Chief Justice and Lord Chancellor of England, Charles Pratt, the Earl of Camden. (Courtesy of Hargrett Rare Book and Manuscript Library/University of Georgia Libraries.)

One

EARLY CAMDEN DAYS

Prior to its colonial parish beginnings in 1758, the heavily wooded forests and swamplands of Camden sustained the Native Americans of the Southeast. They regularly traveled an ancient trail that today is located in the sandhills. By the late 1700s, Puc Puggy (meaning "flower-hunter"), the Quaker naturalist Will Bartram traversed this route. He noted, near the Satilla River, extensive savannahs and described his surroundings as "enchantingly varied and beautiful." Bartram observed large, healthy peach trees, Indian corn, rice, cotton, and indigo thriving along the St. Marys River whose source derived "from a vast lake, or marsh, called Ouaquaphenogaw" (Okefenokee). Into this sparsely settled frontier territory, colonialists came with their cultural baggage. Unlike the remainder of southeast Georgia, Camden's territory hosted Loyalist forts at Wright's Fort and Fort Tonyn during the American Revolution, making Camden unique situated as it is on the borderlands. While the Loyalist Thomas Brown and his foraging Florida Rangers created havoc and devastation, Camden remained uneasy in this continuing struggle within the old debatable land. A few short decades away, agricultural crops such as rice and cotton offered lucrative profits for the planter class whose descendants made judicious decisions.

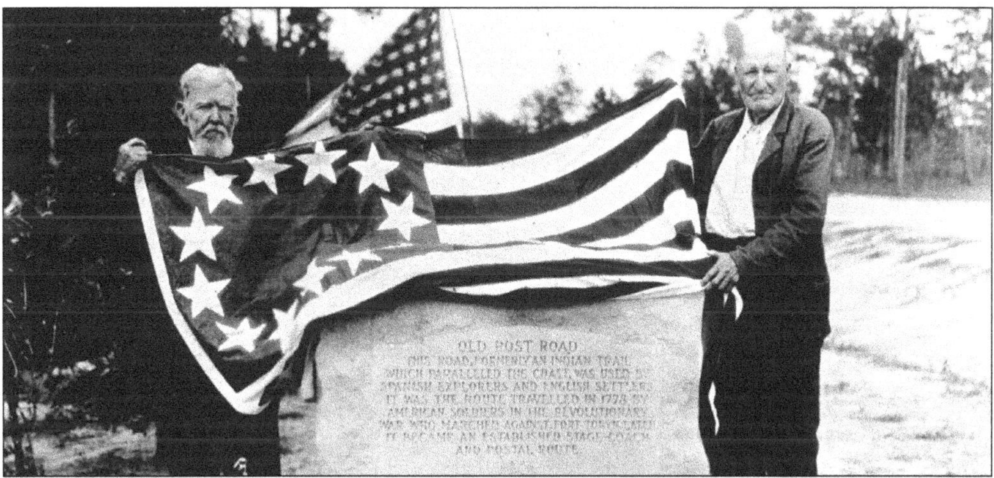

On Flag Day, June 14, 1932, Edmond Howard (1840–1939) and Henderson "Hen" Horton (1841–1936), two CSA veterans who lived along the historic Post Road, unveiled a granite monument erected by ladies of the DAR on the Waycross highway where Glynn and Brantley Counties intersect. The inscription on the "Old Post Road" monument was the vision of coastal historian Margaret Davis Cate (1888–1961). Today, maintained by the Georgia Department of Transportation, this imposing tribute serves as a reminder of this old Indian trail's historic importance as a major north/south corridor. Traveled in Revolutionary War years by foraging rangers and soldiers who marched against the Loyalist Fort Tonyn and Wright's Fort on the St. Marys River, this important road later served as a stagecoach and postal route. (Courtesy of Margaret Davis Cate Collection #997, Fort Frederica National Monument, Georgia Historical Society.)

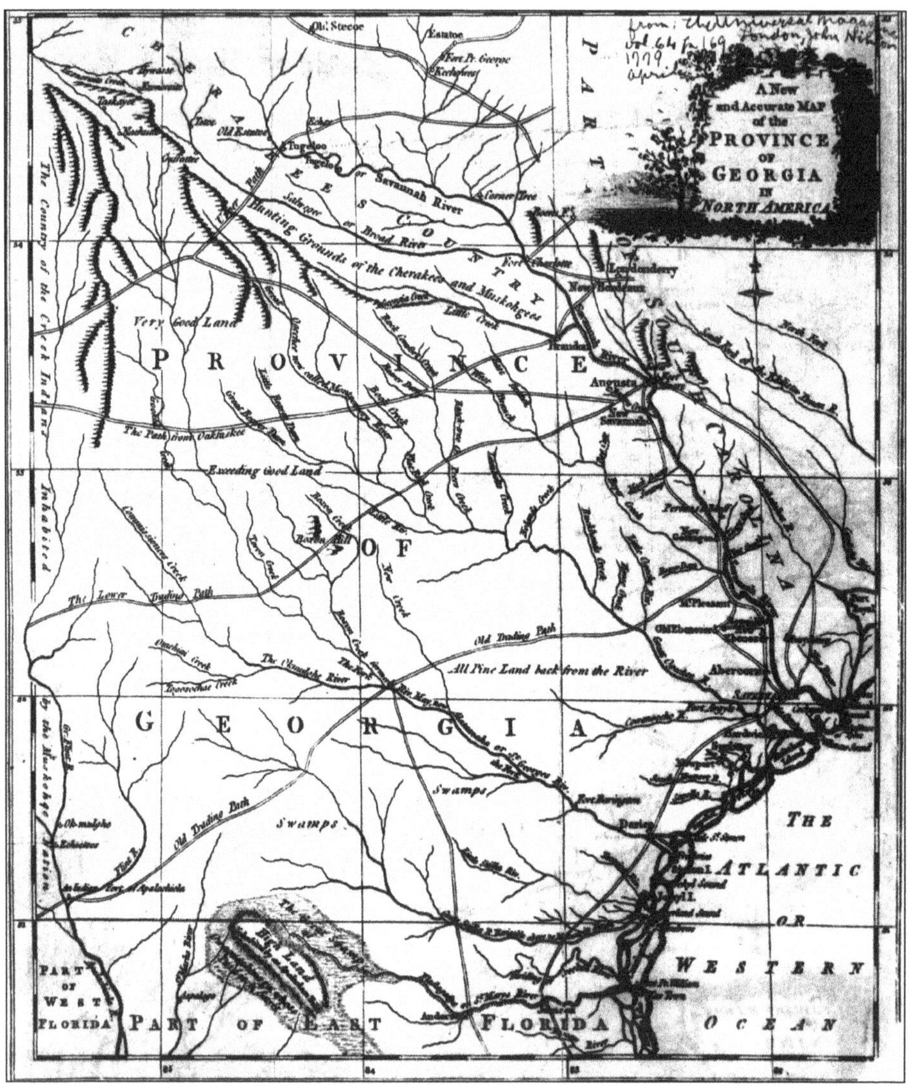

A 1779 map of the State of Georgia provides a graphic view of a wild country, formerly abundant in game animals. Through millennia the Native Americans of the Southeast honed their knowledge, skills, and ability to exploit the abundance of both fauna and flora, used for food and medicine. Georgia was inhabited by traditional arch rivals, the Muskogean-speaking Creek Indians and the Iroquoian-speaking Cherokee, who were forced westward in the 1830s, surrendering their lands as new settlers, who lacked understanding of the customs, habits, and ways of the Native peoples, prosecuted their special interests. The historic trading paths as noted in this important visual provide us with a window of observation on the circumstances that confronted early settlers; the trading paths became important commercial routes followed by Indian traders hawking guns, bullets, knives, hatchets, red and blue stroud cloth, hawks bells, and trade beads. In return, the Southeastern Indians experienced a culture change as they became dependent upon these exotic trade goods. They bartered with pelts and hides—buffalo, beaver, and bear—and especially with the skins of the ubiquitous white tail deer. In the historic period, one of the most important trading posts was located on the St. Marys River at Coleraine. (Courtesy of Hargrett Rare Book and Manuscript Library/University of Georgia Libraries.)

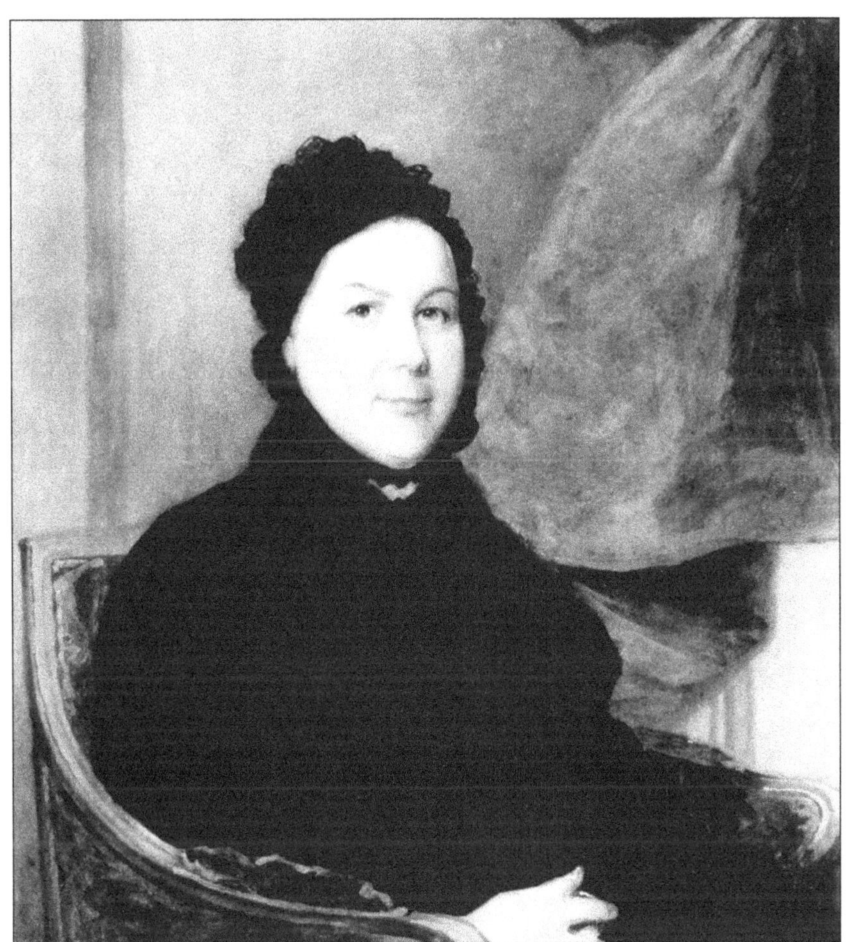

The irrepressible Catharine "Caty" Littlefield Greene (1753–1814) struggled for solvency and indemnification for her deceased husband's expenses, incurred on behalf of his troops in the Revolutionary War. For his military service, Gen. Nathaniel Greene was awarded land in North Carolina, South Carolina, and Georgia where the Greenes settled at a confiscated plantation formerly owned by Loyalists. Beleaguered by debt, the Greenes had moved south to cultivate rice on the Savannah River at Mulberry Grove Plantation. They hired 21-year-old Yale graduate Phineas Miller to tutor their children, and the General dreamed of growing indigo on thousands of Cumberland Island acres he had purchased as an investment. Subsequent to General Greene's death on June 19, 1786, Caty Greene struggled to save her husband's estate by pressing her appeals to Congress. In the 1790s, Eli Whitney came south and, with Phineas Miller, the young genius formed a partnership in which Caty heavily invested to revolutionize the South's economy with a cotton-gin. Heeding the sage advice of friends, in May 1796 Phineas Miller and Caty Littlefield Greene were married in a private ceremony. Clouding their wedded bliss were the substantial investments the couple made in the Yazoo Land Company. This act dearly cost the Millers, and debt hung over Caty like an albatross. By 1800, the Millers moved to Cumberland where contracts were let for harvesting the maritime live oaks, and land was cleared for sugar cane and cotton fields. On the south end of Cumberland, they built a 4-story, 26-room mansion of tabby where they entertained family and friends at the fabled Dungeness. (James Frothingham [Attributed, American, 1786-1863], Catharine Littlefield Greene Miller, c. 1800-1814, Oil on panel, 32 3/4 x 25 3/4 in., Telfair Museum of Art, Savannah, Georgia, Museum purchase, 1947, Erwin Gaspin Photography.)

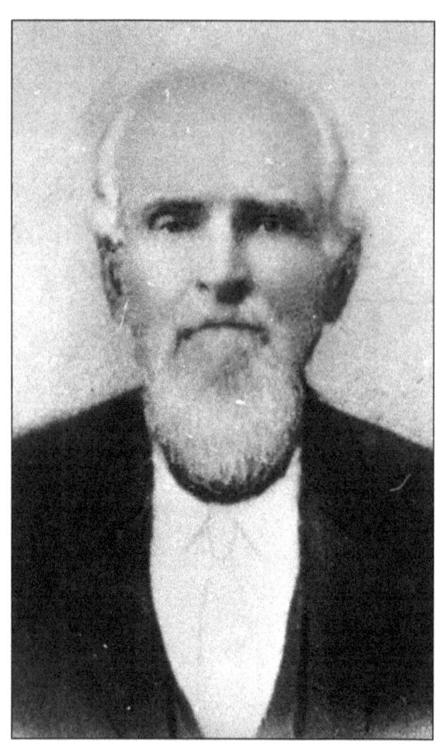

Descended from early Camden pioneer settlers, Claborn Wright Harrell (1825–1902) was born near Tarboro and was the son of Abner Harrell Jr. (1800–1858) whose ancestors migrated to South Georgia from Wayne County, North Carolina. In March 1850, Claborn Wright Harrell married Lucretia Highsmith (1830–1905), and according to that decade's census, Harrell's occupation was listed as a planter. He served in Co. C, Camden Mounted Rifles, 4th GA Cavalry, CSA under Capts. Alexander S. Atkinson and Nathan A. Brown. After the Civil War, he supported his family through farming and selling cross-ties off the land. The Harrells lived on the east side of the old Post Road/ Bartram Trail, land formerly part of a Charles Nevel Drury land grant, purchased from Peter Readdick (b. 1807) and whose ghostly appearance remained on the land and the lane leading from the Bartram Trail. While Lucretia rests in the Bickley Chapel Cemetery with family members, Harrell was buried in the Crum Cemetery near where his son, Abner David Harrell, lived. (Courtesy of Shirley Joiner Thompson.)

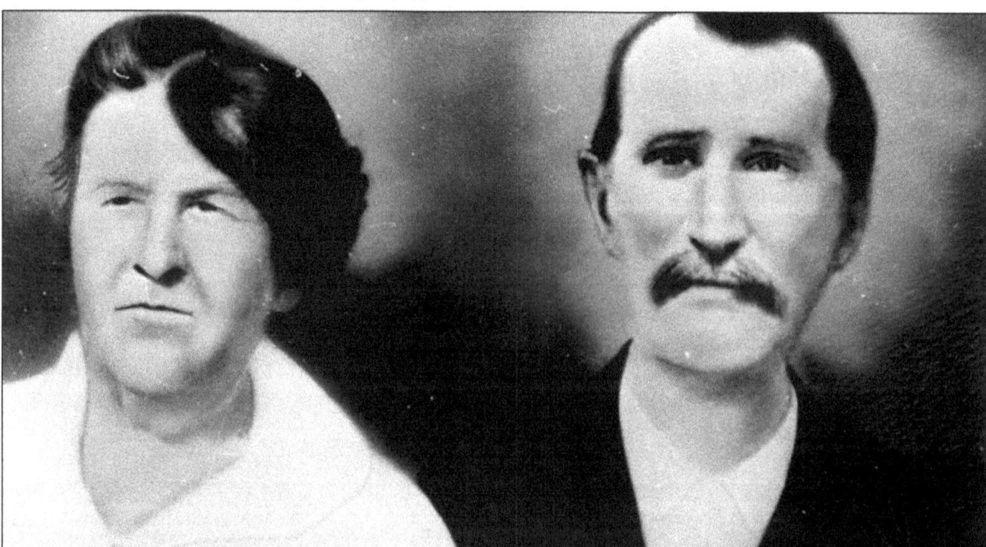

The circumstances of Marian Westann "Sissy" Harrell Joiner (1855–1932) and her husband, Robert Wiley Joiner (1847–1920) typify the hardships and joys of settlers in the sandhills of Camden's old Post Road. At age 13, he joined the CSA army with his father, Jethro (c. 1818–1886) and brother Joseph Baker Joiner. When Wiley's young age was determined, he was sent back home. After their 1872 marriage, the Joiners moved from North Camden to St. Marys, into Florida, and back to the old Peter Readdick home where Sissy's aging, infirm parents, the Claborn W. Harrells, lived, and where the younger Joiner children were born. According to a descendant, church affairs proved "the very core of being for these people." (Courtesy of Shirley Joiner Thompson.)

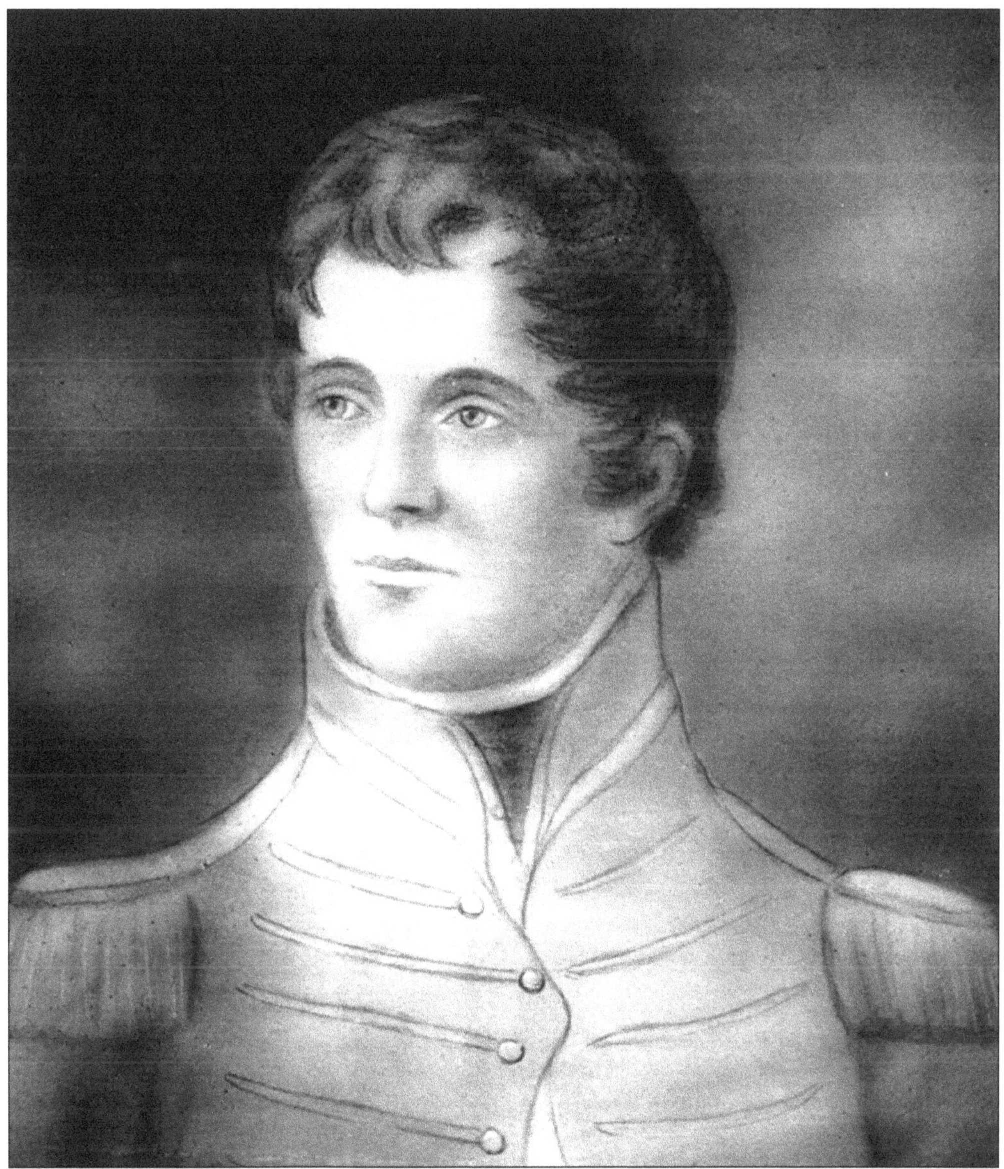

Descended from transplanted Carolinians and the only child of Col. Charles Floyd, a young John Floyd (1813–1838) was apprenticed as a ship's carpenter. The Floyds moved from McIntosh to Camden County, and by 1809, this resourceful family had acquired 5,825 acres at Floyd's Neck where they cultivated cotton, indigo, and rice, as well as a substantial maritime business. Bordering on Todd's Creek, a tributary of the great Satilla River, Bellevue Plantation—where the tabby ruins of an "anchor-shaped" house stand—and Fairfield Plantation were associated with this family. A patriotic John Floyd reserved 200 acres south of Bellevue for a military parade ground and the training of Georgia militiamen in coastal defense. During the War of 1812, General Floyd commanded a force of 600 men at Point Peter, Camden County. He served two terms in the state legislature, both as a representative and a senator, and between 1827 and 1829 represented his district in the 20th Congress. In recognition of his contributions to early Georgia, Floyd County was named in his honor. (Courtesy of Bryan-Lang Historical Library.)

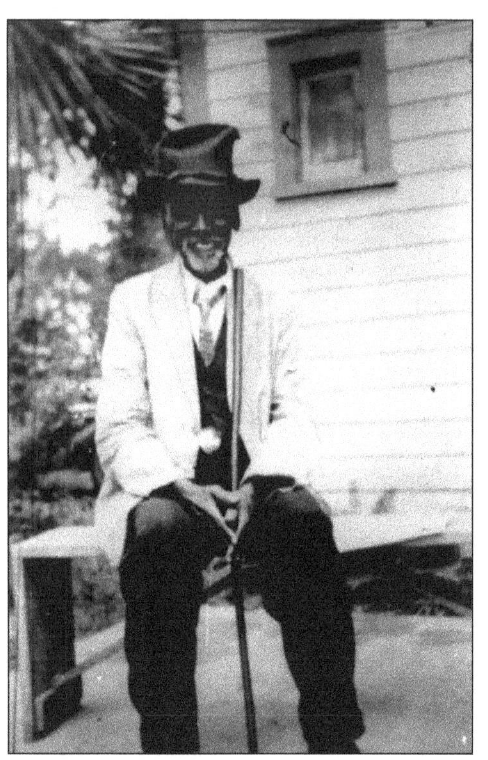

Wearing his signature top hat and holding his walking cane, "Uncle London" Jackson poses for the camera at Island Grove. His quiet dignity belies the fact of his capture as a 12-year-old child somewhere on the coast of West Africa, his crossing of the "middle passage," and his sale at a Savannah auction by slaver Mungin Smith. Throughout his long life, reputedly 125 years, Uncle London was associated with the Lang family; across three generations he advocated civility and a respect for elders and entertained the Lang children with his storytelling abilities. "Auntie's Piano" was the name Uncle London often recalled as his own; Isaac Lang Jr. had traveled to Georgia's founding city on business and was to purchase a piano for his daughter Angeline but instead returned to the Langsbury Plantation with this young African. (Courtesy of Camden County Historical Commission.)

Consisting of three distinct cemeteries—Fader, Alberty, and the Miller-Bunkley burial plots—Half-Moon Bluff Cemetery on Cumberland Island serves as the resting spot for early Cumberland settlers. Located on the north end of this beautiful island between Terrapin Point and a relatively inaccessible Half Moon Bluff, the well-to-do and slaves share common ground. Among others, Primus Mitchell, seen in this *c.* 1917 image, and his wife, Amanda, rest there. Born and reared on the island, they were slaves at Stafford Plantation, and their tombstone records how they were "faithful fieldhands," their lives bound by the seasonal demands of cultivating the lucrative long-staple cotton for planter Robert Stafford. The Mitchells also likely tended gardens of peas, beans, corn, sweet potatoes, Irish potatoes, ribbon sugar cane, figs, lemons, and pomegranates. After emancipation, they lived in a cabin at Banks Field; their seven daughters married and lived at Martin Fishing Camp/The Settlement. (Courtesy of Eloise Bailey Thompson.)

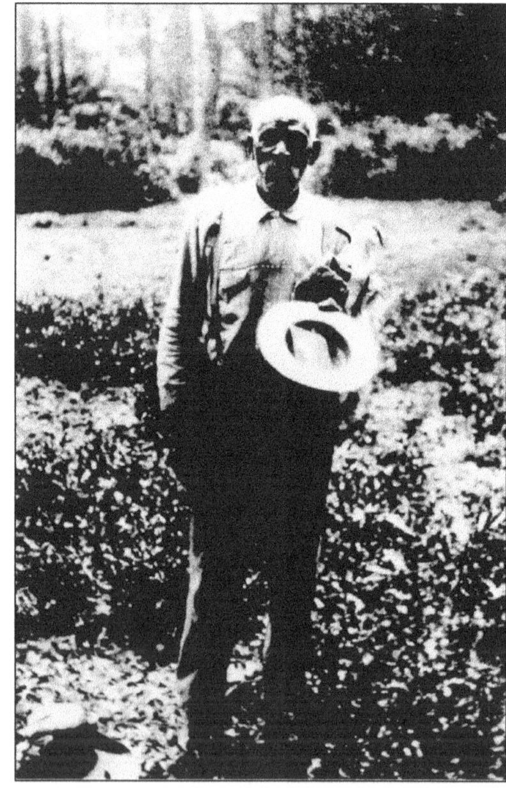

Prominent banker, cotton planter, and land baron Robert Stafford (1790–1877) held sway on Cumberland Island in the 19th century; as a shrewd businessman, he acquired much of his great wealth through foreclosure proceedings and sheriff's sales. He was the son of Lucy T. Stafford and Thomas Stafford, formerly of British East Florida whose move to Camden County was likely in search of a better life and headright land grants. Between 1788 and 1813, the Stafford family worked with the Greene Estate and the Phineas Miller family, and young Robert played with the General's son, Nathaniel "Nat" Ray Greene. Later, his mother was the first Stafford to acquire Cumberland property with an 1800 purchase of 125 acres, and thus began some tangled affairs. By 1850, Robert Stafford's reporting on the slave schedules demonstrated that he owned 348 Africans, making him not only the largest slaveholder on Cumberland, but also part of the small percentage of large slaveholders in Georgia. (Courtesy of Eloise Bailey Thompson.)

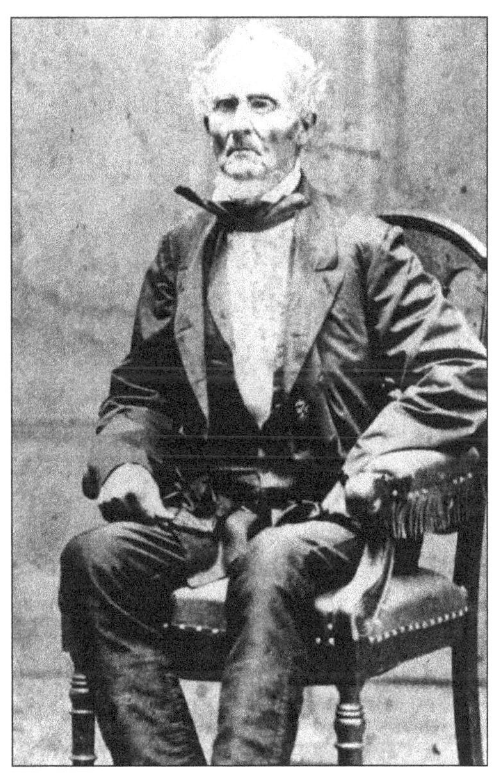

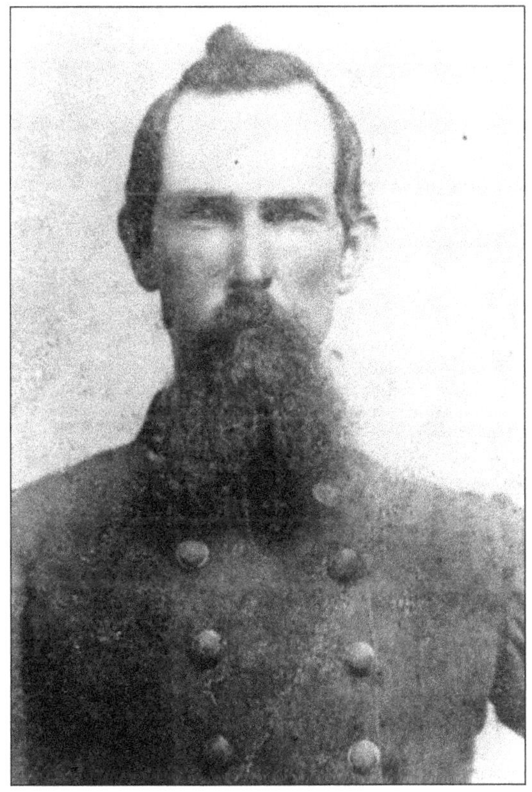

Sporting a lean and hungry look, Robert Newton King's (1821–1897) piercing eyes stare into the camera. Clothed in a handsome Confederate uniform befitting him as captain, Co. E, 4th GA Cavalry, CSA under the command of Col. Duncan Clinch, King has a demeanor that suggests the deprivation and hard times suffered by the people of Camden. The son of James King (1776–1861), Robert's lineal ancestor was John King (c. 1740–1804), one of the largest landowners in the county. The elder King was a North Carolina Revolutionary War veteran, one of five commissioners at St. Marys founding, justice of the Inferior Court from 1794 to 1804, state senator, and collector for the port of St. Marys. Some of the lands owned by the King family included the Cherry Point area, as well as Woodlawn Plantation west of the present Kingsland. (Courtesy of Eloise Bailey Thompson.)

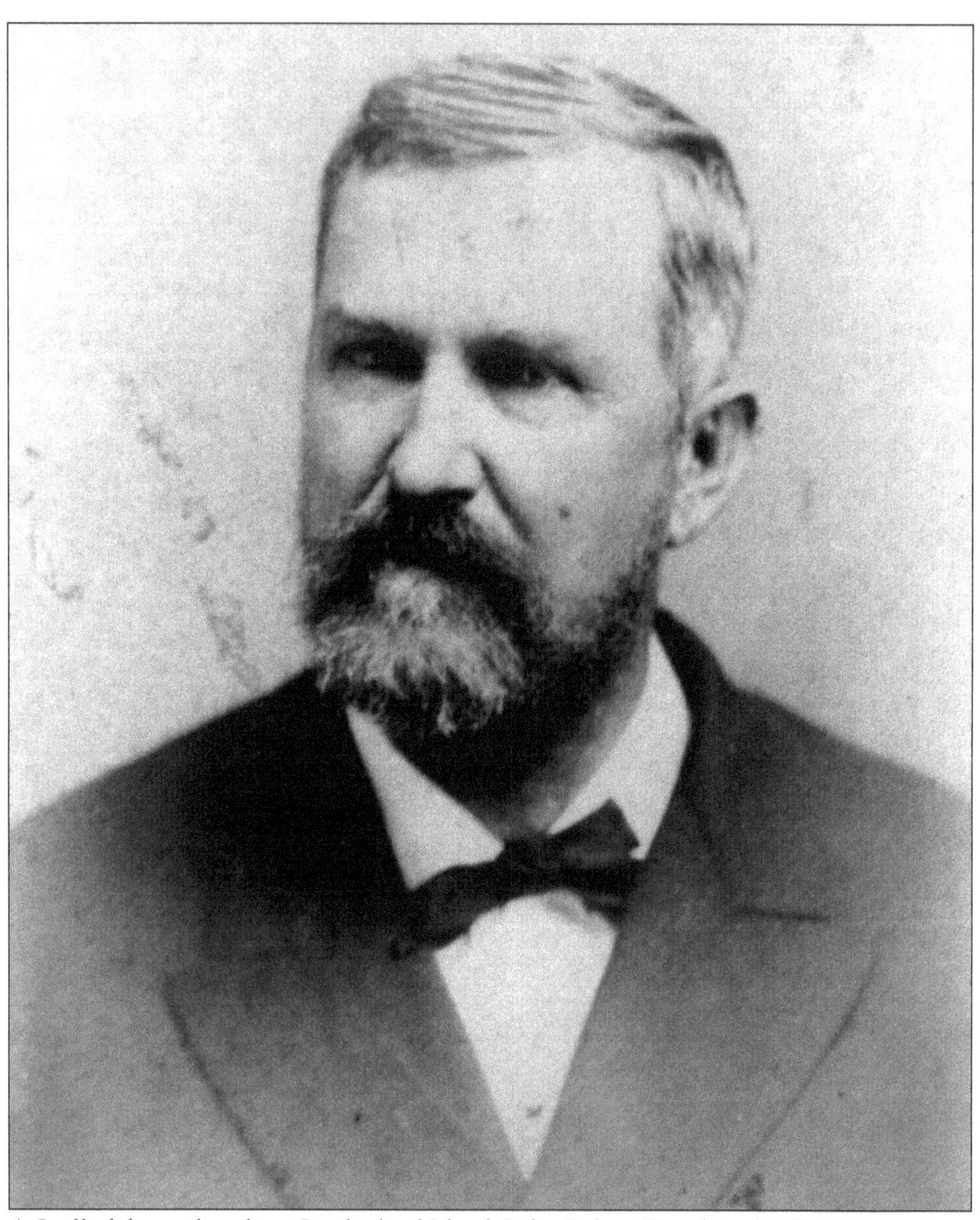

A Stafford descendant from Cumberland Island, Judge Robert Tompkins (1825–1904) was born in the Rose Creek area of Camden County and was eulogized in the newspaper at his death for defining characteristics. He held quick sympathies for the plight of his fellow man and possessed unstinted liberality of mind. His first wife was Emily Lang, seen on page 71, whom he married in 1854; subsequently in August 1881, he married Madena Bunkley (1858–1959) of Cumberland Island, daughter of the resort owners at The Cumberland Hotel, William R. Bunkley and Isabel Miller Bunkley (1832–1917). During their marriage, the Tompkins were devout members of the St. Marys United Methodist Church, reserving a room in their home for the comfort of circuit riding Methodist ministers who came to St. Marys. After her husband's death, Madena B. Tompkins remarried in 1908 and can be seen on page 116 as Madena B. Kemp. (Courtesy of Eloise Bailey Thompson.)

Two

PORT OF ST. MARYS, VILLAGES, AND RAIL TRANSPORT

Envisioned as a city by Georgia's third royal governor James Wright (1760–1775) and encouraged by planter Jonathan Bryan, St. Marys dates from the 1780s as a planned community. Across the years, the port has been prosperous and, because of its geographic location, bound to the affairs of East Florida. Buffeted by wars and yellow fever epidemics, panics and depressions, pillaging, looting, and burning during the American Civil War, St. Marys sets an example. The small city endures and prospers due to the foresight and commitment of its citizenry—many of whom invest in the past through preservation of historic structures—as well as cultivating a booming economy. Connected to main corridors and Kingsland via Highway 40, a St. Marys and Kingsland Railroad provided impetus for growth with its coming. Growth and development issues remain high priorities for government officials who seek common ground for resolving the challenges confronting Camden.

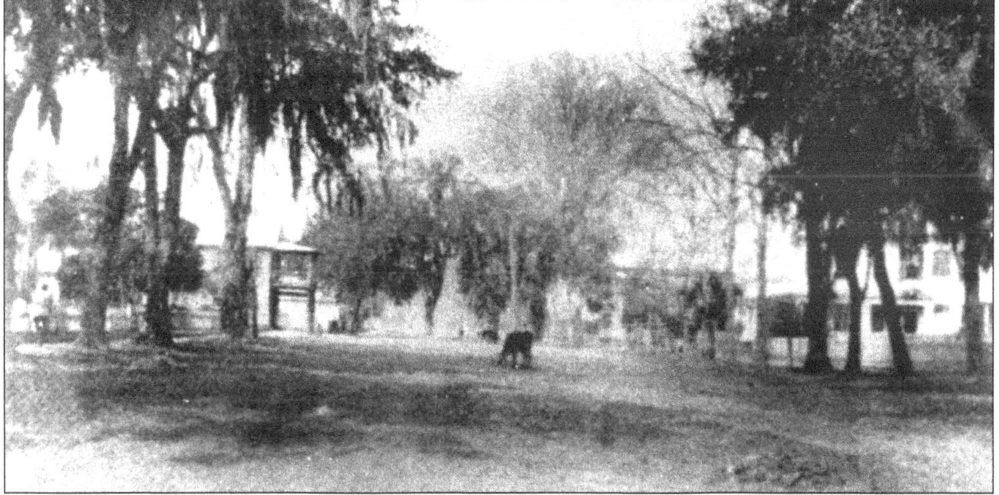

In an early 20th-century setting, St. Marys "main street"—Osborne—appears as a dirt road with a cow grazing in its center. On the left is Sterling's Store and on the right is the Bachlott House. Business records of the Hernandez family document the operation of St. Marys "longest continuing establishment" since its beginning after the American Civil War. When the Hernandez family sold the grocery business to Dave Sterling in 1884 it was located on the corner of Weed and Osborne Streets, seen in the image. After it burned in 1896, Sterling's Store was rebuilt in its present location and remodeled in 1955. Enjoyed by aficionados of bed-and-breakfast inns, the Spencer House, built c. 1872 nearby in the heart of St. Marys downtown, is another Reconstruction-era structure. (Courtesy of Eloise Bailey Thompson.)

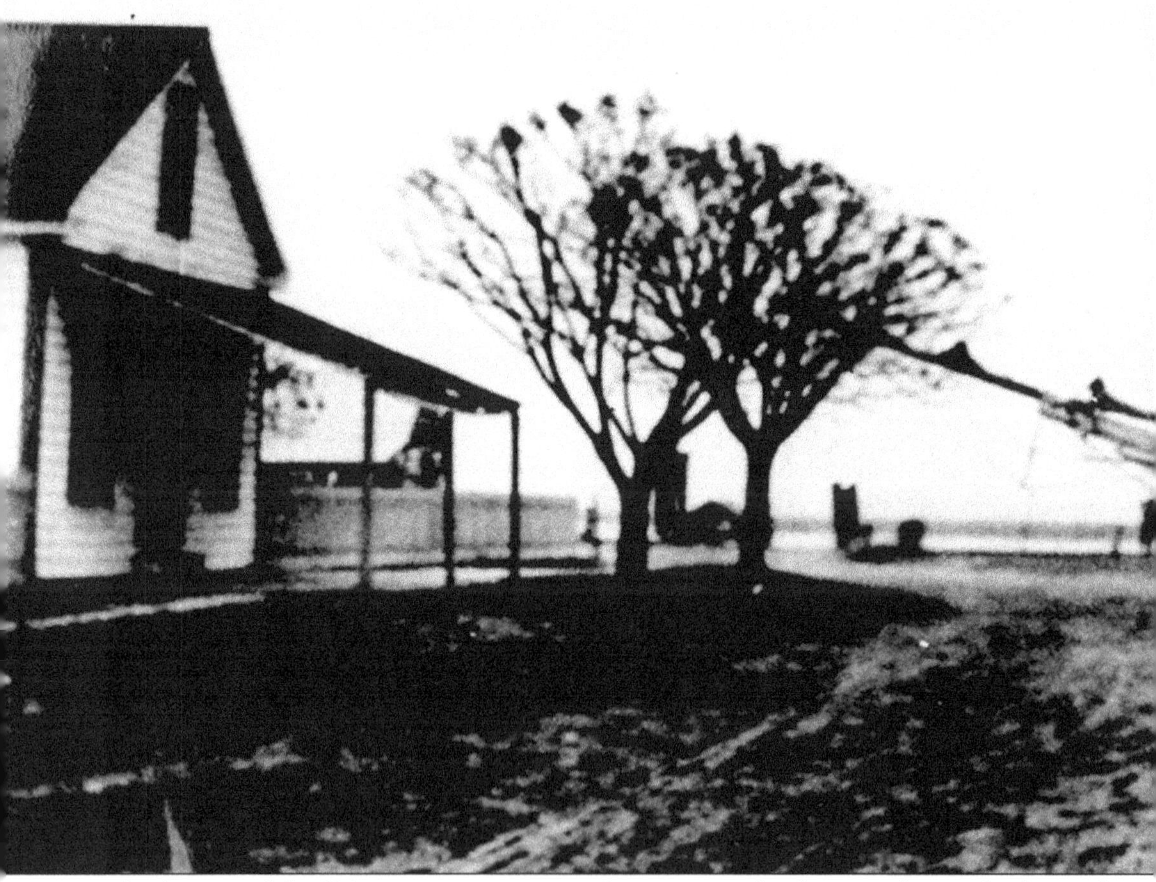

In this turn-of-the-20th-century image, a wooden two-masted sailing vessel awaits loading and can be seen docked at the St. Marys waterfront. During the heyday of the mills (1872–1910), logs were rafted down the rivers and placed near a vessel's bow to be skillfully loaded into the mouth of the hold. Notice several buildings: The Register House; the warehouse of Capt. John Richardson, a co-owner of the steamer *Hildegarde* along with Steve Chadwick, John Bachlott,

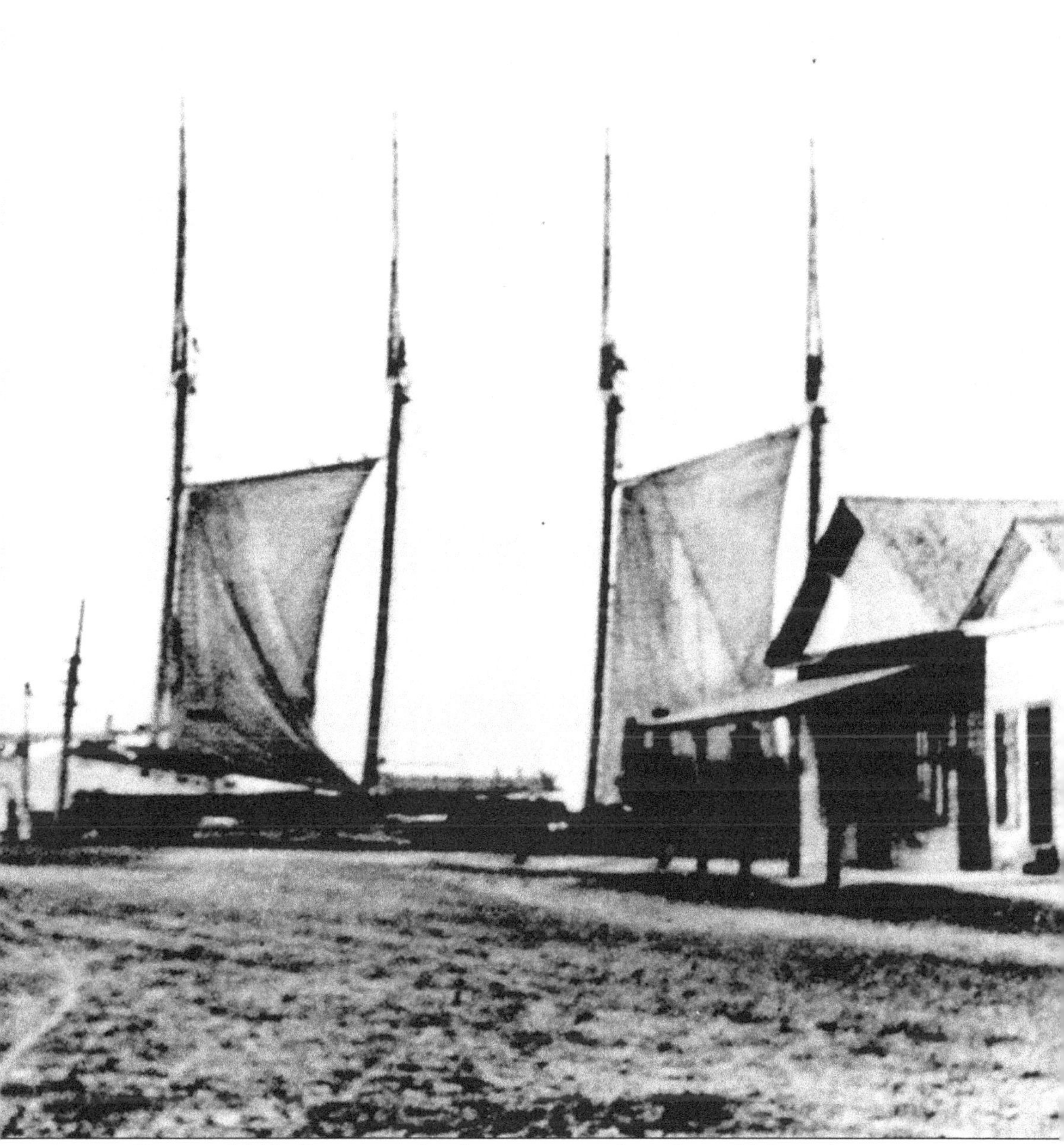

Captain Yates, and Mike Register; railroad entrepreneur Capt. Lemuel Johnson's commissary and the city market converted to Johnson's railroad office. After his death, city residents memorialized Johnson with the Lemuel Johnson Park located in the median at the foot of Osborne Street where a plaque recognizes him as a "Confederate veteran and benefactor of this city, 1918." (Courtesy of Bryan-Lang Historical Library.)

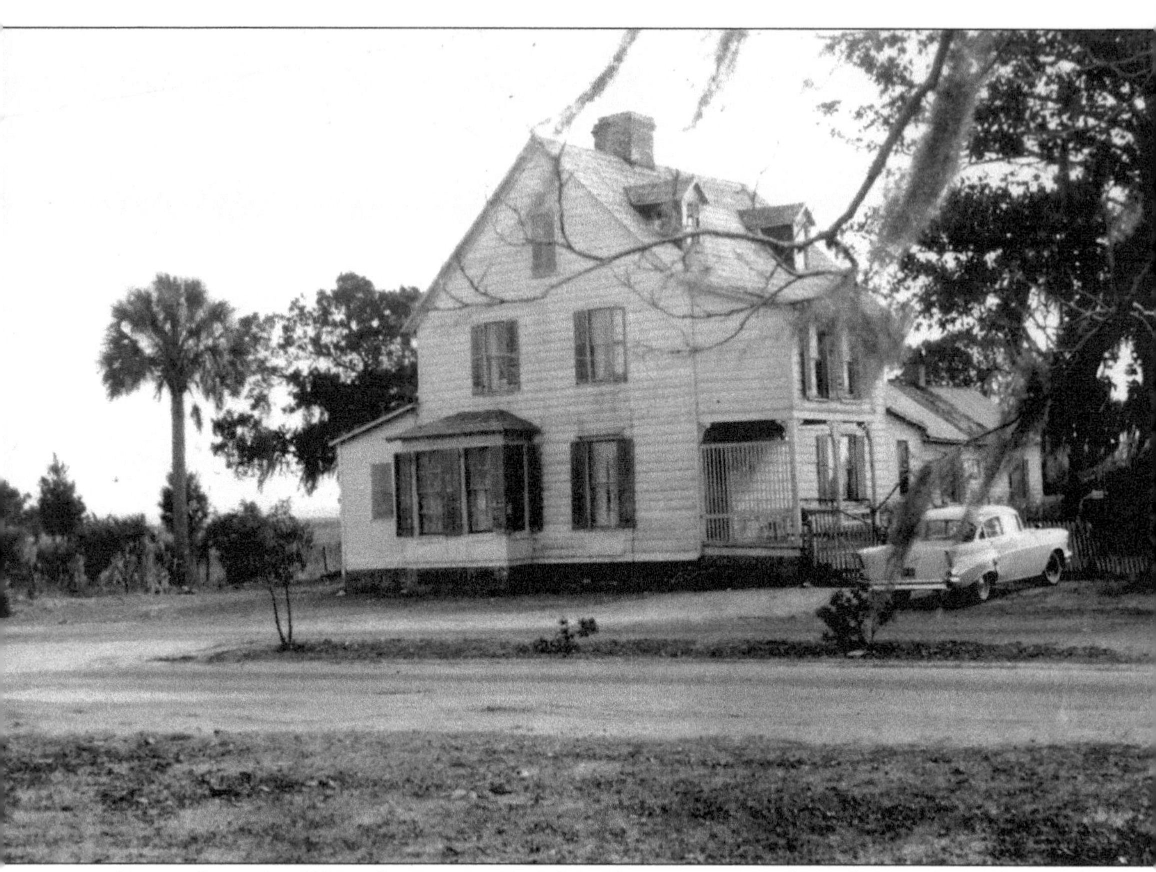

Dating from the 1780s, the historic Rudulph House once stood on the marshes' edge at the east end of Bryant Street. Gone but not forgotten, this historic landmark served as a beacon for mariners sailing in the St. Marys River until it was demolished, after severe storm damage, in April 1966 by a Rudulph descendant. The home's third floor offered a commanding view of Cumberland Sound and the Atlantic Ocean and was formerly operated as the St. Marys Inn, sometimes referred to as the Ross Inn. Built of hand-hewn lumber, the home was constructed with wooden pegs in place of iron nails. A loss to historic preservationists, this pre-Revolutionary War structure featured hand-carved doors and mantles and wide plank floorboards. Secret passageways or hideaways beneath east and west dormer windows led to great speculation upon which creative imaginations held free rein. When this large frame house was operated as an inn, guests reported ghostly bumps, thumps, and groans in the night. Some saw a shadowy figure; others recalled tales of buried treasure and the inn's use as a swash-buckling pirates den. (Courtesy of Herbert Rowland.)

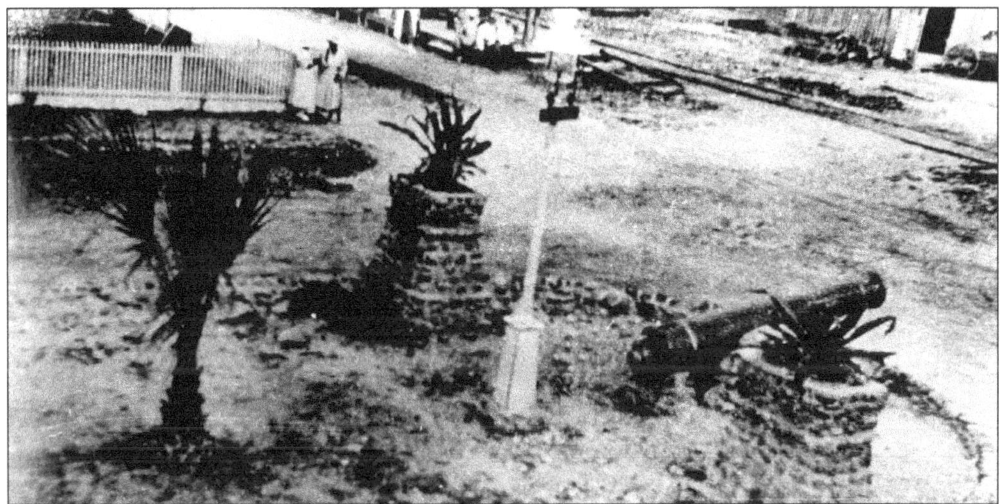

In a street scene image taken after 1916 from an upper level of the Riverview Hotel, one may glimpse the intersection of St. Marys and Osborne Streets where the cannon points toward the waterfront. Ballast stones, useful for weighing down and stabilizing tall-masted sailing vessels engaged in international commerce, can be seen on the small wall framing the median. Notice a relic of yesteryear in the carbide lamp, at front center, and, at top right, the turntable located by the railroad station for motor cars traveling on the St. Marys Railroad. (Courtesy of Eloise Bailey Thompson.)

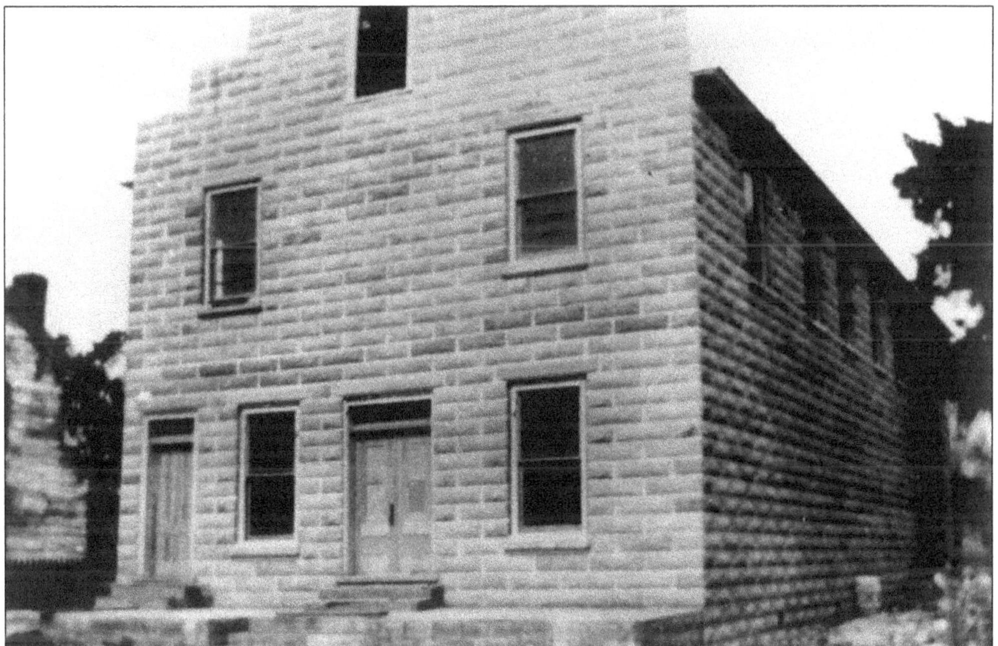

Dating from 1910–1911, the two-story Lucas Memorial Building on the St. Marys waterfront was constructed of cement block and was originally operated as a general merchandise business by the venerable J.K. Bedell. Later, this structure was cut down to one and one-half story and converted to a movie theatre; today, the St. Marys Submarine Museum, Inc. can be found in this historic building. This non-profit supports the presence of Naval Submarine Base Kings Bay and provides outreach to the community. (Courtesy of Eloise Bailey Thompson.)

The Riverview, St. Mary's, Ga.

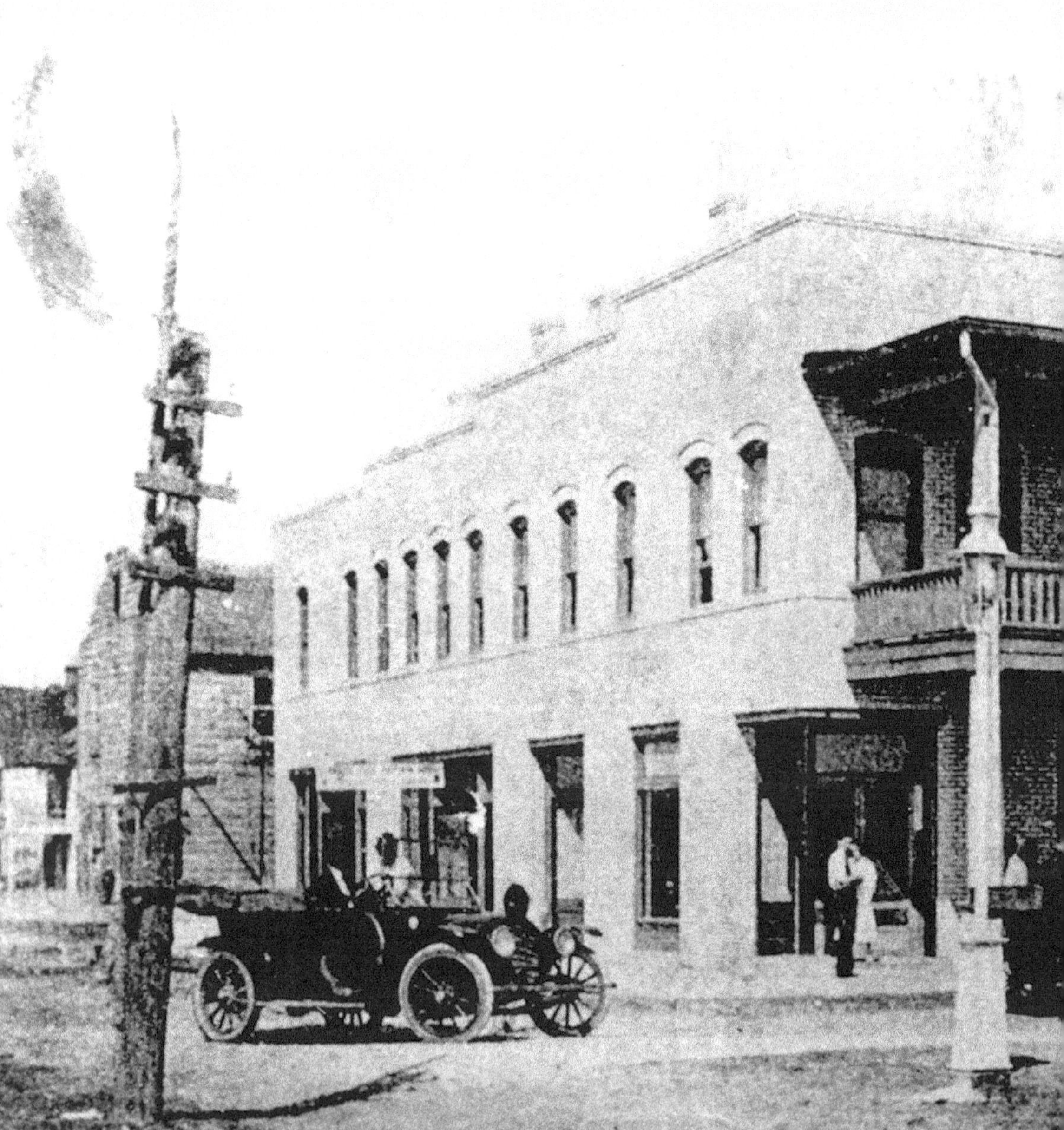

The grand Riverview Hotel on St. Marys waterfront offered pleasing views and cooling breezes for hotel patrons. Contractor J.H. Banks supervised the hotel's construction, with plans for 20 rooms and 8 baths, for Mrs. K.J. Wadley. A lobby and large dining room on the ground floor invited guests when the Riverview Hotel opened for business in 1916; Wadley's brother George L. Johnson served as manager. Subsequently, Sally Brandon bought the hotel and with the able

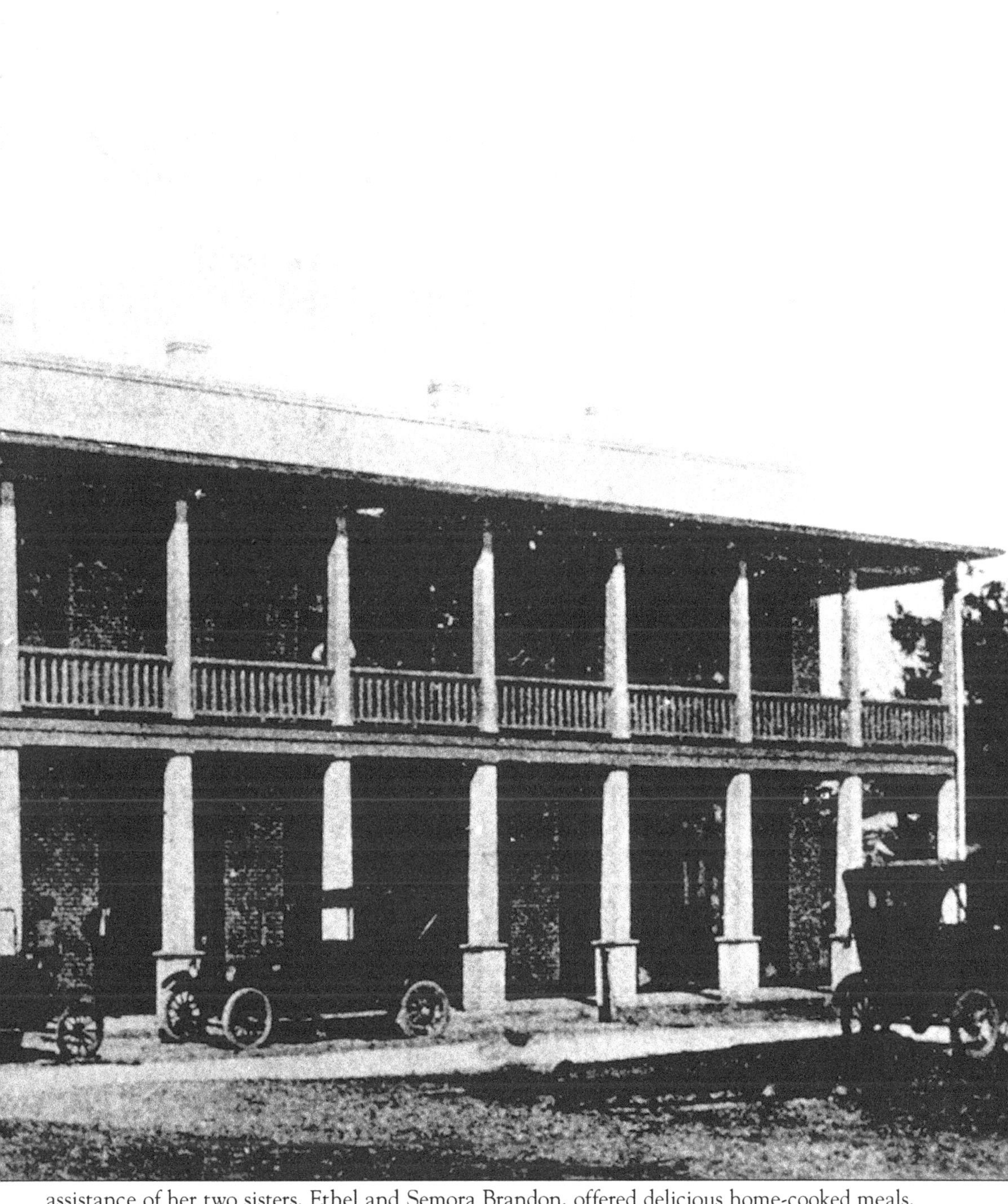

assistance of her two sisters, Ethel and Semora Brandon, offered delicious home-cooked meals. Saturday night entertainment and dances attracted not only hotel guests but also Camden Countians eager for good food and good company; among others, the Cross Creek, Florida 1939 Pulitzer prize-winning author Marjorie Kinnan Rawlings visited at the Riverview and heaped accolades in tribute to St. Marys. (Courtesy of Eloise Bailey Thompson.)

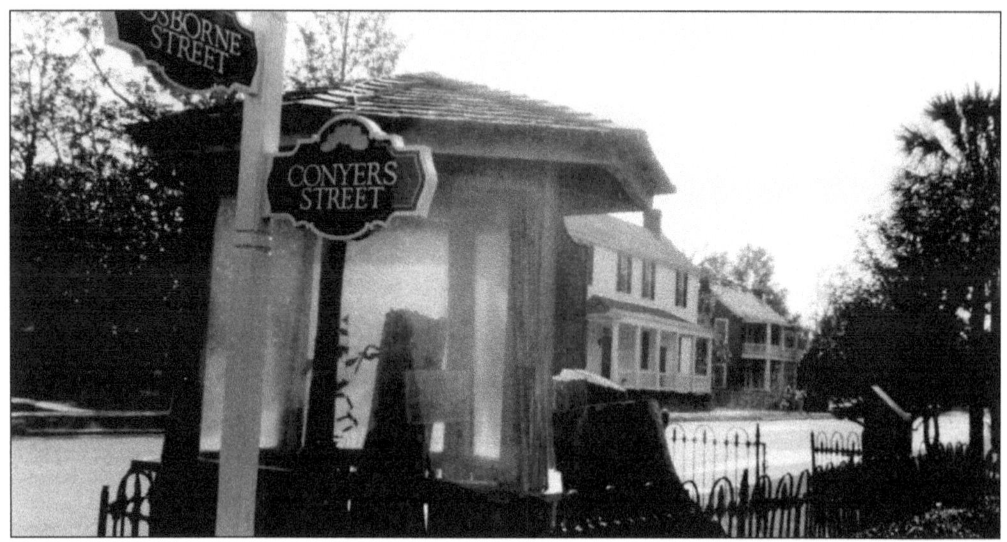

Located at the intersection of Osborne and Conyers Streets, the Washington Pump has served as a St. Marys landmark since 1799. The old cypress pump with hand-forged iron handle and spout was one of six public wells for each of the squares, serving the needs of thirsty citizens; this is the only one remaining. The late Miss R. Lee Russell of St. Marys and Incachee Plantation at Waverly recalled how the pump got its name. When our country's first president died, the citizens of St. Marys held a commemorative event honoring his interment at Mount Vernon, including planting four oak trees. A mock funeral ceremony proceeded from the St. Marys waterfront, to the public square, and a casket was buried where later a street well was installed; hence the name "Washington Pump." Until recent years, the oaks grew near the public well. (Courtesy of Eloise Bailey Thompson.)

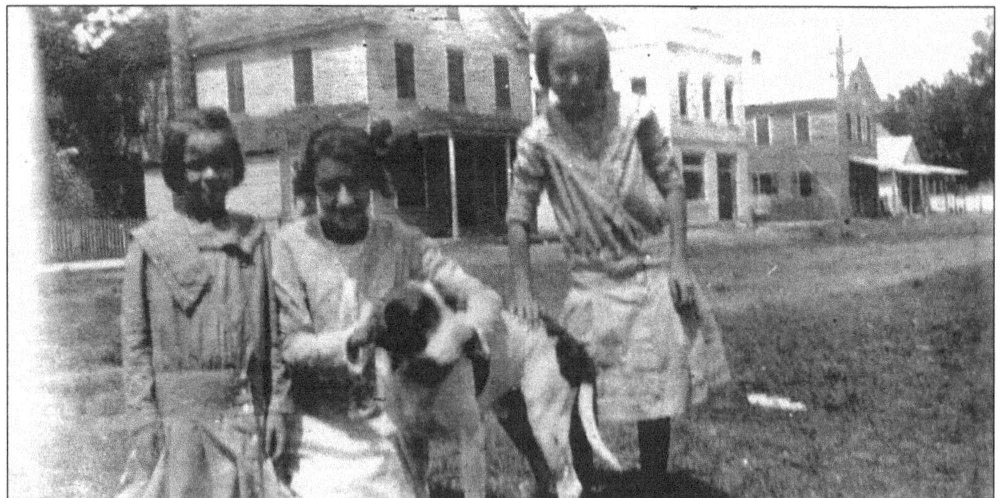

Leona Register (center) pets the family bird dog with two unidentified girls. Her parents, Michael and Isabella Proctor Register, married on July 1, 1885, suggesting that this photograph dates to the second decade of the 20th century. In the background are several businesses that once operated in St. Marys, including, from left to right, the Rudulph Brothers' store (the attached post office is where John J. Rudulph served as postmaster, 1883–1898, and Herbert F. Rudulph, 1898–1924); next, the Camden Bank, which stands today; the headquarters for *The Southeast Georgian* newspaper; and Vocelle's store. (Courtesy of Eloise Bailey Thompson.)

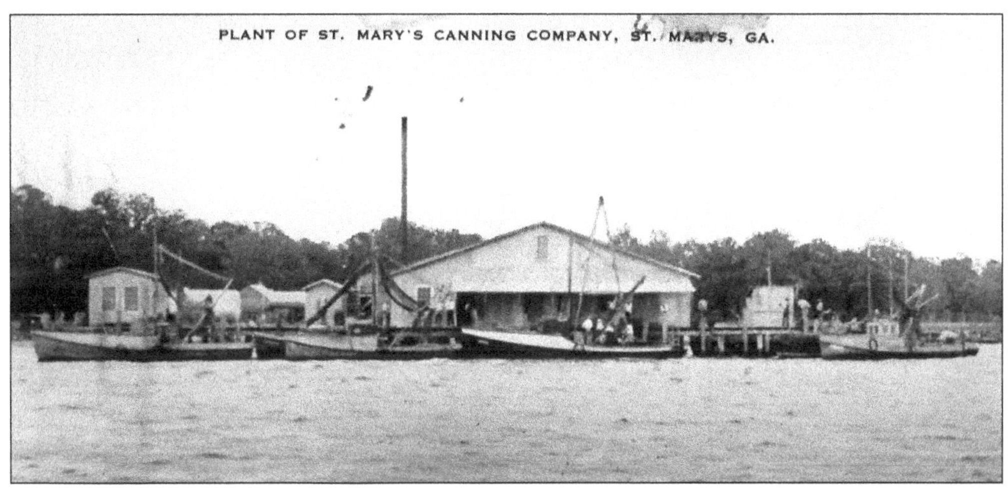

During the early 1900s, a number of canning plants located in St. Marys. After purchasing Lemuel Johnson's sawmill location, J.S.N. Davis Jr. and George W. Brandon opened a canning business, specializing in canned shrimp, sweet potatoes, and string beans. Their presence provided economic opportunity for local women who snapped beans while tending to their home fires. A special courier retrieved the vegetables for further processing at the cannery. By 1912, Davis and Brandon faced stiff competition when three other canning businesses opened. Fernandina brothers John, Charles, and Noble Hardee opened a waterfront shrimp canning plant, seen in an E.C. Kropp Co. postcard image. Later, their business was sold to prominent businessman Clyde A. Taylor Sr. (1871–1954). He was vice-president of the St. Marys Railroad, was president of the Bank of Camden County, served on the Camden Board of Education, and was active politically as mayor of St. Marys. He lived in Brunswick after 1952. Following in his father's footsteps, Clyde A. Taylor Jr. served as mayor of Brunswick (1972–1978). (Courtesy of Eloise Bailey Thompson.)

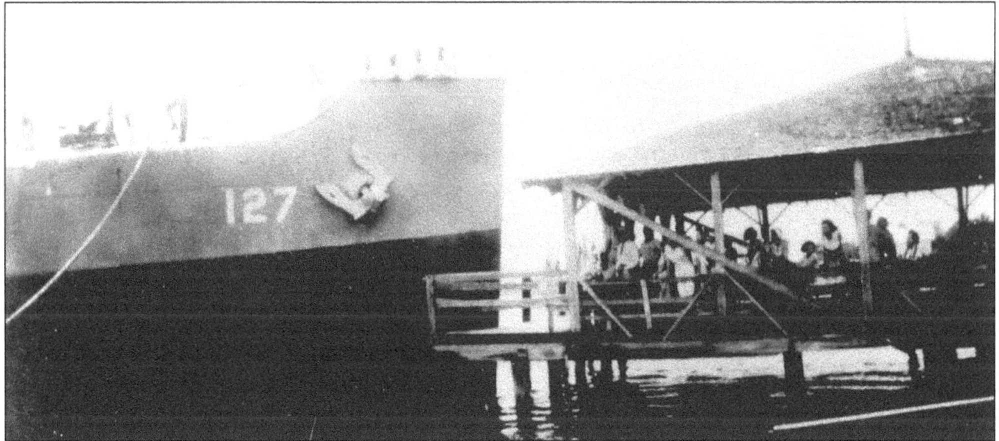

On the pavilion where a nickelodeon once played, crowds danced the night away, and new acquaintances became lifelong partnerships. Seen in this image, a U.S. Navy minesweeper has arrived for the July 4, 1946 Independence Day celebration. A small gathering has assembled to watch the vessel tie up at the pavilion. Nearby stood the Will Carnegie home. Carnegie stayed aboard his vessel, the *Lucinda*, built in 1934 by A.H. MacDonell's shipyard at Major Moore Creek, while his winter home was under construction. Located at the foot of Osborne Street, today Lang Seafood Company operates one of several waterfront businesses at Carnegie's former home. (Courtesy of Maxine Wells.)

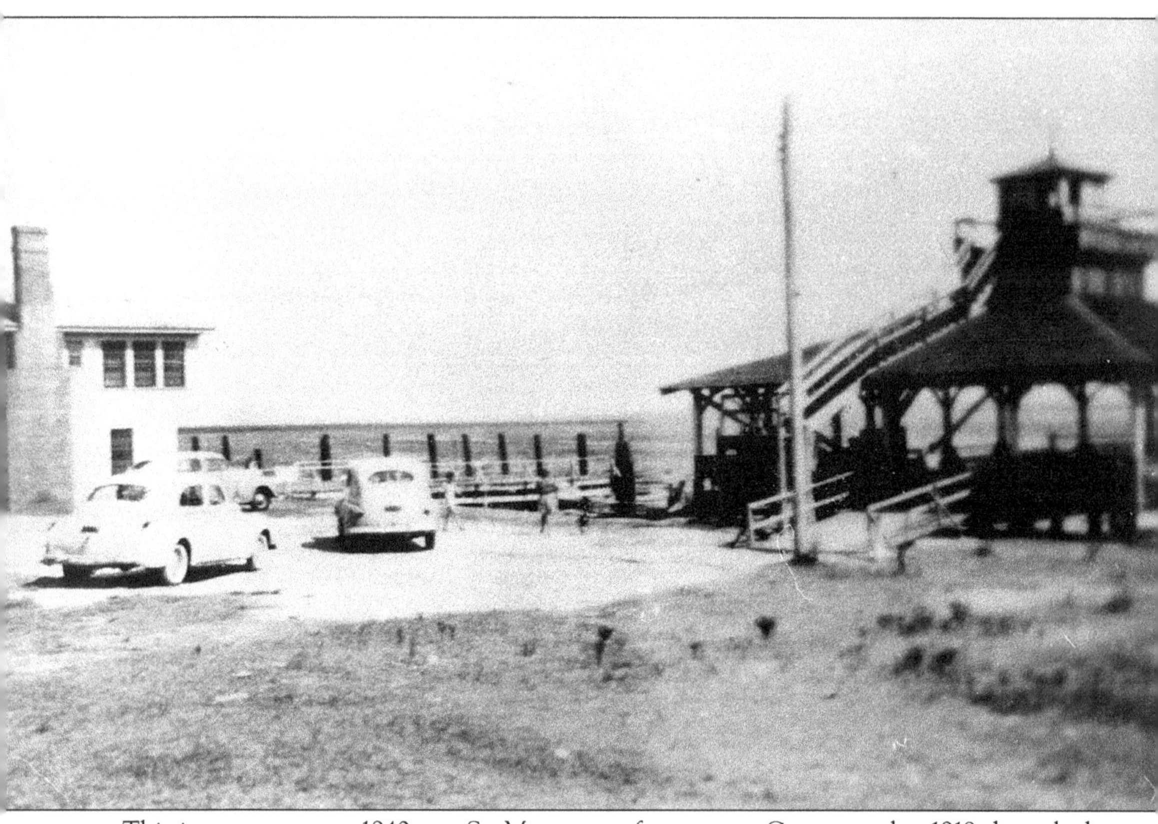

This image captures a 1940s-era St. Marys waterfront scene. Constructed c. 1918 through the civic-mindedness and vision of John Bachlott, a waterfront pavilion offered respite from the day's toil and trouble. Vintage automobiles are parked near the old pavilion, once a favored gathering place for St. Marys citizenry seeking balmy, cooling sea breezes. Notice the plane-watching tower for vigilant citizens who, as plane spotters, took two- to four-hour shifts in support of the war effort. As civilian participants, these volunteers searched the skies for enemy planes in a coastal Georgia beset by World War II rationing, coastal blackouts, and offshore German submarines. Due to time, deterioration, and the ravages of an unforgiving sub-tropical climate, this landmark structure was dismantled in June 1963 and replaced in the 1970s with a newer pavilion. Today, city government and St. Marys residents once again invest in preserving important landmarks and an accessible waterfront park with several amenities catering to large segments of the population and visiting public. Backed by ambitious plans, more than ten years in staging, a new St. Marys riverside park creates a pleasing setting for enjoying a revitalized waterfront. Features include new piers, a 1,400-foot boardwalk, bike paths, a kayak launching ramp, and a lengthy marsh walk. Honoring a community benefactor, the waterfront park was dedicated on June 30, 2001 as the Howard Gilman Memorial Park. (Courtesy of Maxine Wells.)

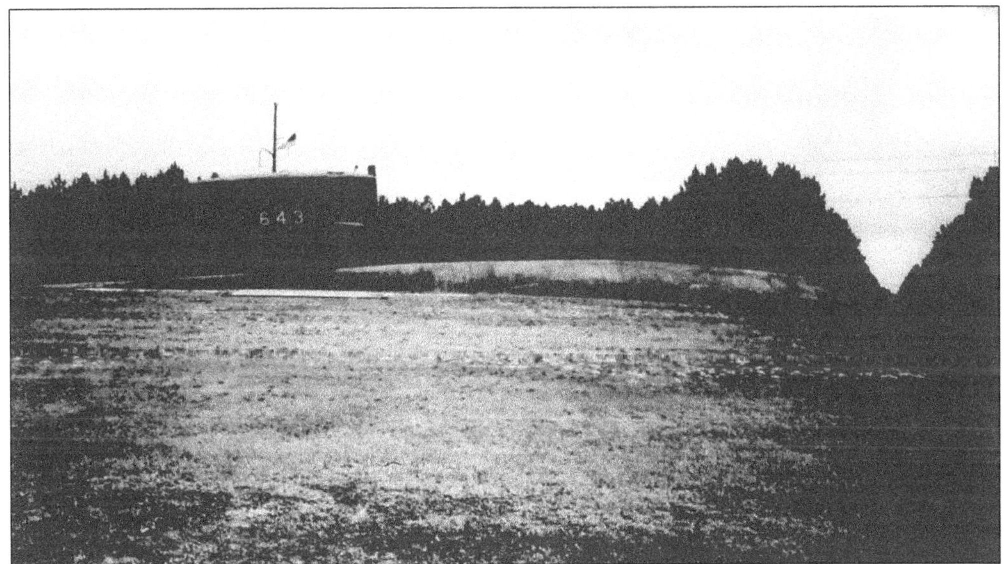

Built in partnership with the St. Marys Submarine Museum and SUBVETS who raised $60,000 for the construction of a full-scale SSBN, this exhibit was dedicated on April 17, 2000, kicking off a two-day event and celebration that attracted thousands of participants. Located on over 16,000 acres, Naval Submarine Base, Kings Bay began on July 1, 1978 and achieved its current status in April 1982. The base serves as homeport for ten Atlantic Fleet Trident Submarines and logistics support for the Trident II (D-5) Missile, employing more than 9,700 people with an annual total payroll of just over $225 million. (Courtesy of Forrest "Frosty" Barefoot.)

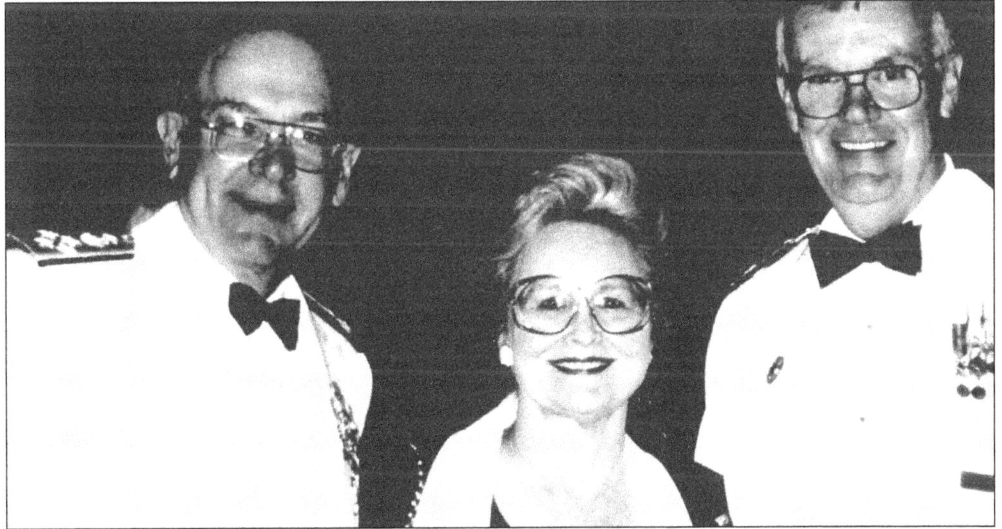

Pictured here, from left to right, Adm. Vern Clark, chief of naval operations; Sheila M. McNeill, 2003–2004 national president, Navy League of the United States; and Adm. James Loy, commandant of the U.S. Coast Guard, pose for the cameraman. Owner of a St. Marys business, McNeill has been active in community affairs in support of the economic contributions made by the presence of Naval Submarine Base, Kings Bay. The Navy League is a civilian organization dedicated to the education of civilians and supports the sea services and families through a variety of outreach programs and lobbying efforts. (Courtesy of Sheila M. McNeill.)

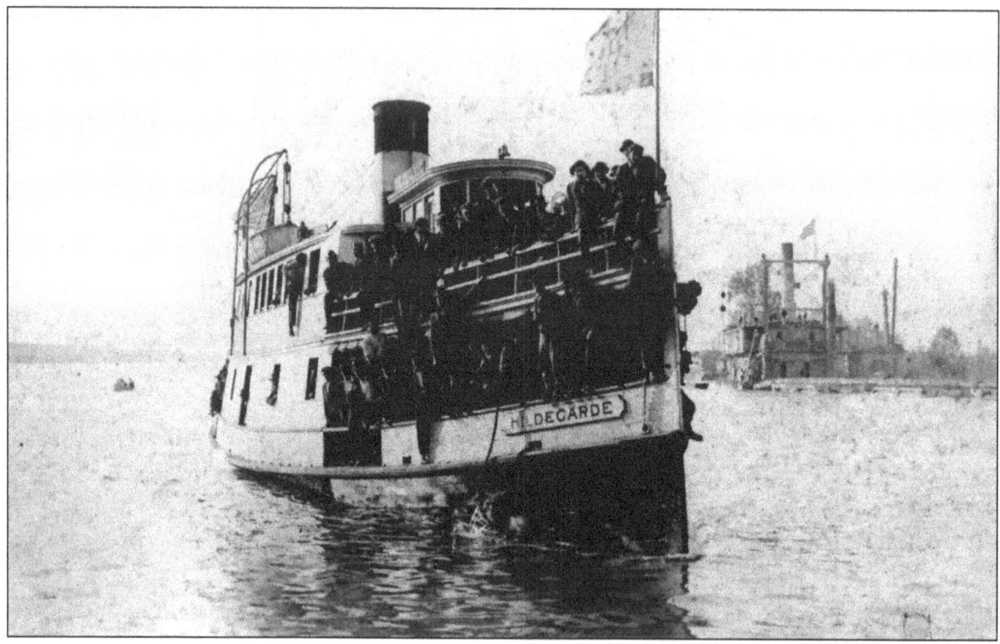

Prior to the coming of the railroad, steamboats offered transport on the Cumberland Route between Brunswick, Fernandina, and Jacksonville, as well as a lifeline to the remote river settlements. Along the way, passengers were discharged to enjoy the amenities of an early resort hotel on the north end of Cumberland Island. When the 105-foot, locally owned steamer *Atlantic* burned at Burnt Fort, another replaced it. The *Hildegarde* was used for hauling not only passengers but also general merchandise and other freight, such as barrels of rosin. Later, railroads offered more efficient and less costly transport, ringing the death knell for the romantic steamboat era when Americans began to explore the wild and exotic Deep South and Florida. (Courtesy of Bryan-Lang Historical Library.)

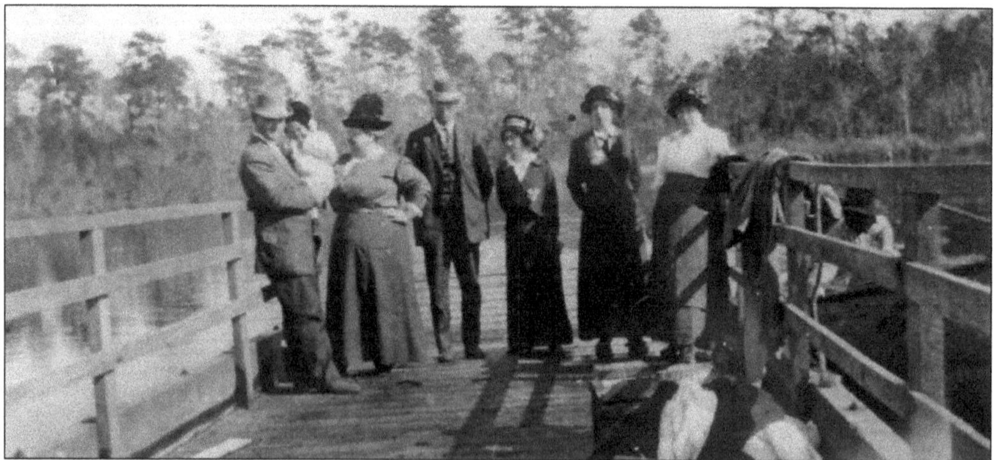

In a 1912 image, S.C. Sheffield (left) holding his baby Ida West, and his sister postmistress Sally S. Westbrook (second from left) await the steamer *Hildegarde* on the St. Marys River with four unidentified passengers. While in the past the Satilla and St. Marys Rivers served as vital transportation and commodity corridors, today they serve as recreation outlets. Locals and visitors pursuing eco-tourism interests express great fascination with the uniqueness of the marshy coast, its flora and fauna. (Courtesy of Rodney Sheffield.)

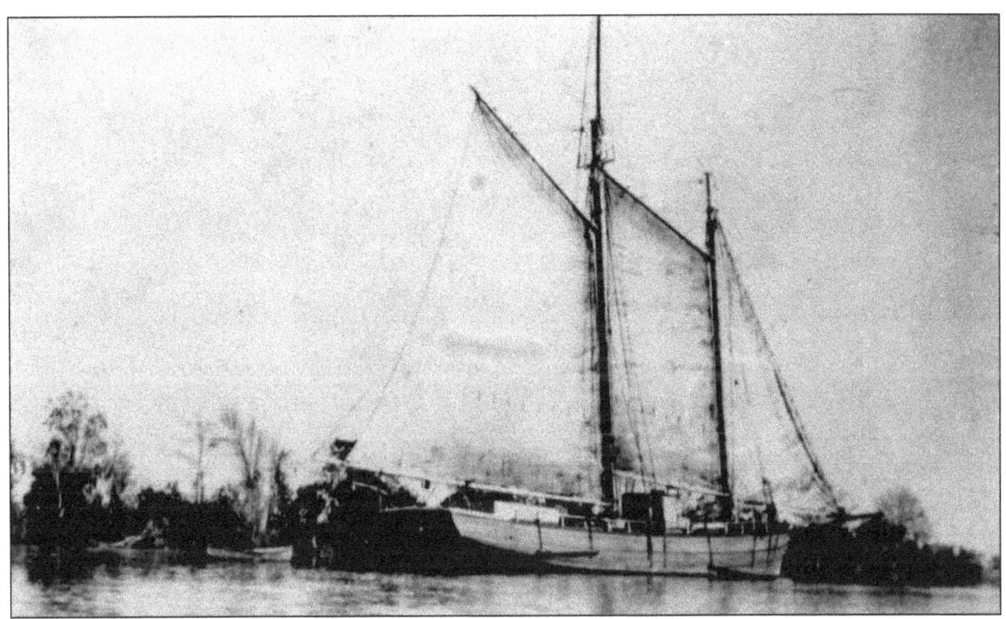

On the Satilla River a section known as Owen's Ferry has had many names to its claim: the Cattleford, Leman's Ferry, Mills's Ferry, Brown's Ferry, and Ivanhoe. Numerous accounts agree that the crossing was part of an old Native American trail traveled by the Quaker naturalist Will Bartram. Through various changes in ownership, enormous tracts of land were cultivated in a grainy crop of rice, an attraction for migratory waterfowl in another era. Hugh Crawford Brown served as an overseer at the Owen's Ferry rice plantation, and his daughter Allie Brown Carmichael recalled how vessels lined up at the docks for loading the golden grain to be transported to Savannah and beyond for sale. Seen in the image, a two-masted wooden sailing vessel has arrived for loading rice at Owen's Ferry, located up the great Satilla River. (Courtesy of Charles K. Perry.)

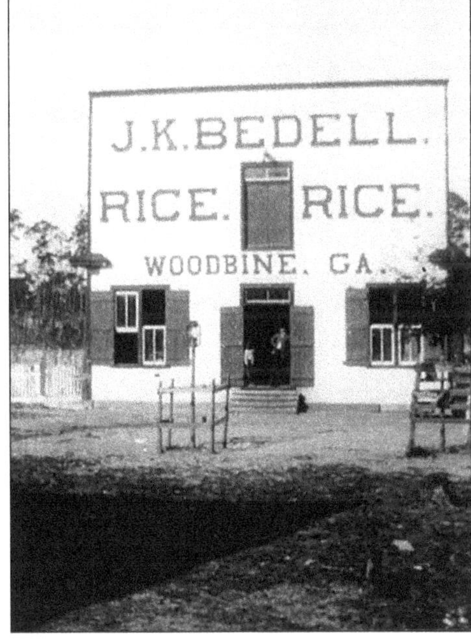

Conveyed from John Bailey to his son Henry and from Henry to his three children, Woodbine Plantation was operated on the Satilla River as a tidal rice plantation, where this grainy crop proved a lucrative agricultural product. Subsequently, James King Bedell (1849–1923) purchased the property from Bailey heirs and continued growing rice on about 300 acres of tidal lands. He farmed, cut timber, and operated a commissary for his workers on the Woodbine Plantation. Heralded as Woodbine's founder, J.K. Bedell sold rights of way to the railroad with the stipulation that the new railroad community be named "Woodbine" after the twining vine or trumpet honeysuckle seen in area woods. In this intriguing pre–railroad era image, Bedell advertised in a succinct manner leaving no doubt in anyone's mind about the nature of his business in Satilla River rice. (Courtesy of Eloise Bailey Thompson.)

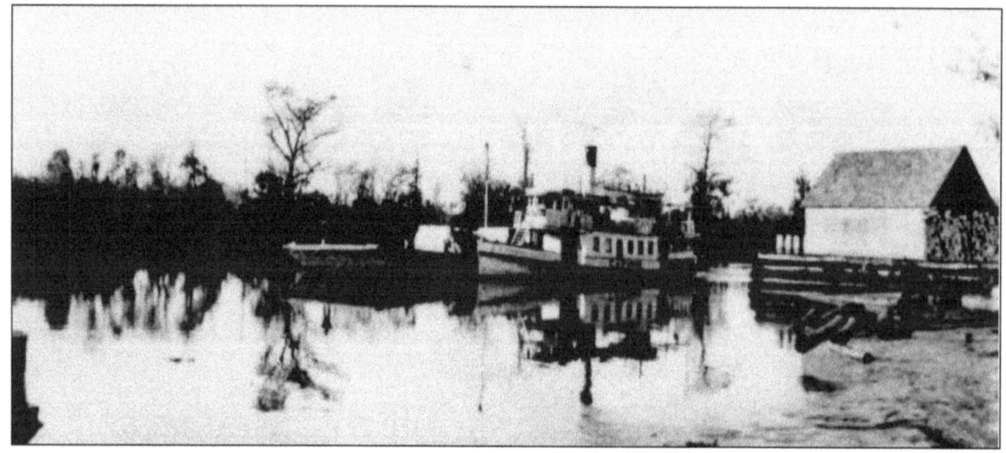

Built in 1903, the steamer *C.H. Evans* plied the waters of the Brunswick and Satilla Route leaving the Mallory line wharf on the waterfront each Monday, Wednesday, and Friday at 9:30 a.m. On its return trip, the vessel arrived back in the City by the Sea on alternate days at 2 p.m. from its regularly scheduled calls. The steamer captain stopped at Jekyll Island before heading up the Satilla River to Ceylon, Satilla Bluff, Halifax, Woodbine, Refuge, Owen's Ferry, Clark's Bluff, Bailey's Mill, Silco, and Burnt Fort. Managing owner Capt. Benjamin A. White worked with general manager and passenger agent J.O. Dyal of Owen's Ferry to accommodate freight and passenger service, in addition to lighters (barges). By 1907, Captain White had over 20 years experience plying the tannic waters of the great Satilla River and had captained other steamers, such as the *Cracker Boy* and the *Falcon*. Seen in this image is the steamer *C.H. Evans* and, on the vessel's starboard side, a lighter filled with lumber. (Courtesy of Charles K. Perry.)

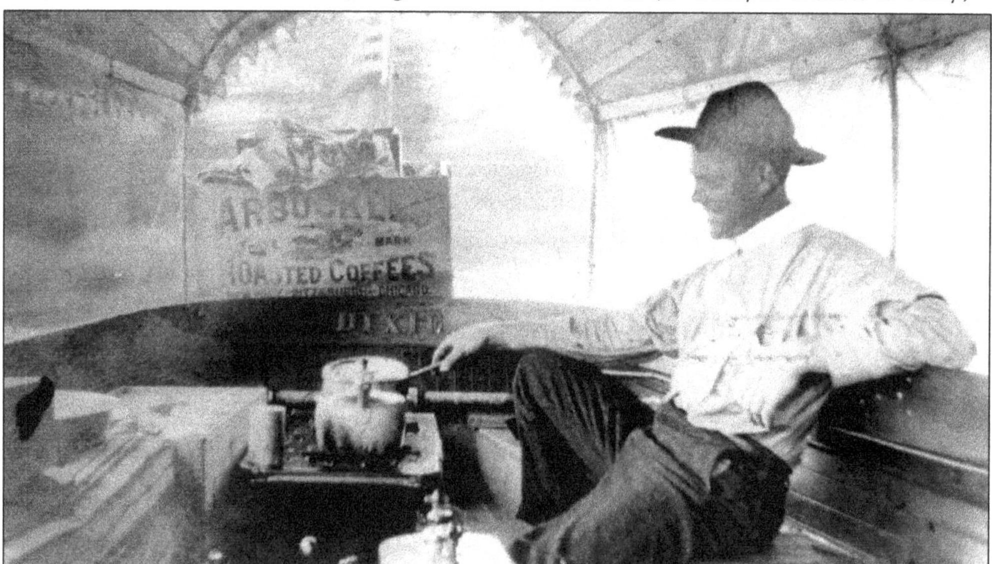

In an image salvaged from obscurity by the late Catherine MacDonell, her father, Fernandina native A.H. MacDonell (1879–1954), is seated on a river launch. In what appears to be a canvas-covered vessel MacDonell cooks on the stove in the center of the image. Notice the Arbuckles Toasted Coffees advertisement. Launches such as this one were useful for servicing the needs of the settlements on the great Satilla River. Alexander Henry MacDonell's wife, Ria, and son John are seen in other images on page 70. Today, some of their descendants live in St. Marys and have remained active in community affairs. (Courtesy of Eloise Bailey Thompson.)

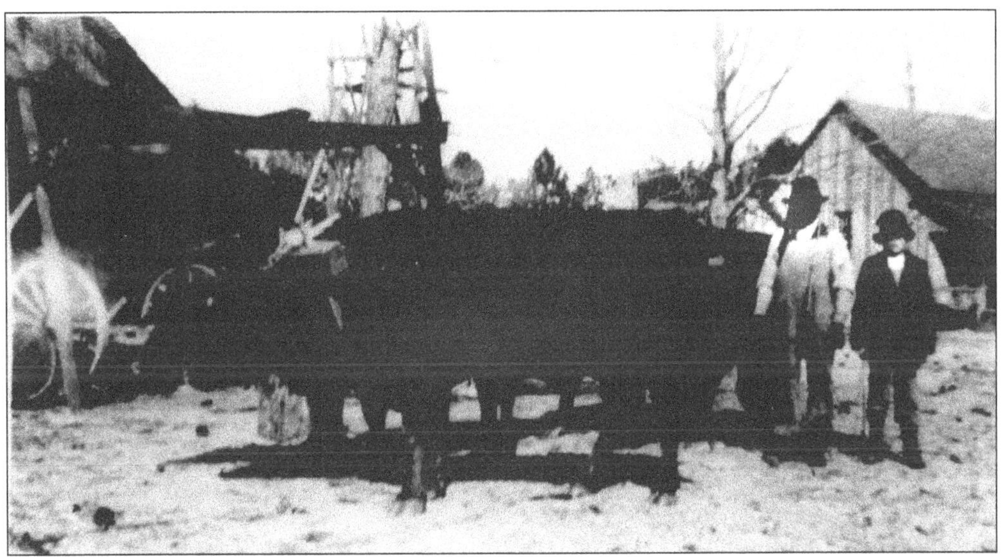

Ox teams were used for transportation and, in the deep woods, for hauling out crossties. In this image taken at Silco, two unidentified people stand next to the team. Naval stores operations were scattered throughout southeast Georgia in an earlier era, and the livelihood of many Camden families was dependent upon this hard work. They were woodsriders, box chippers, and gum-dippers, and commissaries offered allied support services and commodities. Certain men were known for their expertise as a stiller within the turpentine community. A skillful turpentine stiller knew how to build the fires under the raw gum, run off the charges, distill the rosin into the vats, and read the signs of when the charge was ready to be run in this risky business. (Courtesy of Camden County Historical Commission.)

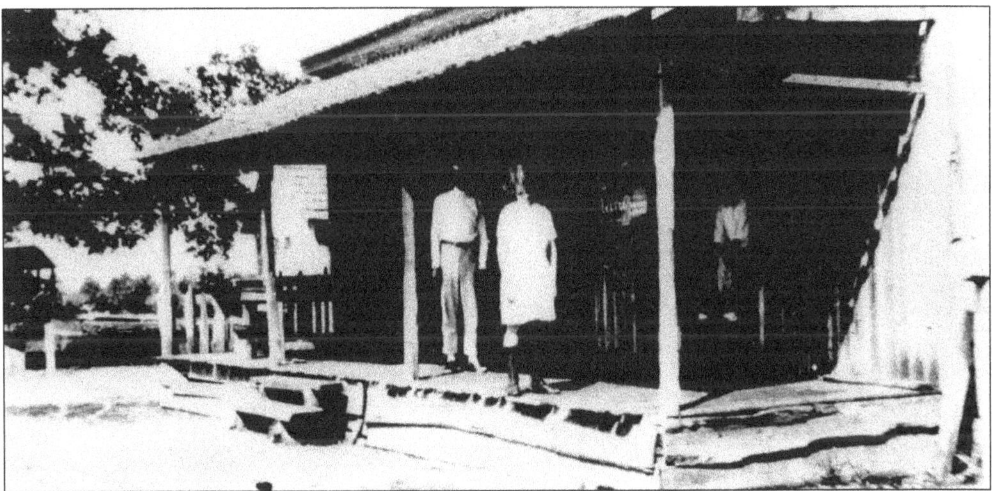

In an undated image, Luther Readdick and his first cousin Carolyn R. Boring (1911–2000) stand on the porch of the commissary at the turpentine community of Silco. Carolyn's father, Horace Blair Readdick (1877–1954), and his wife, Elizabeth Cobb Lang Readdick (1888–1985), had moved there in 1910. Readdick managed the Silco Commissary for J.S.N. Davis and George Brandon, and his nephew Luther worked as a storekeeper. Later, Horace Readdick purchased the business and maintained a well-stocked store until selling to Georgia Forest Products Company; this was later owned by Union Camp Corporation. (Courtesy of Eloise Bailey Thompson.)

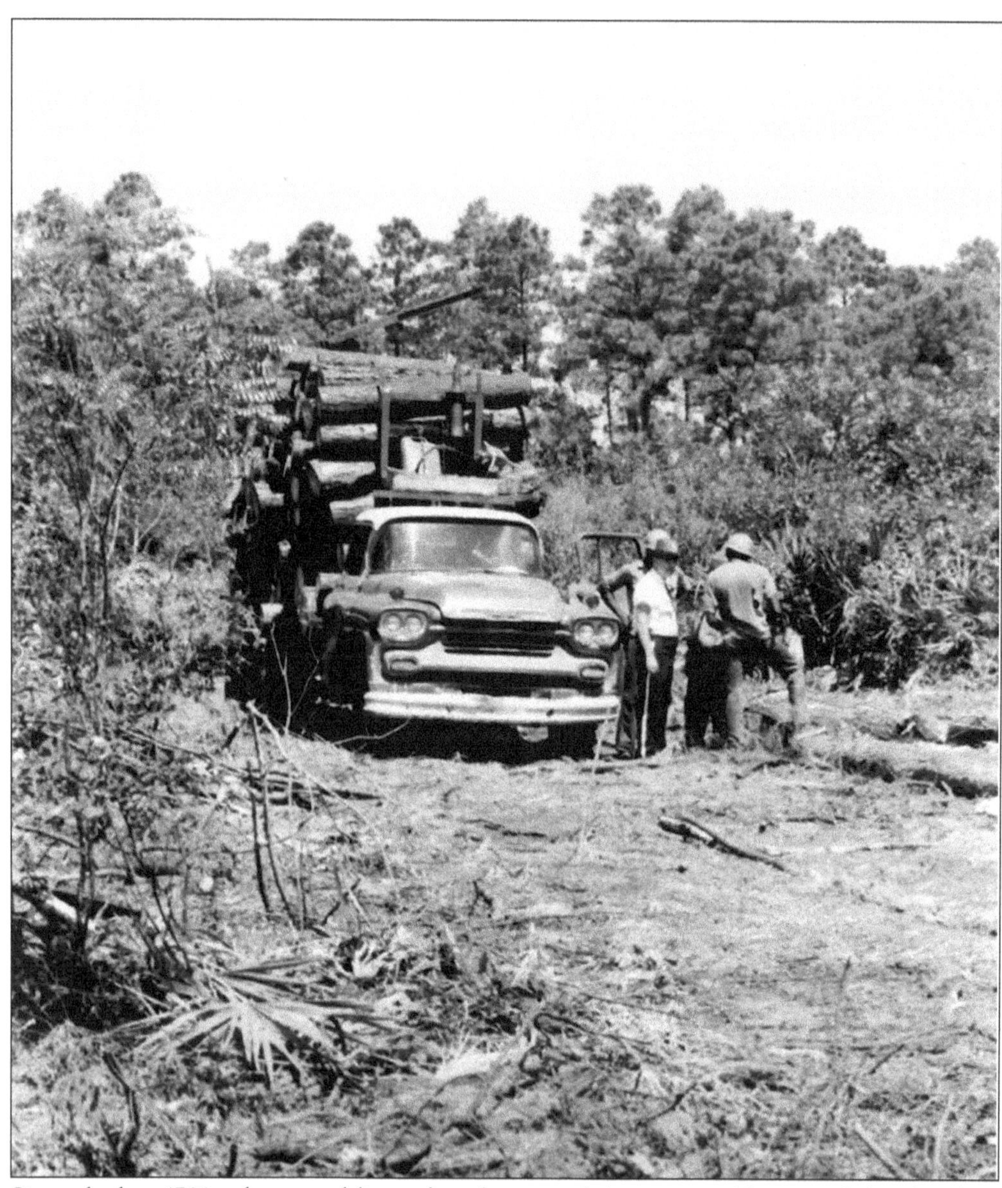

Since the late 1700s when naval live oakers frequented the coast and harvested the abundant evergreen oaks for a fledgling country's naval shipbuilding needs, Camden lands have been exploited for timbering and naval stores production. River mill villages were numerous along the rivers. Turpentine camps dotted the woodsy setting at Colesburg, Scotchville, and Silco, where large stills produced turpentine and other naval stores. Davis and Brandon Lumber Company and the Proctor Timber Company offered employment for a large segment of Camden's population. In 1941, a family-owned Gilman Paper Company opened its St. Marys Kraft Corporation Plant on 250 acres, and until the arrival of the Naval Submarine Base at Kings Bay, it was the largest employer in Camden County. After its sale, the mill operated in St. Marys as Durango-Georgia Paper Company but closed in November 2002. Names within Camden County's forestry-related industries include McKinnon, McCarthy, Wilson, Price, Grainger, Meschke, Proctor, Gross, Paschall, Lang, Middleton, Russell, Buie, and Peeples. (Courtesy of Rodney Sheffield.)

Largely dependent upon watery connections with the outside world, St. Marys experienced several failed attempts at bringing a rail connection to the port. Notably, in March 1856 prominent businessmen were issued a charter by state authorities for a St. Marys Rail Road Company. They included Henry Bacon, Julius Baratte, John Dufour, John L. King, Samuel Burns, William Temple, A.J. Bessent, Gideon Mallette, David Bailey, and Robert Stafford. Proposals in 1871 and 1882 failed, and in 1887 the formidable Henry Plant eliminated competing interests of his Plant System. Finally, in the early 1900s Capt. Lemuel "Lem" Johnson (1844–1918) was granted land by the city of St. Marys for his railroad, the Waycross Air Line Company, later the St. Marys and Kingsland Railroad, bringing the rails to port of St. Marys. Canneries, seafood processing, a pogy plant, and, dating from Reconstruction, sawmills continued to offer economic opportunity. (Courtesy of Eloise Bailey Thompson.)

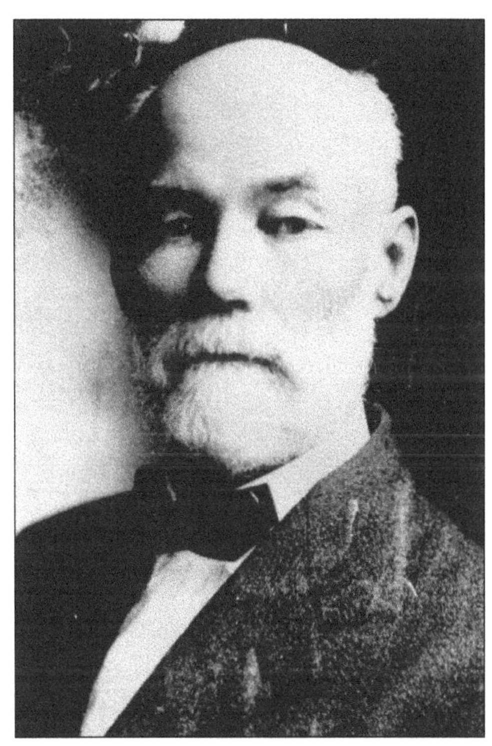

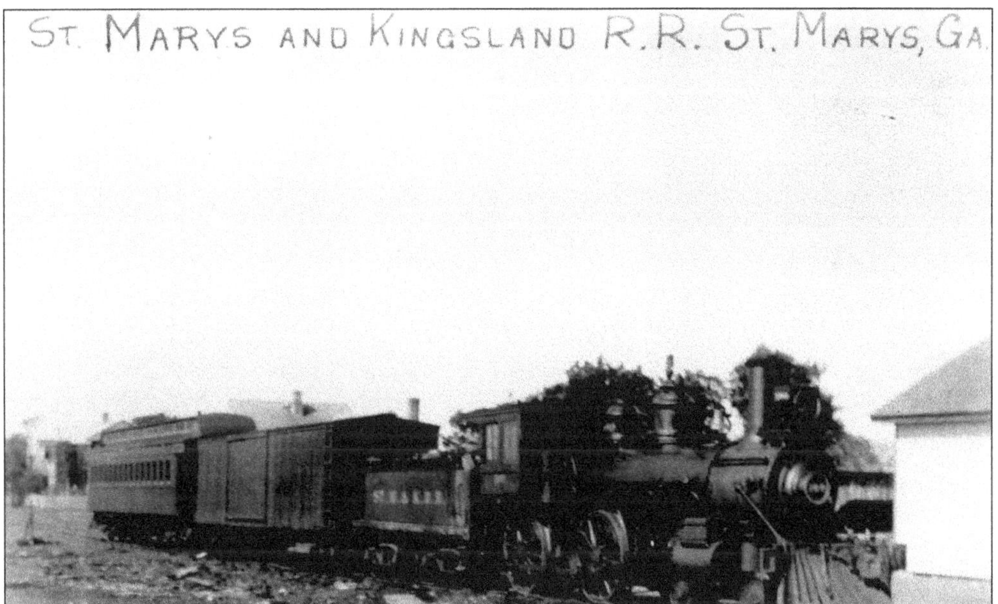

Chugging along, a wood-burning locomotive offered passenger service that began on the St. Marys and Kingsland Railroad on July 11, 1908. Eventually a regular passenger car was used for transport, but in the interim, travelers sometimes shared space with the flotsam and jetsam of assorted cargo loaded onto hand-crafted vehicles. After Lemuel Johnson's death, the railroad's name changed to the Atlantic, Waycross and Northern Railroad. When Savannah's Southern Fertilizer and Chemical Company purchased the controlling stock in 1924, it changed the name to the St. Marys Railroad Company. (Courtesy of Bryan-Lang Historical Library.)

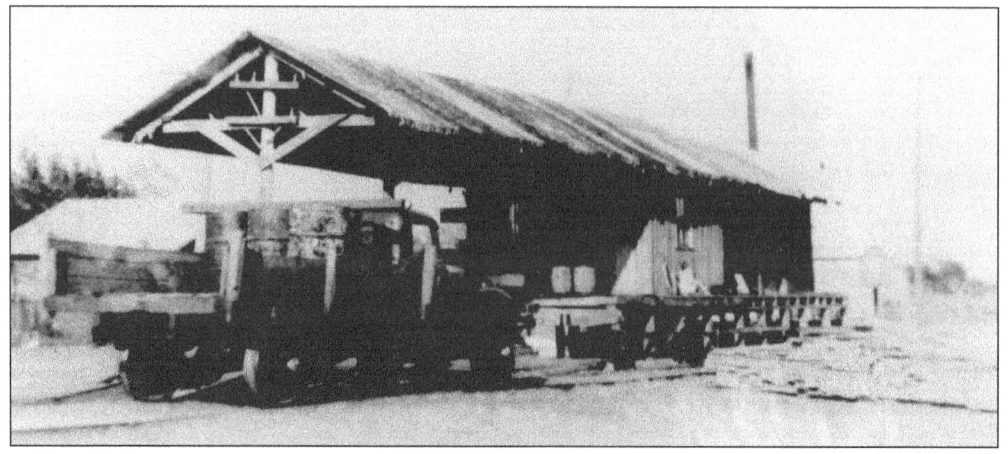

A late 1930s image captured a waterfront view of the St. Marys Railroad office and the nearby turntable. Notice the truck mounted on railroad wheels awaiting loading before beginning a slow return trip to Kingsland. When the St. Marys Railroad purchased a Ford truck with a V-8 engine, an earlier era ended. Hopper's ingenious contrivance, the Model T contraption was retired from passenger and freight service and remains enshrined in the memories of Camden Countians of those earlier days. (Courtesy of Eloise Bailey Thompson.)

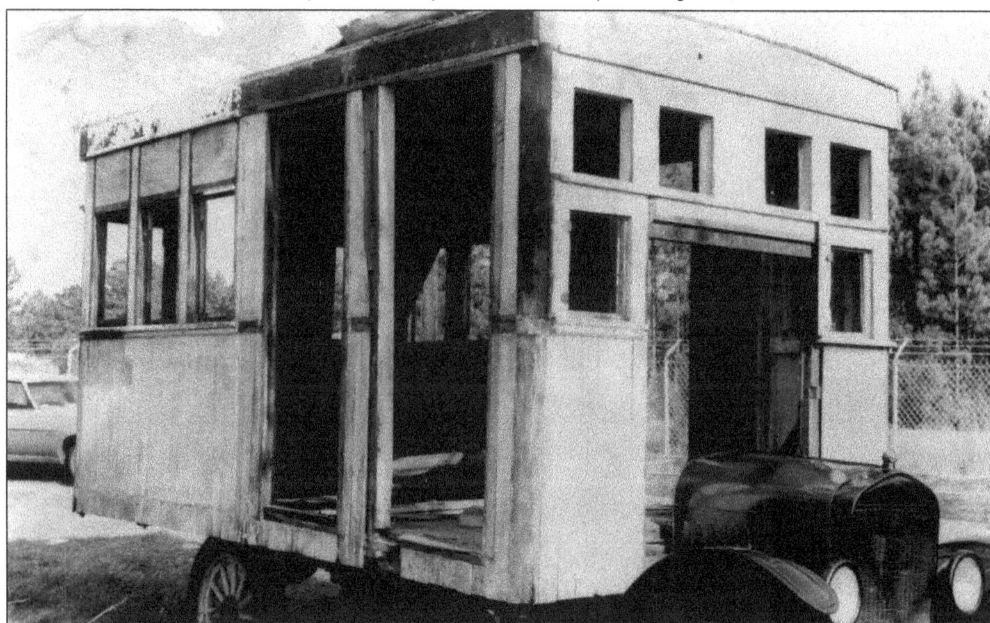

Designed by Phil Hopper, a boxlike contraption mounted on a Model T truck chassis became popular in the late 1920s and holds a nostalgic place in the memories of Camden Countians. Seen in the image is Hopper's invention, which, when mounted on rails, was useful for traveling back and forth from St. Marys to Kingsland and for hauling the mail. Later, it was replaced by a Ford truck and then by *The Doodle Bug*, which was a single railroad car operated from either end. *The Doodle Bug* featured a passenger compartment, hauled the mail train, and served as an express carrier. In 1935, the St. Marys Railroad used the engine for heating tar and paving Highway 40 connecting Kingsland with St Marys. With this completed, the two small cities were more accessible and the commute an easier ride for travelers as well as those employed by the mill. (Courtesy of Eloise Bailey Thompson.)

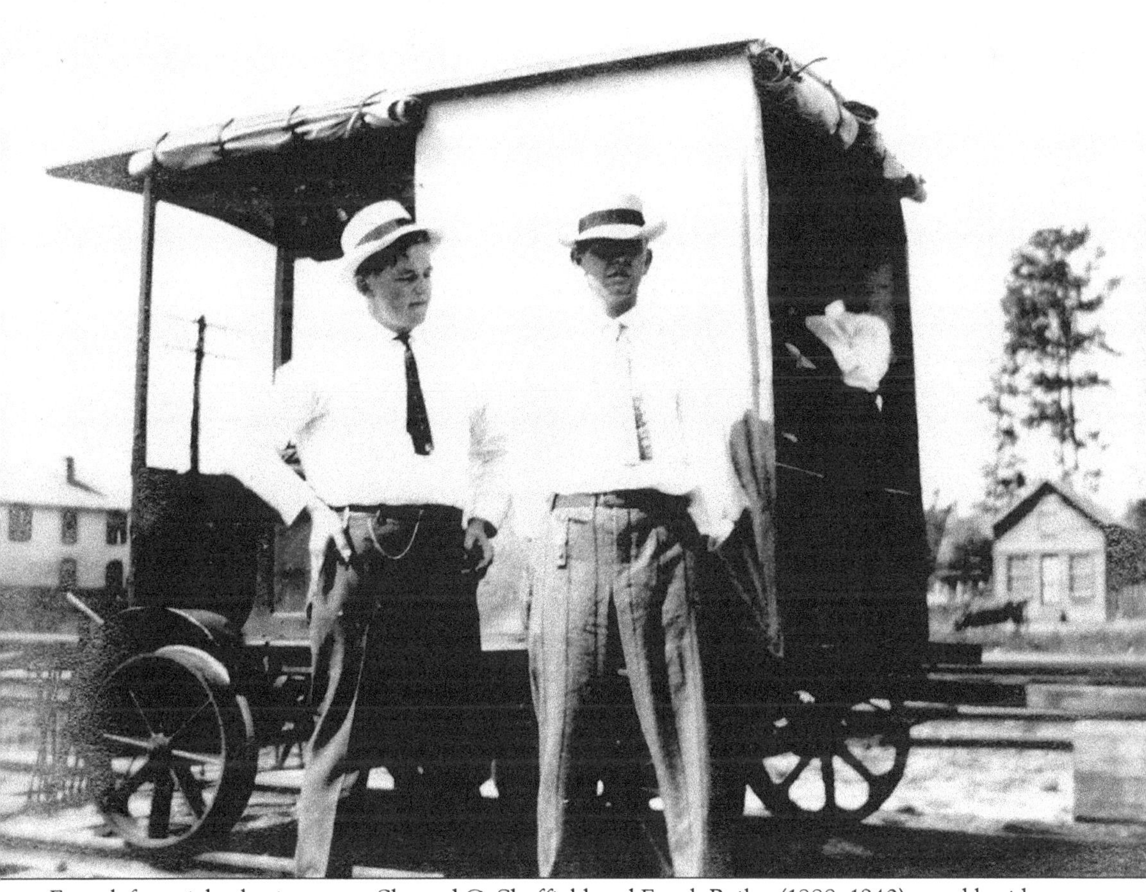

From left to right, businessmen Sherard C. Sheffield and Frank Bailey (1888–1940) stand beside a mechanized motor car put into operation prior to 1911 on the St. Marys to Kingsland rail line. Travelers initially rode in a regular passenger car pulled behind an engine. Subsequently, handcrafted vehicles carried both passengers and freight on the line. Bailey served as general manager of the St. Marys Railroad and owner of the St. Marys and Kingsland Telephone Company, which, under the ownership of Bailey's sons, became the Camden Telephone Company. Bailey was politically active as mayor of St. Marys from 1926 to 1940. Shown in the background on the far left, the W.H. Peeples' Store was one of the first businesses to operate along the new railroad line at Kingsland; Peeples offered the first postal service in town. In 1910, his daughter Shirley Everdine married S.C. Sheffield, uniting two of Camden's oldest pioneer families. (Courtesy of Rodney Sheffield.)

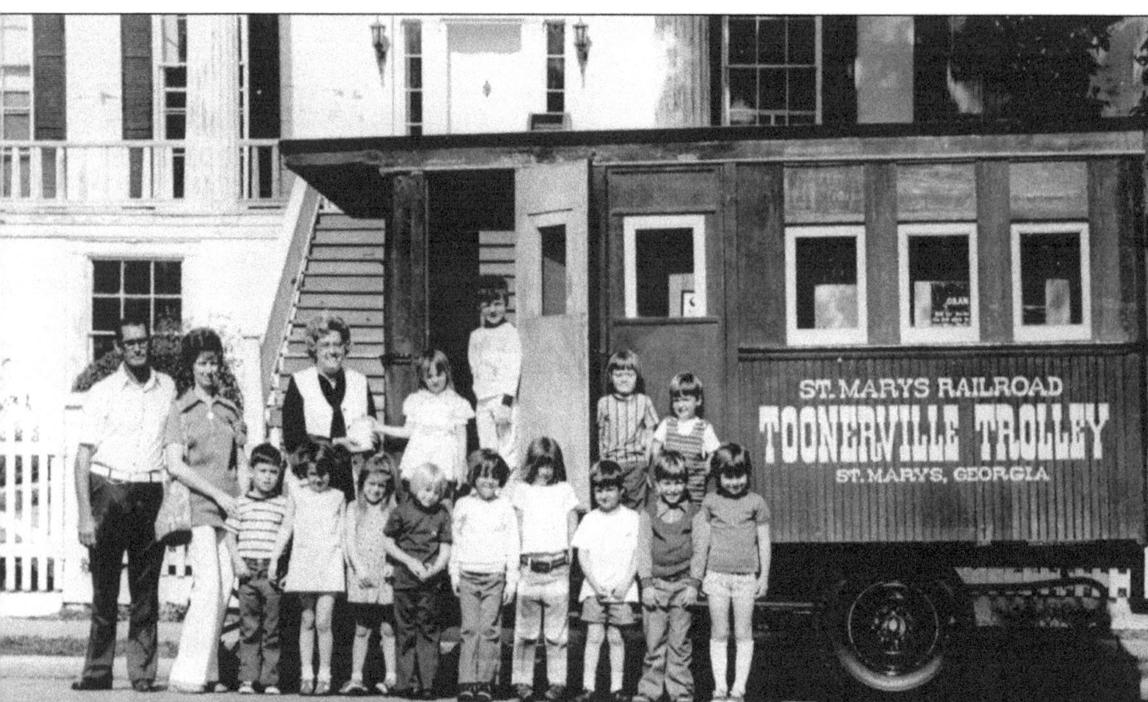

In a contemporary image, the St. Marys Railroad Trolley has stopped on Osborne Street in front of the Orange Hall mansion. Phil Hopper's motor car was restored by Jake Chapman (far left) through the interest of the Kiwanis Club of St. Marys. Kindergarten teacher Camay Howell (second from left) and her children stand beside Dot Barker, a longtime supporter of historic interests and St. Marys tourism. In 1935, cartoonist Roy Crane stayed at the Riverview Hotel. While in St. Marys he sketched historic landmarks, including the Hotel, and later used his sketches in his "Wash Tubbs" comic strip. Two cartoon characters, Wash Tubbs and Easy, were transported aboard this trolley. Crane's syndicated cartoon recognized the uniqueness of St. Marys and put the small city on the map. Subsequently, in 1975, St. Marys tourism officials used the St. Marys Railroad Trolley for visitors touring the port's historic district. (Courtesy of Eloise Bailey Thompson.)

Three

Landmarks and Historic Structures

Dotted with historic landmarks, Camden's three small cities each boast of abundant historic sites. Dating from their National Register designations, St. Marys, Kingsland, and Woodbine recognize their historic structures and invest in preserving special attributes of the past. While Kingsland's limits were plantation-size tracts, the coming of the railroad vastly altered William Henry King's old Longwood Plantation and Camden Sheffield's Beauvoir Plantation. Across these pages are more than a few relics of the historic past, some of which remain only as memories. Through yesteryear's treasures and the ruins of an earlier era, one may gain a greater insight and appreciation for those who came before us and whose lives facilitated a valuable "sense of place" within a transient world.

In April 1912, ladies of the Lyman Hall Chapter, National Society of the Daughters of the American Revolution erected an impressive monument at Coleraine, located in southwest Camden County. Their act commemorated a June 29, 1796 "Treaty of Peace and Friendship" signed by 400 mostly Upper Creek Indians reaffirming a boundary line and perpetuated the widespread myth that the Coleraine Treaty was "one of the few treaties recorded in which the Indians did not lose land." Not so, this important 1796 gathering cemented the Treaty of New York, signed on August 7, 1790 with Creek Indians over the Georgia cession of their beloved "Oconee lands" or about 3 million acres lying between the Ogeechee and Oconee Rivers in middle Georgia. Coleraine's location on the St. Marys River was of strategic importance both as a "cultural crossroads" and as a bustling trading post. (Courtesy of the Author.)

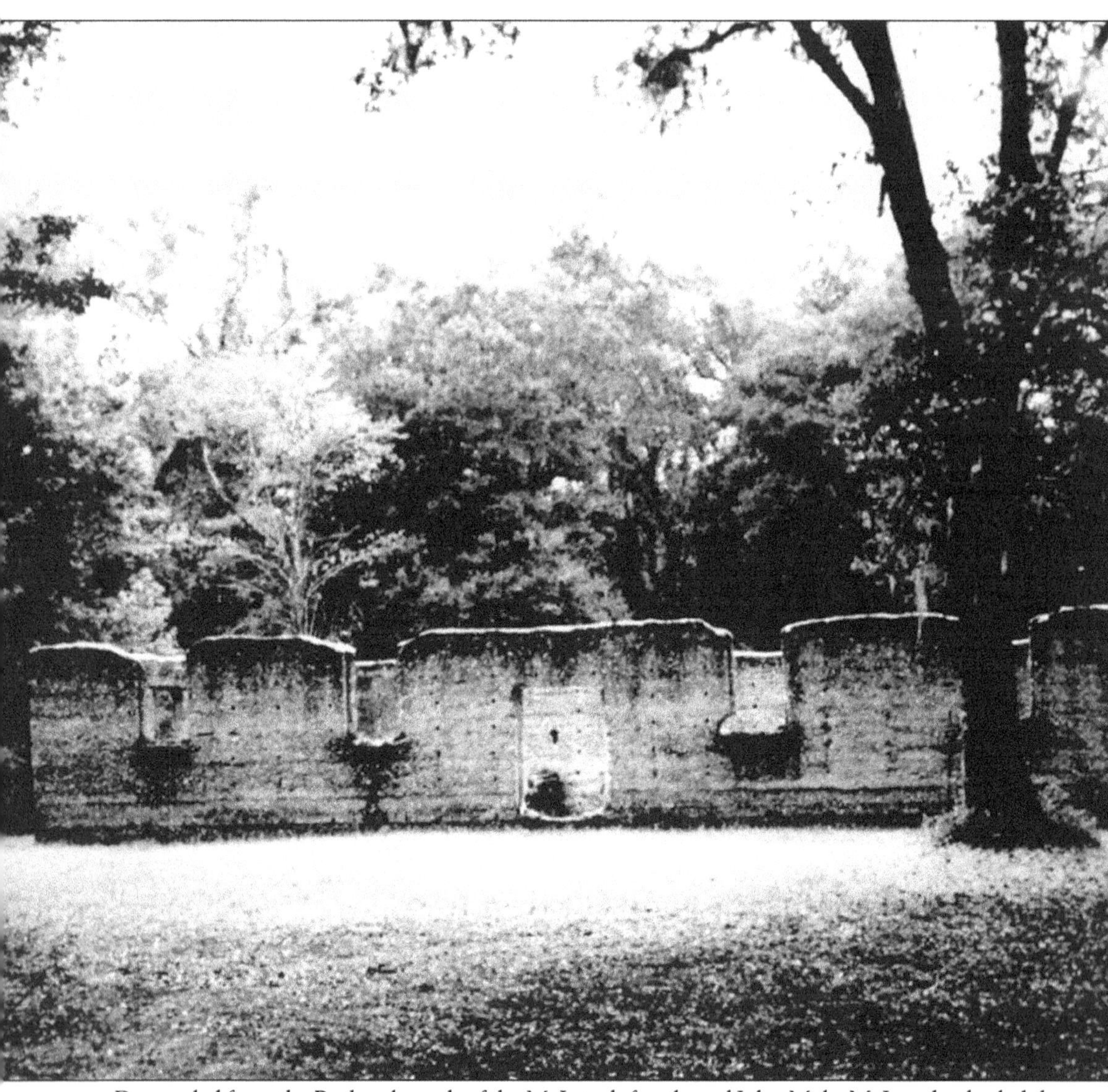

Descended from the Borlum branch of the McIntosh family and John Mohr McIntosh who led the Scot Highlanders to early Georgia, settling in Darien, John Houstoun McIntosh demonstrated a penchant for business, proved an innovative planter, and possessed great leadership ability. He was only seven years of age when his father, George, died, but only after devising land and bequeathing great wealth to his young son. Three plantations in Camden County bear the mark of John Houstoun McIntosh: Refuge, Marianna, and New Canaan Plantations. In 1792, he brought his bride, Elizabeth Bayard, to live on a 500-acre tidal rice plantation at Refuge—named for its use as sanctuary during periods of Indian raids, storms, and other threats. In Spanish East Florida, McIntosh acquired large tracts of land where he continued his planter activities and lived at Fort George Island. After being involved in a sensitive political imbroglio, McIntosh abandoned East Florida lands and removed to the St. Marys area where he built an impressive plantation home at Marianna Plantation. Not far away, he planted sugar cane at New Canaan in the vicinity of where a state commission marker stands today, as well as the tabby ruins shown in this contemporary image. (Courtesy of the Author.)

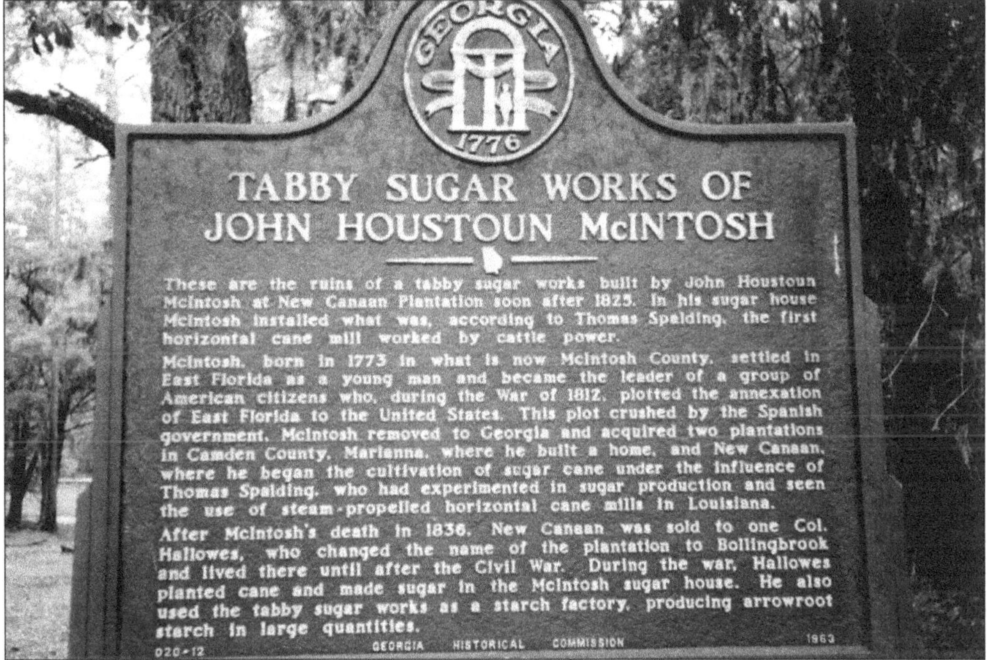

While Marianna Plantation was mostly absorbed by the development of Kings Bay Naval Submarine Base, the tabby walls of McIntosh's impressive sugar works still stand. The 14-foot-high walls surround the rectangular building, which once featured three large rooms and two porches. Dating to 1825–1826, the tabby walls were attributed in the early 20th century to a 17th-century Spanish mission site and played a key role in the "tabby mission myth" concerning ruins in McIntosh, Glynn, and Camden Counties. In the Dexter Press postcard, a "Santa Maria Mission near Kingsland, Georgia" represents an early 20th-century misidentification of McIntosh's sugar works for a mission site. McIntosh was credited with building the first animal-powered horizontal sugar mill in Georgia, and his sugar works were done on the "Spalding method," in which whole oyster shells were used, a method advocated by his first cousin and agriculturist Thomas Spalding (1774–1851) of Sapelo Island. (Courtesy of Eloise Bailey Thompson.)

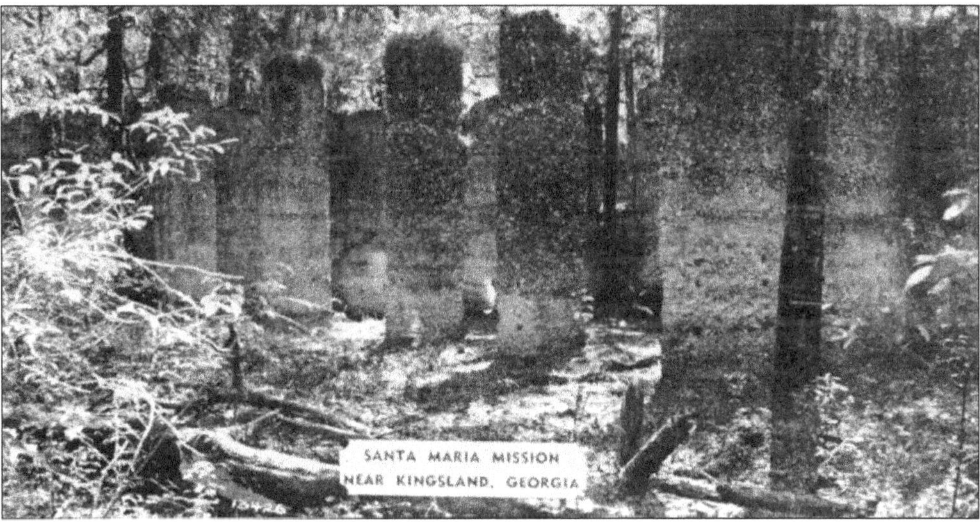

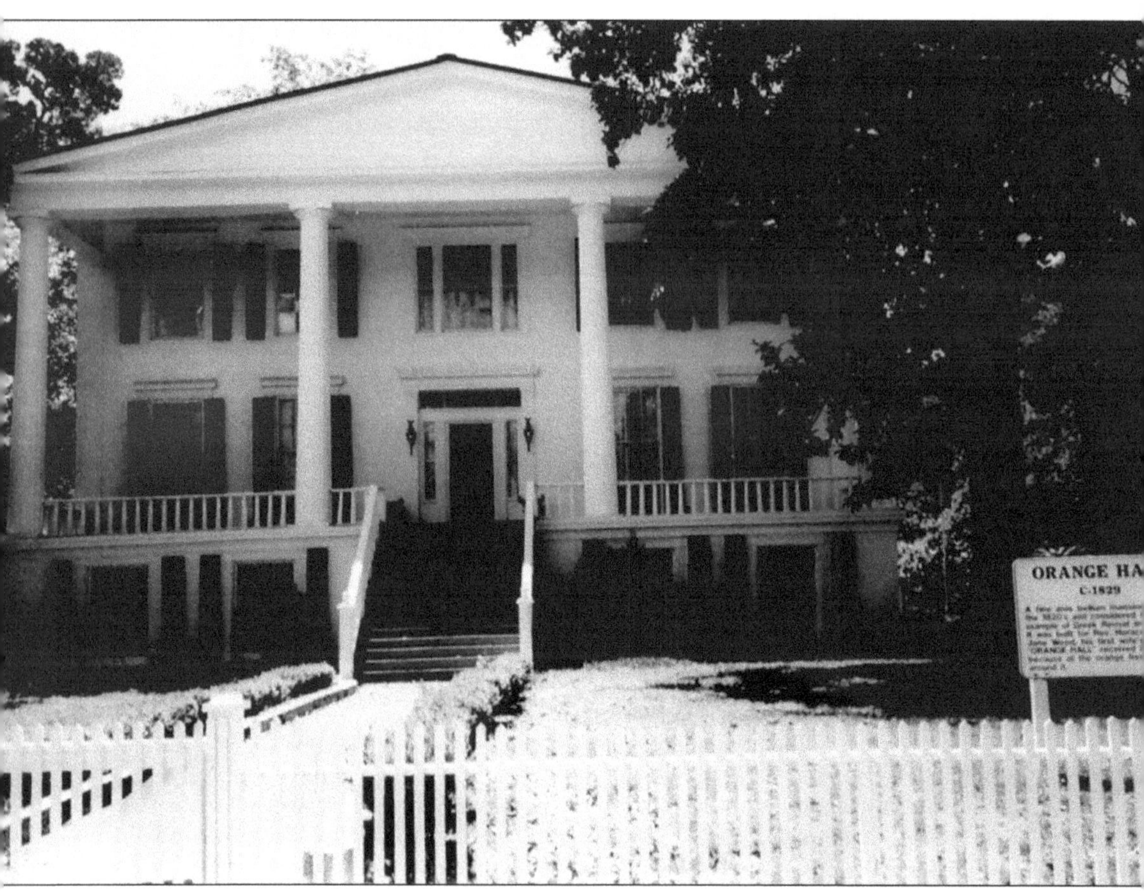

Listed on the National Register in May 1973, a restored Orange Hall welcomes both preservationists and visitors to St. Marys. This elegantly furnished, three-story Greek Revival mansion stands prominently on Block 43 in the Historic District on St. Marys "main street"—Osborne Street, dominating the setting and overlooking the Archibald Clark House. The property was granted originally to William Ashley, one of St. Marys 20 founders, and passed to Phineas Miller, Ethan Clarke, and John Wood. Wood's son-in-law Rev. Horace Pratt, pastor of the Presbyterian Church seen on page 123, has been credited with the construction of this manse, which began perhaps as early as 1829. Across the years, Orange Hall has been occupied not only by Pratt family members, but also by a number of other illustrious owners. This magnificent structure has served the community as a school, library, apartment building, and, since its loving restoration, as St. Marys Welcome Center and a house museum often hosting cultural activities, such as serving as headquarters for the annual St. Marys Candlelight Tour. Through a generous Georgia Historic Garden Grant and matching city funds, Orange Hall's landscape faces redesign, reflecting the occupancy of the J.H. Becker family from 1919 to 1925, when terraced gardens and flowering trees embellished the grand home. (Courtesy of Forrest "Frosty" Barefoot.)

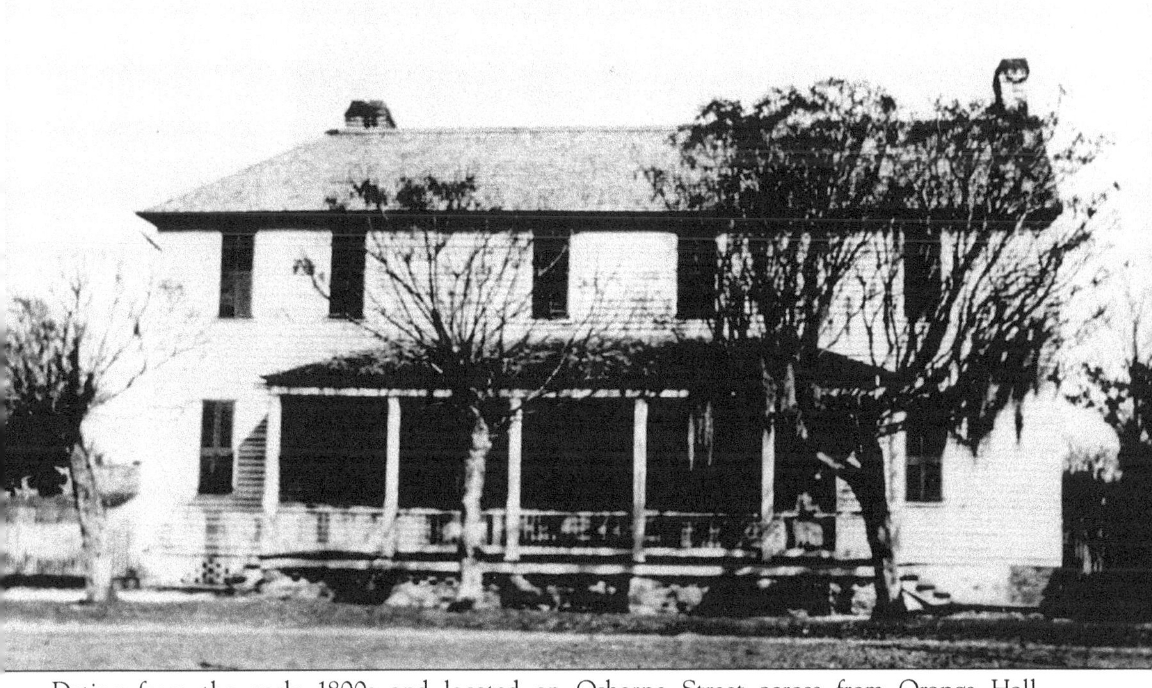

Dating from the early 1800s and located on Osborne Street across from Orange Hall, Maj. Archibald B. Clark's historic house has been occupied by four generations of the MacDonell family. Ria and A.H. MacDonell's only daughter, Catherine, lived there until her death in 1999 at age 97. In 1800, as a young attorney, Archibald Clark (1780–1848) arrived in St. Marys and, by 1807, was appointed customs collector for port of St. Marys, holding this position until his death. He served in the state militia, as a state representative for Camden County, as justice of inferior court, and as mayor of St. Marys for several years. Clark's lucrative sawmills on Spanish Creek were threatened by the British during the War of 1812, but an intrepid fighter, Capt. William Cone accompanied by 28 men successfully challenged their onslaught and overwhelming number. While fleeing authorities and spurned by Caty L. Miller of Cumberland Island, Aaron Burr visited with the Clarks in 1804. Other notable guests included Gen. Winfield Scott, who was entertained by the Clarks after his failed Florida campaign against the Seminole Indians during the Second Seminole War (1835–1842). (Courtesy of Bryan-Lang Historical Library.)

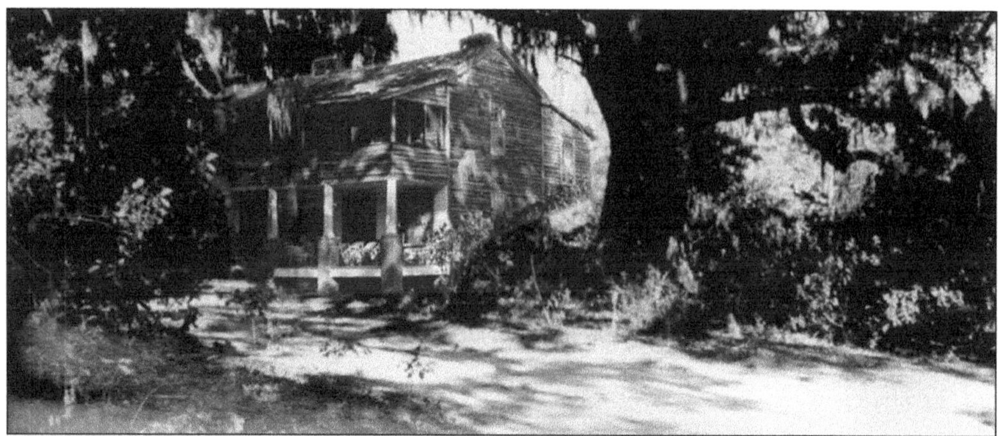

When Burwell Atkinson (1848–1931) and his wife, Ann Felder Atkinson (1775–1838), lived at Wayside Plantation they grew food crops and raised long-staple cotton. Located in the sandhill section of northwest Camden County, the Wayside Plantation House was used as a stagecoach stop, and the historic building is one of the last of its kind still standing. Supported by piers of yellow brick, hand-hewn yellow pine timbers frame a two-story structure that features a central hallway, 14-foot ceilings, two chimneys, and fireplaces for eight rooms. During a 1920s storm, the original 63-foot-long piazza was destroyed by a fallen live oak tree, and an L-shaped detached kitchen was later moved about 100 feet behind the house. The Nathaniel Lang family traded property at Hickory Hill near Muximo for Wayside, near where rumors suggested the railroad planned to lay track. Three generations of the Lang family lived there, planting big gardens of vegetables for home consumption. They raised chickens, hogs, sheep, and kept "woods cattle" that roamed before the 1940s range laws were passed by state authorities. "Uncle London" Jackson titillated the imaginations of the Lang children with his tale about an Indian attack on the old stagecoach house. (Courtesy of Jasper N. Lang.)

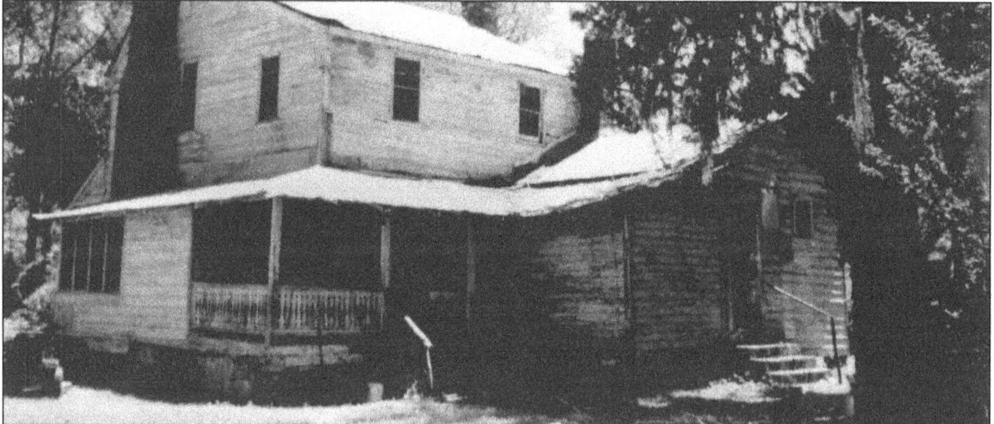

Formerly the home of the William Lang family, Cambray Plantation dates from 1820 and was established on the south side of the Satilla River near the mill village at Satilla Bluff. Built by Sheriff William Lang and his wife, Nancy Atkinson Lang (1801–1877) of Black Hammock, this two-story home remains in the Lang family, and the original owners rest in the small family graveyard on site. After her husband's untimely death in 1826 and with four children to rear, Nancy Lang successfully continued in her role as a plantation mistress and assumed greater responsibility for producing a profit through farming. Built of old growth timber and featuring hand-formed bricks, Cambray Plantation House is one of Camden's historic treasures and one of the oldest standing residences in the county. (Courtesy of Bryan-Lang Historical Library.)

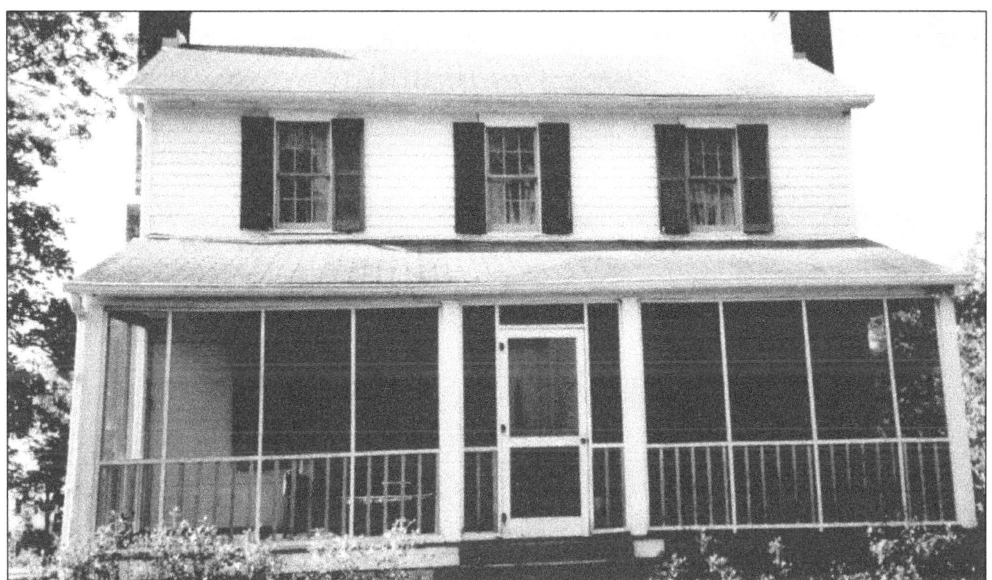

Located at the mouth of the Little Satilla River in north Camden at Hazzard's Neck, Black Hammock was granted to John Tompkins in the late 1700s as a 500-acre plantation tract. In 1800, planter Nathan Atkinson (1758–1817) acquired the property and lived there until his death. The estate was left to his children: John, Alexander, Nancy, and Edmond. Subsequently, Alexander Atkinson (1796–1840) lived and planted at Black Hammock until his ill-fated purchase in 1837 of Boggy Swamp Plantation. A number of Atkinson family members rest in the small cemetery located to the east of the plantation house, including Nathan and his son, but many ancestors of this distinguished family rest at historic Homeward Cemetery. (Courtesy of the Author.)

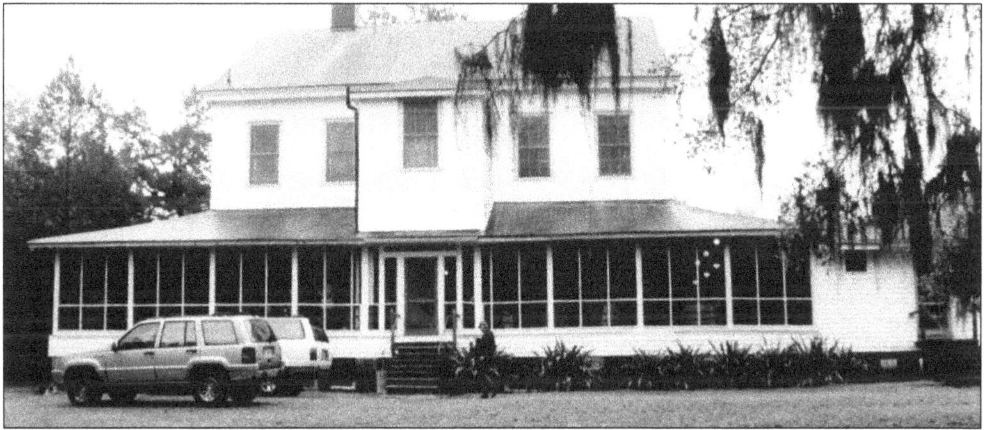

Guests have arrived at the Satilla River Club—the historic Linda Plantation, formerly home to Revolutionary War veteran West Sheffield (1747–1830) and his family. Sheffield constructed a simple log cabin and sold the property to James Fort. Ownership then passed into the King family when Fort's only daughter, Mary, married her tutor Stephen Clay King. Later, S.C. King's brother Thomas Butler King, moved south from their Massachusetts home, and married Anna Matilda Page of Retreat Plantation, St. Simons Island. The King brothers fared well and, through marriage alliances, bettered their circumstances. When Archibald Clark's daughter Louisa married James Fort King, the couple built a wood frame home, seen here, c. 1854. (Courtesy of Rodney Sheffield.)

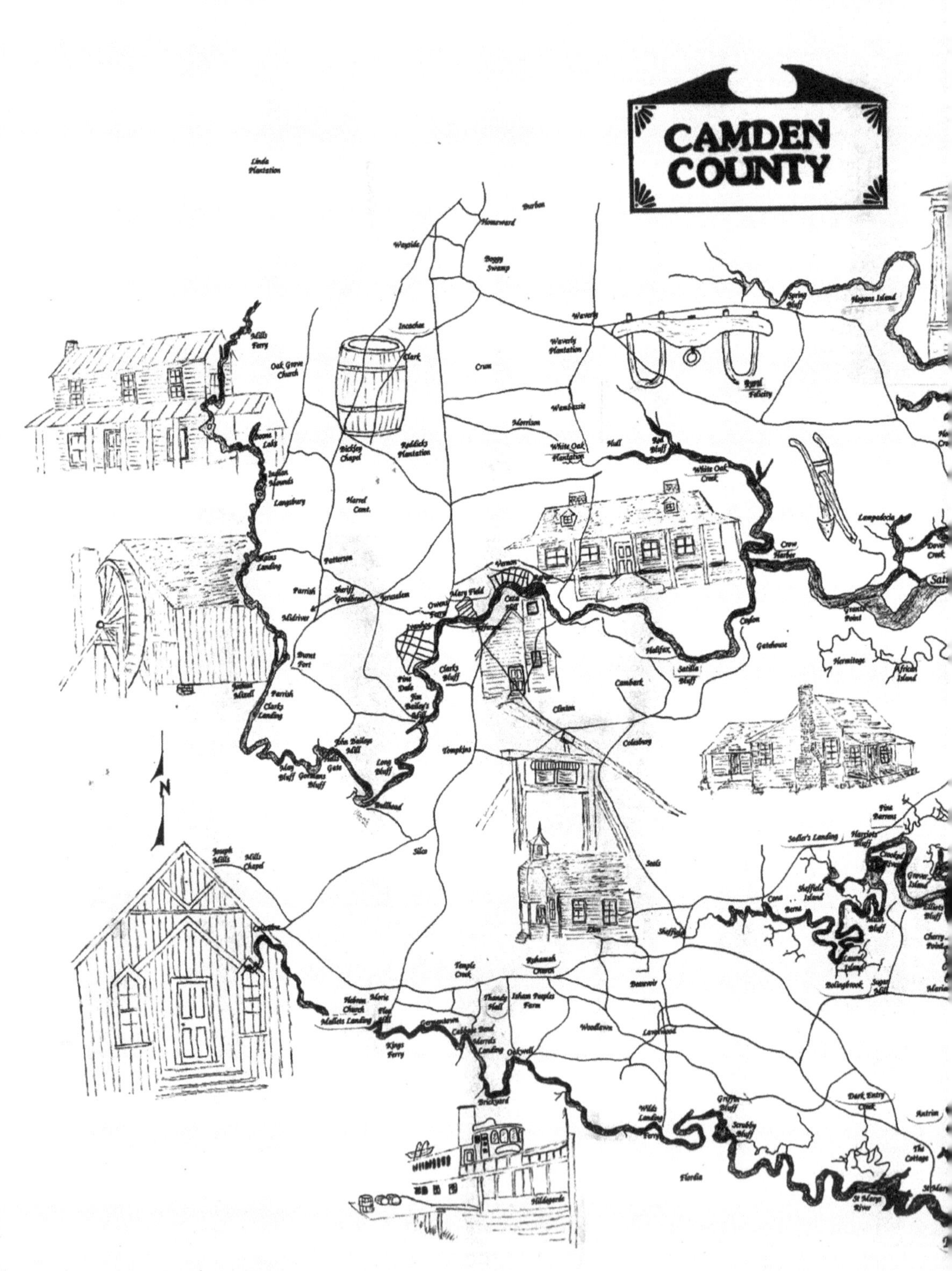
CAMDEN
COUNTY
N
Linda Plantation
Burbon
Homeward
Wayside
Boggy Swamp
Waverly
Mills Ferry
Oak Grove Church
Incachee
Clark
Crum
Waverly Plantation
Spring Bluff
Hogans Island
Ryral
Felicity
Wambassie
Morrison
Boone's Lake
Bickley Chapel
Reddicks Plantation
White Oak Plantation
Hull
Red Bluff
White Oak Creek
Indian Mounds
Langsbury
Harrel Cemt.
Patterson
Vernon
Crow Harbor
Lampadocia
Parrish
Sheriff Goodbread
Jerusalem
Owens Ferry
Mary Field
Midriver
Burnt Fort
Clarks Bluff
Pine Dale
Jim Bailey's Mill
Grants Point
Cydon
Gatehouse
Halifax
Satilla Bluff
Hermitage
African Island
Cambark
Clinton
Parrish
Clarks Landing
Colesburg
John Baileys Mill
Tompkins
Long Bluff
May Bluff
Gormans Bluff
Bullhead
Pine Barrens
Sadler's Landing
Harriots Bluff
Joseph Mills
Mills Chapel
Silco
Seals
Sheffield Island
Cona
Berne
Grover Island
Elliotts Bluff
Cherry Point
Laurel Island
Bolingbrook
Sugar Mill
Sheffield
Zion
Temple Creek
Rehamah Church
Beauvoir
Hebron Church
Morie
Mallets Landing
Thandy Hall
Isham Peoples Farm
Woodlawn
Germantown
Cabbage Bend
Kings Ferry
Marrels Landing
Oakwell
Brickyard
Wilds Landing
Ferry
Griffin Bluff
Scrubby Bluff
Dark Entry Creek
Antrim
The Cottage
Flordia
St Marys River
Hildegarde

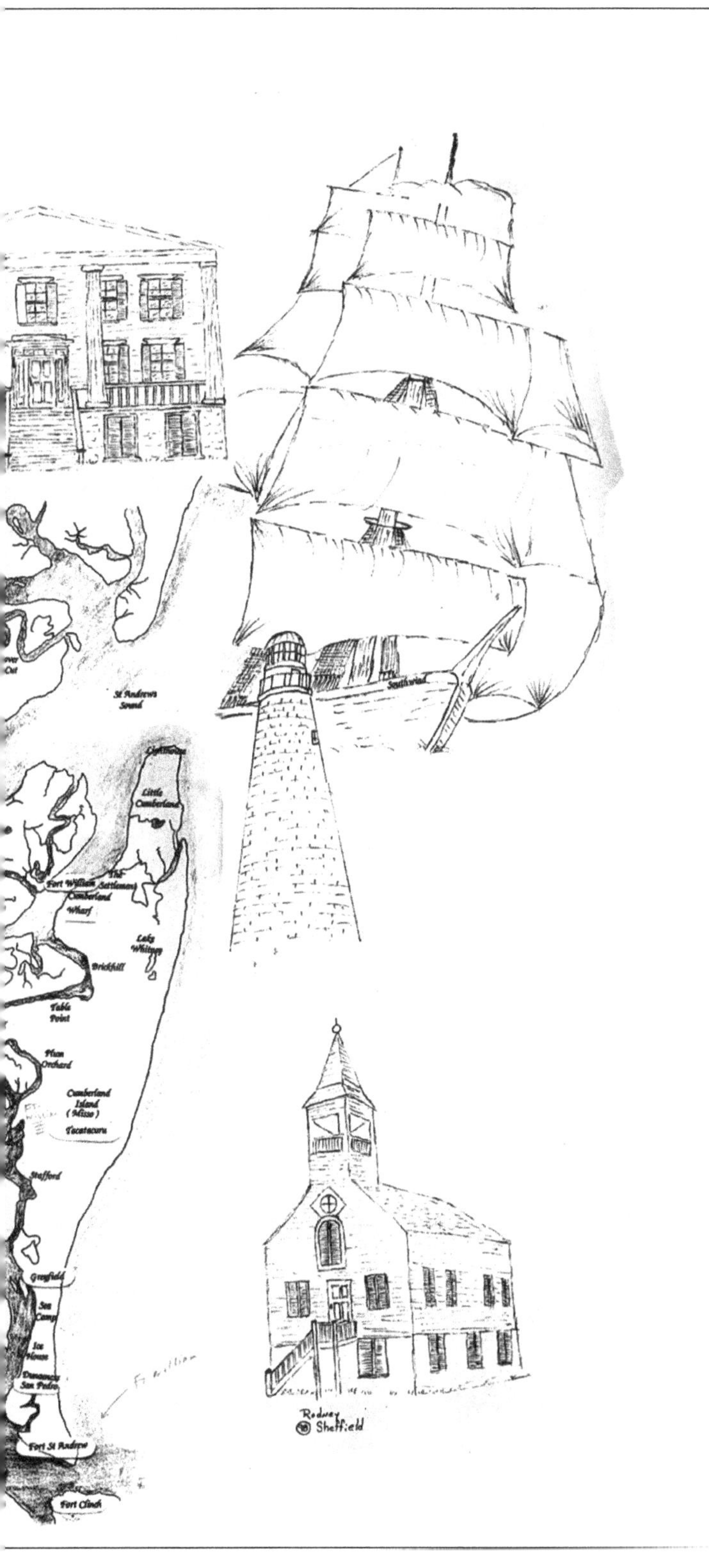

Drawn from a wellspring of knowledge about southeast Georgia history, artist Rodney Sheffield's map provides an overview of the county and the antebellum era when over 70 plantation sites spread across Camden. He traced the map and embellished it with an estimate of roadways and with fanciful tracings of the historic structures that grace the landscape, such as St. Marys Orange Hall and the Little Cumberland Island Lighthouse (upper right), the old Refuge Plantation House (center), historic churches, the steamer *Hildegarde*, and a gristmill, this map suggests the richness of Camden's history. Dramatic etchings of the three primary river corridors—the Little Satilla River, the Satilla River, and the St. Marys River—frame this original Georgia county. (Courtesy of Rodney Sheffield.)

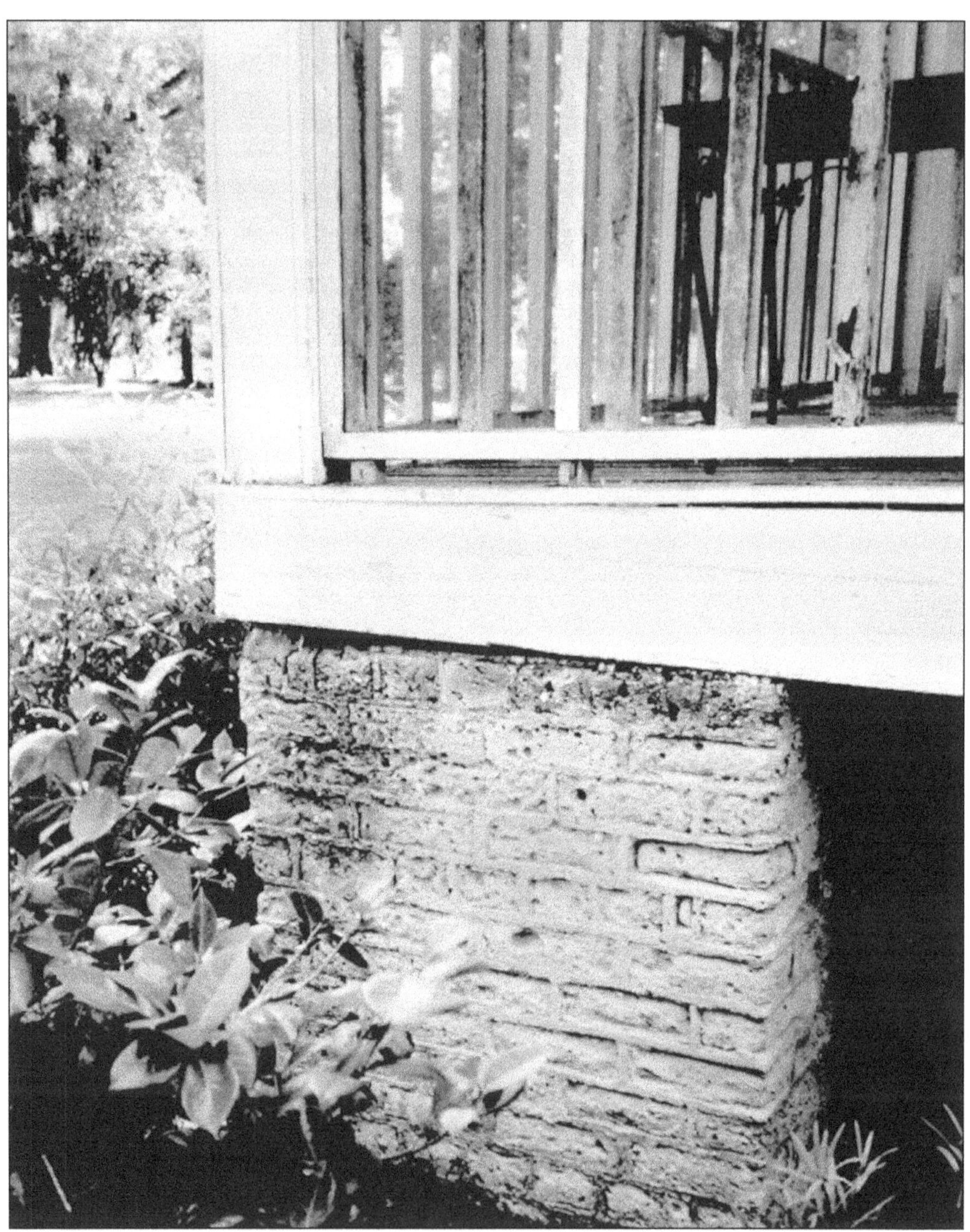

What a laborious task to produce the tabby bricks used for foundation pillars, seen in this image. Gathered from Indian shell middens, oyster shells were burned in a lime rick and the resulting product, calcium carbonate or lime, was mixed with sand, water, and more oyster shells to produce this coastal concrete, or tabby. Although tabby ruins dot the coastal landscape and fascinate historians, in general, it is unusual to find bricks made of tabby. This handsome two-story, plain-style wood frame home was built of the finest timbers by the Atkinson family in whose possession this property remained until the 1940s when Mr. and Mrs. W.C. Kirby Jr. purchased the property and restored the home. One of Camden's historic treasures, Black Hammock House may be the oldest standing residence in Camden County. (Courtesy of the Author.)

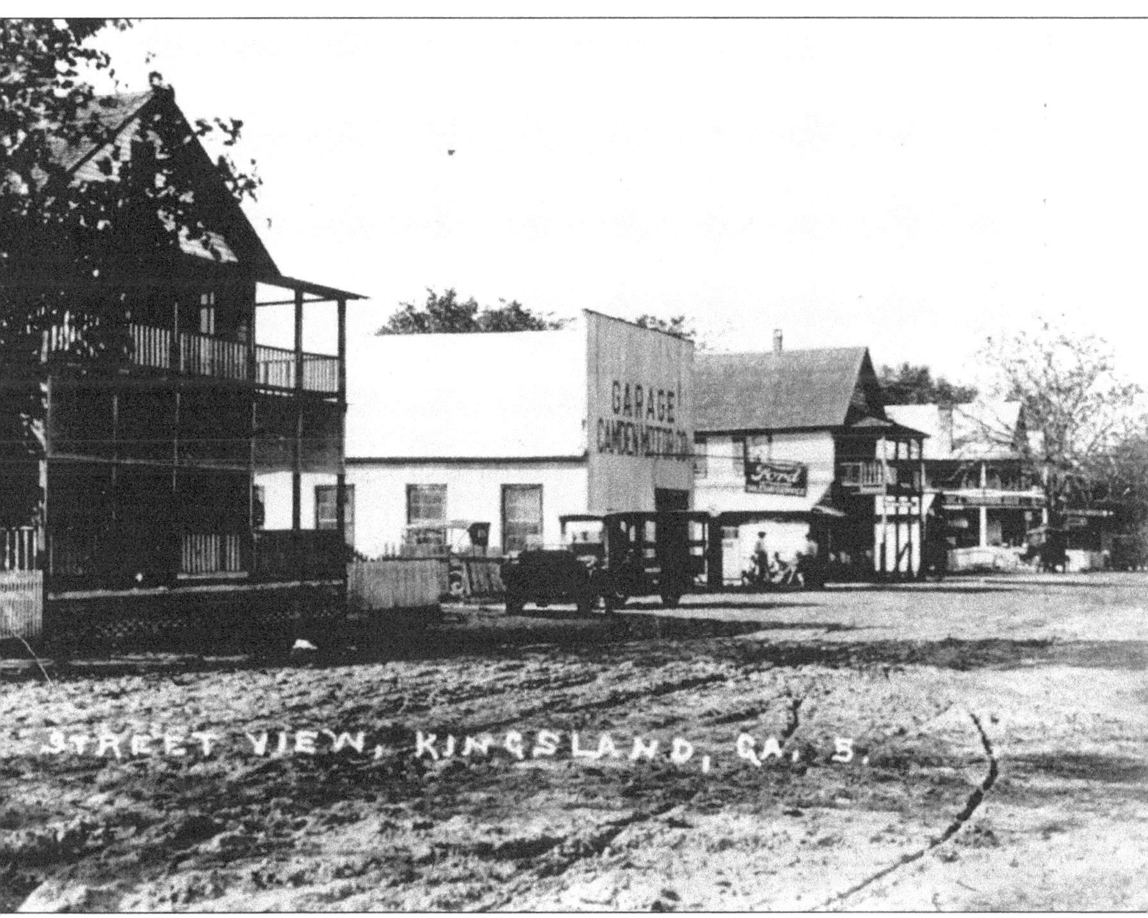

Taken in the 1920s, Kingsland's "main street" view provides a window on the downtown's former circumstances when businesses were situated on Railroad Avenue close to the tracks. Located on a dirt rutted Railroad Avenue, just west of the railroad between William and King Streets, glimpse the Old Dixie Highway built in 1912 which led from Maine to Miami. In this image are, from left to right, the two-story wood frame H.F. Whildon home; the Camden Ford Motor Company Garage, owned and operated by H.F. Whildon and formerly located near the present State Highway 40 railroad crossing; W.H. Peeples' Store; and the Hotel Kingsland. (Courtesy of Maxine Wells.)

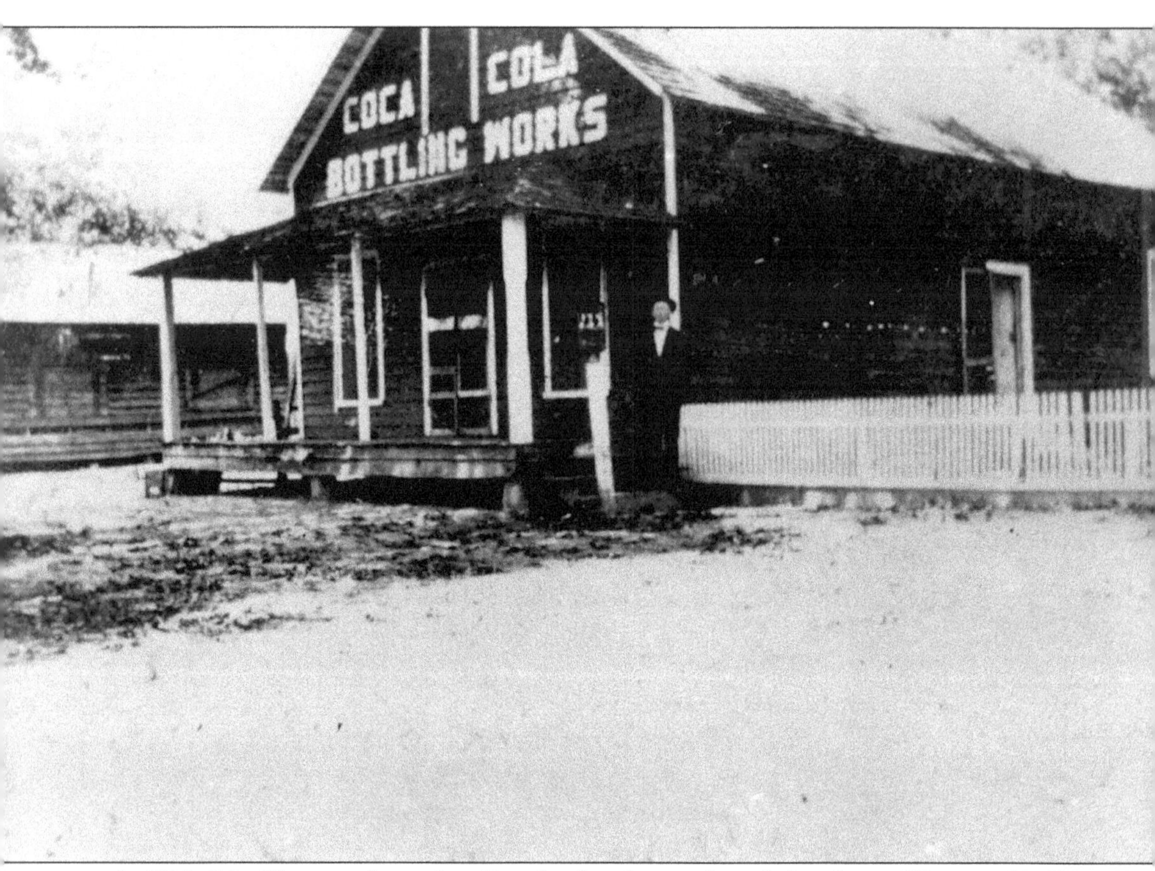

In 1915, Q.L. Claxton relocated to Kingsland and opened a sub-franchise of Brunswick's Coca-Cola Company. In 1920, Kingsland's Coca-Cola Bottling Works was located on Railroad Avenue and offered refreshing sodas and employment for young men in the Kingsland area. By 1927 Claxton's franchise was not renewed, and the Bottling Works became Claxton Bottling Works, which bottled and sold a variety of cola drinks and soda waters until ceasing operation in 1953. Standing in front of his business, Q.L. Claxton, proprietor, proudly poses for the cameraman and contributes to the visual history of the City of Royal Treatment. (Courtesy of Eloise Bailey Thompson.)

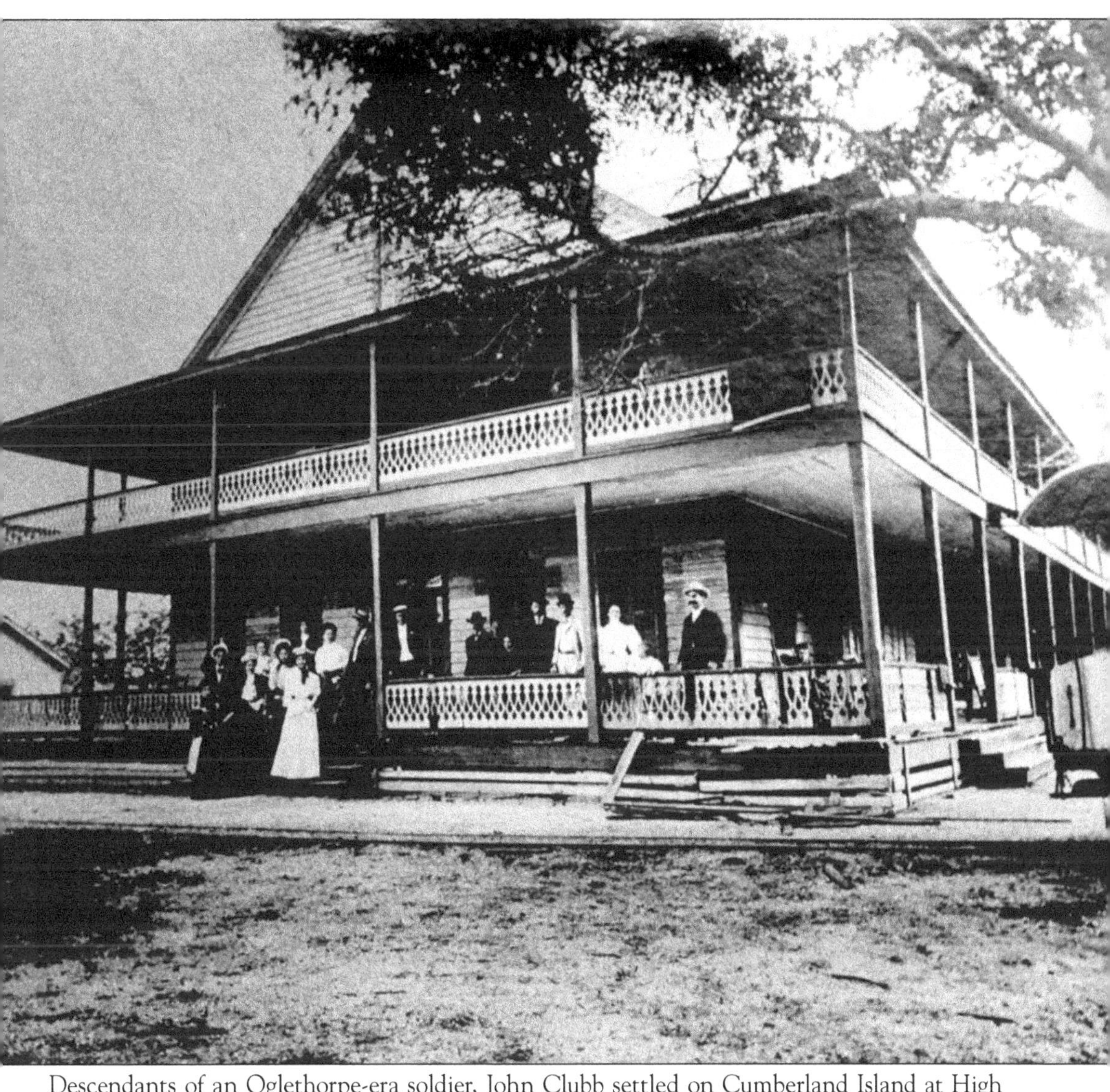

Descendants of an Oglethorpe-era soldier, John Clubb settled on Cumberland Island at High Point where some of the men engaged in seafaring activities. James and William Clubb served as harbor pilots through a treacherous St. Andrew's Sound. James's claim to fame derived from piloting, at gunpoint, the infamous *Wanderer* in 1859 into the south end of Jekyll Island, landing the last cargo of enslaved Africans transported to North America. He served a stint as lightkeeper and captained several of the steamers plying the Cumberland Route. Passengers seeking "restful pleasure" stayed at the Oriental House operated as a seaside resort in the 1870s by James Clubb and later his son Elias. Subsequently, the name was changed to High Point House, and its expansion followed the demand for roomier accommodations. Praised by the world traveling and irrepressible Miss Mary Miller (1903–1999) in several of her books, the Cumberland Island Hotel, seen here, ushered in coastal Georgia's golden resort era. Innkeepers catered to guests who swam, seined, crabbed, gigged for flounder, fished, hunted, played billiards, and relaxed on a beautiful beach. Times changed, and in 1918, the executors of the W.R. Bunkley estate sold the property at public auction in St. Marys. (Courtesy of Eloise Bailey Thompson.)

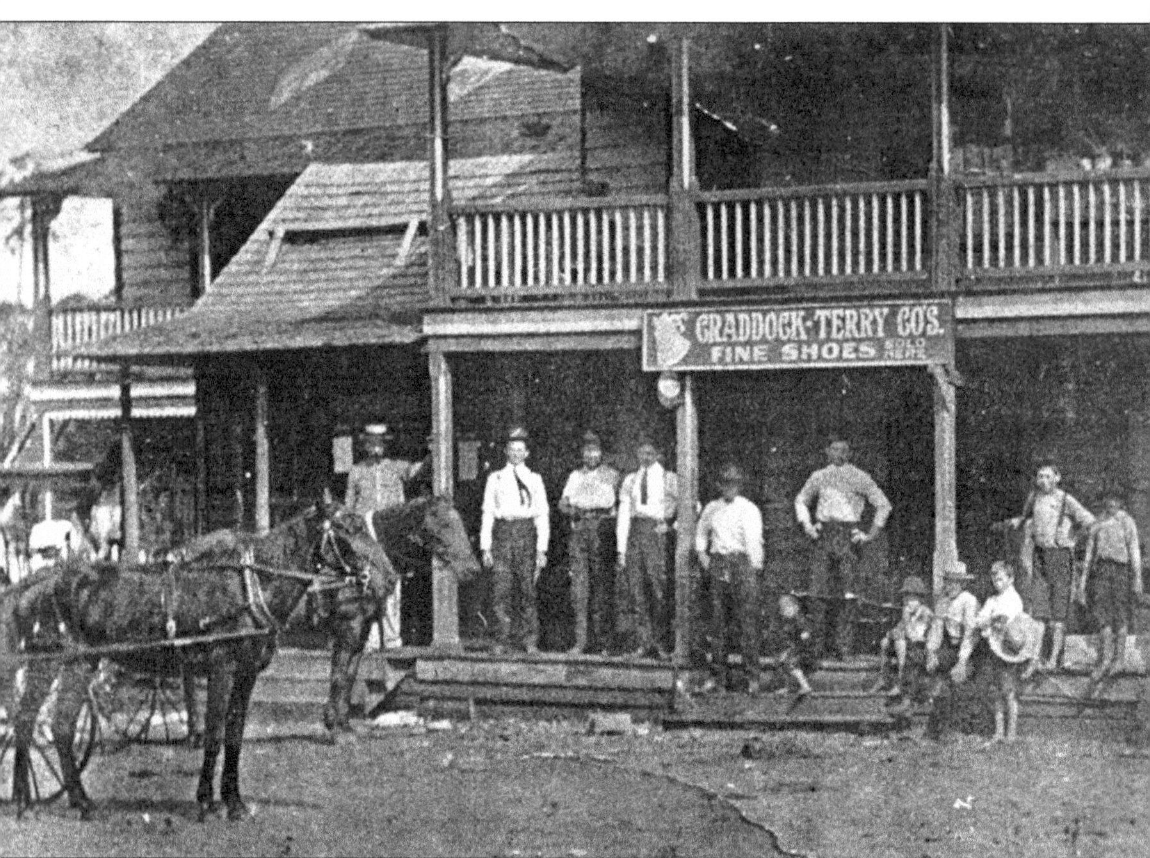

Townspeople have gathered at Sheffield's General Merchandise Store located on the northwest corner of Railroad Avenue and King Street. The cameraman captured this image about 1908 when horse-drawn buggies provided a major means of transportation. Part owner S.C. Sheffield, with hands on his hips, stands directly under the sign advertising fine shoes. Sporting a watch fob and white beard, his prosperous father (far right), Cam Sheffield (1841–1912), leans against a supporting porch column, above which hangs an upper-story balcony. The small boy standing far right and below Sheffield was a young J. Nolan Wells (1900–1963). He worked 30 years for Seaboard Airline Railway, built Camden's first movie theatre in Kingsland in 1942, and was politically active on a local and state level. (Courtesy of Maxine Wells and Rodney Sheffield.)

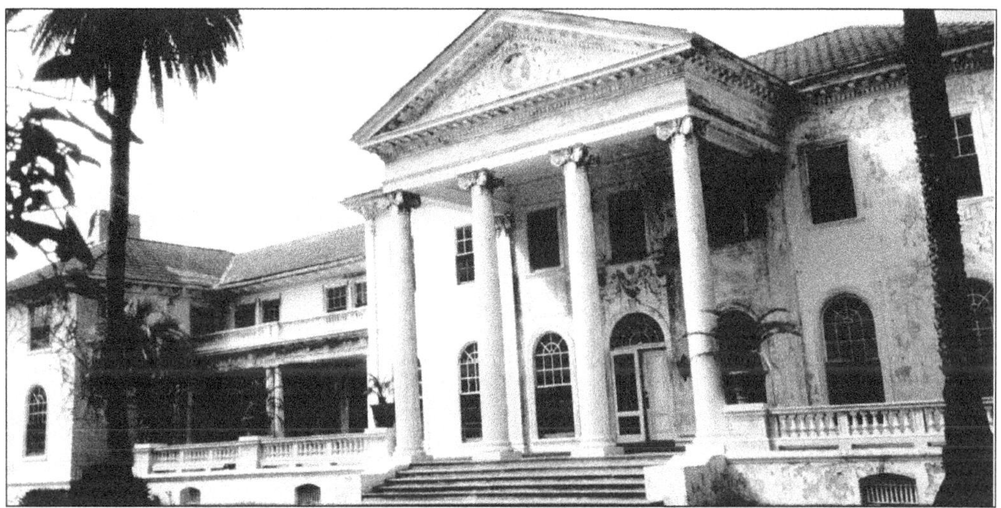

After building the Dungeness mansion, Lucy Coleman Carnegie (1846–1916) continued with construction projects on Cumberland Island, building homes for her children—Greyfield, a three-storied mansion, and the Cottage, a 29-room home. Stafford Place plantation had been given to another son. Designed by the Boston architectural firm of Peabody and Stearns, Plum Orchard was built in 1898. George Lauder Carnegie and Margaret Thaw celebrated their marriage in the mansion in the same year. Located nine miles north of the elder Mrs. Carnegie's Dungeness mansion, "Plum" was constructed as a square to which wings were added in 1906. Recognized as one of the finest examples of Georgian Revival–style architecture in America, Plum Orchard poses challenging preservation concerns for the National Park Service, and current work continues stabilization while government authorities determine the fate of an architectural treasure and the Carnegie's legacy. (Courtesy of the Author.)

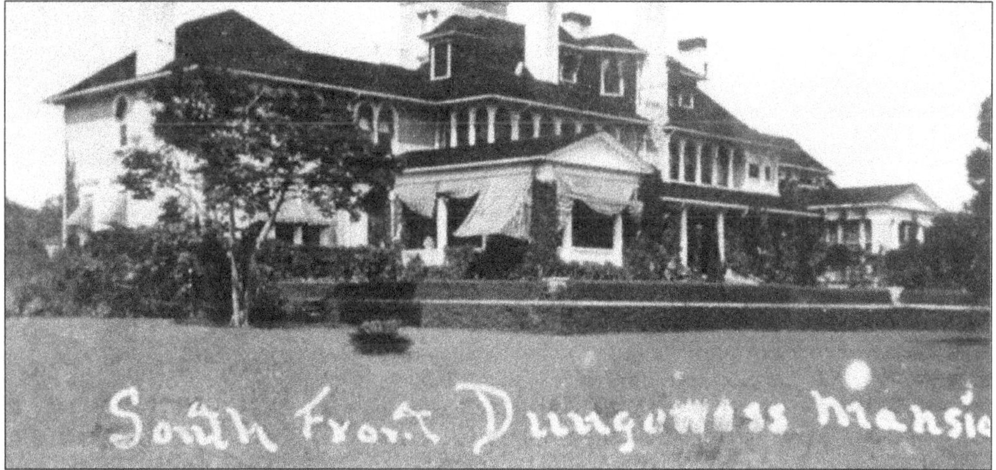

In the following two images, the fabled Dungeness dominates its south Cumberland setting. Planned by Thomas Morrison Carnegie (1843–1886) and completed by his widow, Lucy Coleman Carnegie, the 44-room mansion was enjoyed by the family until it was vacated in 1925. Subsequently, poachers and trespassers posed threats to the Carnegie holdings, and on June 24, 1959 an arsonist responded in fiery ways to a May 1959 encounter with a gamekeeper. Islanders were unable to save this grand Victorian-era home, and engulfed in flames, Dungeness tragically burned. Today, visitors to Cumberland Island National Seashore can walk the Main Road/Grand Avenue to view the ruins of Dungeness. (Courtesy of Herbert Rowland.)

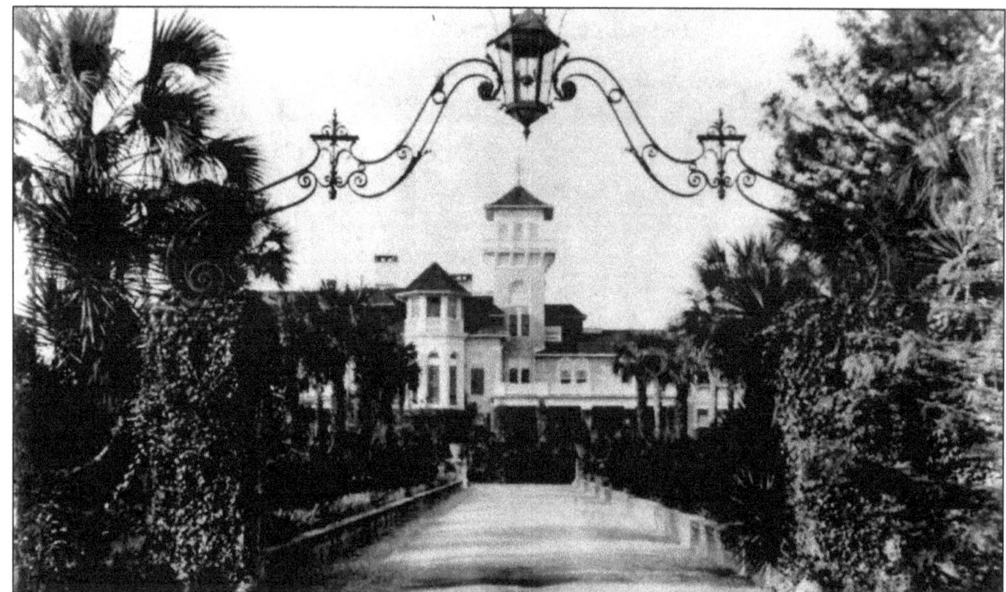

Seen in its heyday, Dungeness tower rises 100 feet into the sky, and Carnegie family, friends, and visitors enter this magical world through imposing wrought-iron gates. Possessed of fortunes made from coal and iron manufacturing interests in Pennsylvania, the Thomas Morrison Carnegies married in June 1866. They made their home in Pittsburgh where their nine children were born: William, Frank, Andrew II, Margaret, Thomas, George, Florence, Coleman, and Nancy. Later, they acquired property on Cumberland Island's south end, where the vivacious Caty Greene Miller formerly lived, and created their own Dungeness, expanded and elaborated to an Italianate style after the senior Carnegie's death. (Courtesy of Eloise Bailey Thompson.)

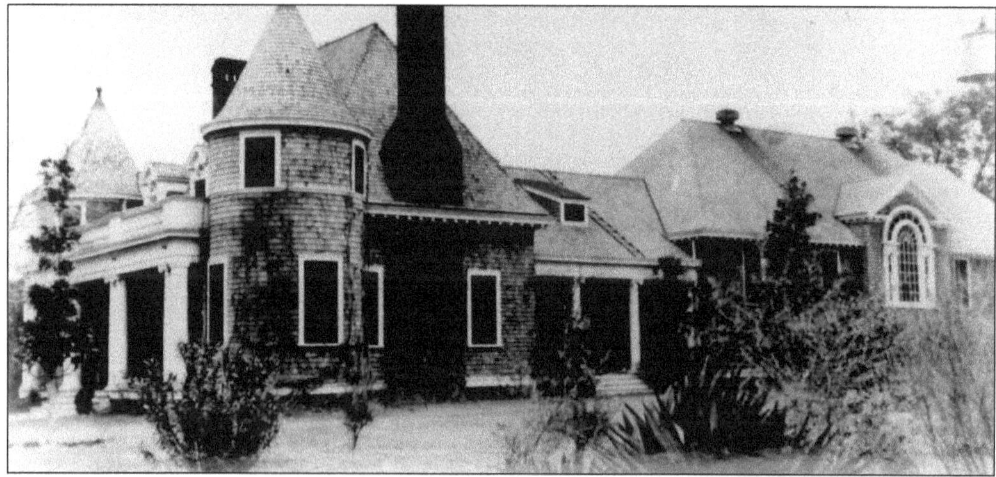

Designed by New York architect John W. Ingle, the Carnegie's poolhouse dates from 1900, and although in ruins today, was built in the popular Victorian-era Queen Anne style; construction was supervised by contractor James McGiffin at a projected cost of $10,000. Located near Dungeness mansion, this imposing structure was of wood frame, 150 feet in length with flanking turrets, clad with cedar shingles, and provided the following amenities: heated tile swimming pool, steamroom, baths, recreation room, and squash court. Guest rooms were situated on the second floor and the poolhouse/playhouse served as a "bachelor's house" for Carnegie's sons. (Courtesy of Eloise Bailey Thompson.)

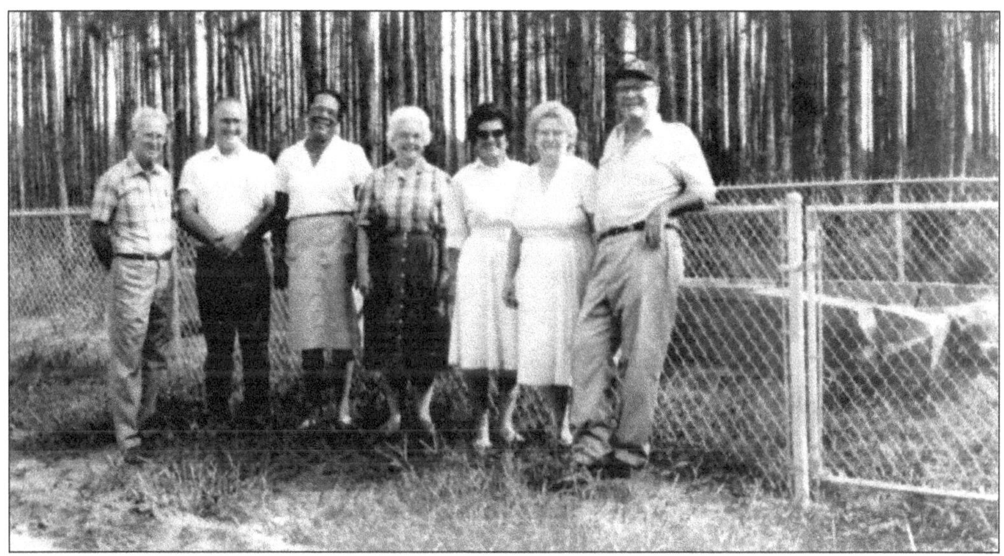

In July 1986 members of the Camden County Historical Commission, Guale Historical Society, and Camden County Commissioner E.B. Herrin (second from left) stand beside one of two cow dipping vats remaining in Camden. Through partnering preservation interests, the cow dipping vat on the Bullhead Bluff Road was cleaned out and fenced. Camden County constructed 40 of these oblong concrete vats, costing $120 each, in the early 20th century when the dread Texas Tick Fever devastated the Georgia cattle industry with a $6.5 million loss. On July 1, 1906, federal authorities initiated a quarantine program in 985 counties throughout the affected states. Shown here, from left to right, Henry Williams, Herrin, Edna Armstrong, Virginia Proctor, Bebe C. Williams, Dolly Horne, and Howard Horne stand near the vat on the Bullhead Bluff Road located west of Woodbine. (Courtesy of Eloise Bailey Thompson.)

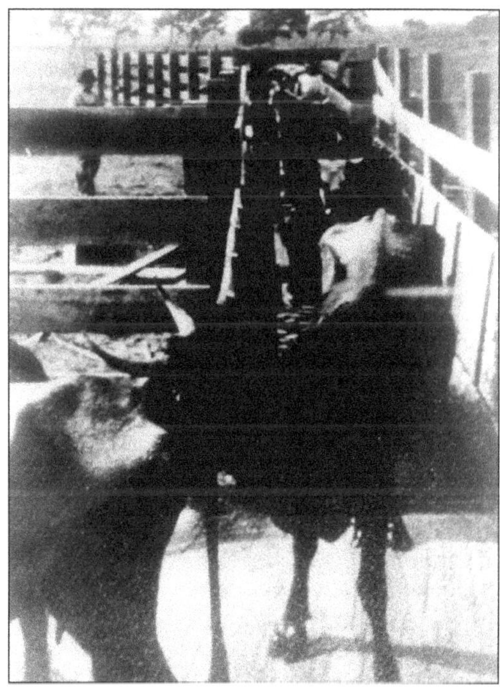

Prior to the 1940s range laws, cattle roamed freely throughout Camden County. For this reason, in the early 1900s, a massive tick eradication program targeted those pesky, disease-bearing arthropods. In 1914, the first cattle vat or tank was operated at the Refuge Plantation where 50 local cattlemen assembled to observe the procedure of herding cattle through a wooden chute, down into a vat with a ramp or steps leading out into another chute. To combat this ravaging parasite that produced bloody urine, or "red water fever," cattle were dipped every 14 to 30 days from April through September. Camden County's precarious position as a border state confronted the hesitancy of Florida authorities to implement quarantine; that state's eradication program began in 1923. Seen in this image is a cow dipping vat on Cumberland Island where a dipping vat was used at Stafford by 1913. (Courtesy of Eloise Bailey Thompson.)

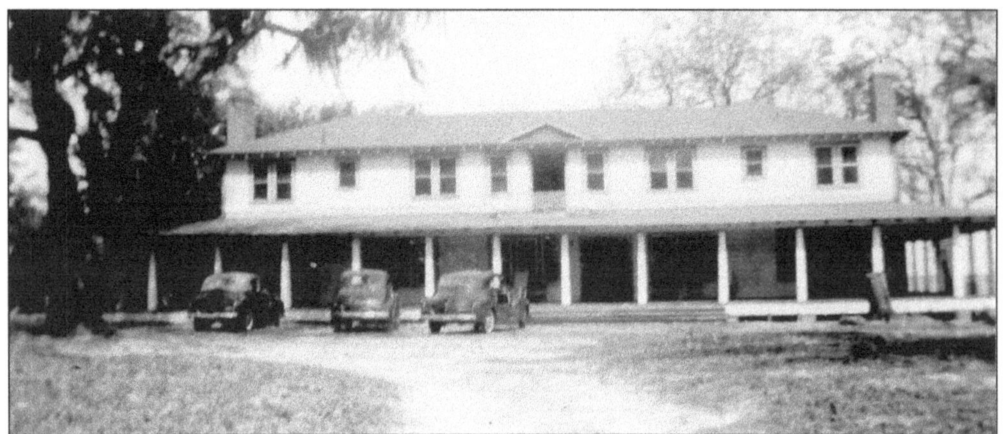

Seen in a 1940s-era image, the Crooked River Club overlooked the winding river that gave the private club its name. The two-story clubhouse featured a wrap-around porch, 14-15 bedrooms, and a large dining room and den suitable for entertaining parties of 25 or more. Names associated with its ownership include Waycross, Macon, and Tifton families such as the Hiers, Moodys, and Blalocks. They hunted for the clacking clapper rails, or marsh hens, and fished the inshore waters of the beautiful Crooked River. For many years, Rosalie Readdick (1897–1977) managed the club. After it was torn down, Marianna Club House was moved to the site in the 1970s from Kings Bay. Located on property adjacent to the Crooked River State Park (which is administered by the Georgia Department of Natural Resources), the former Marianna Club House today serves as a private residence. (Courtesy of Helen R. Peeples.)

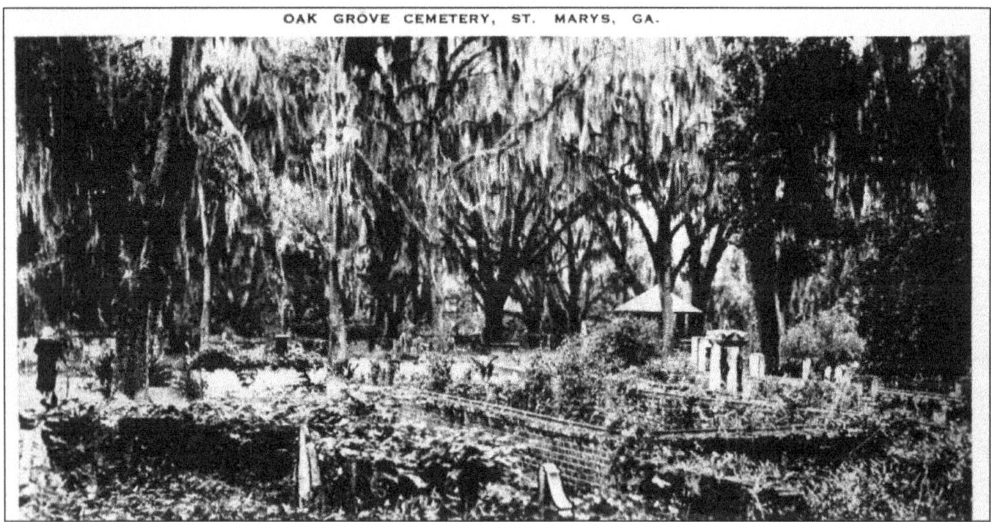

An E.C. Kropp Company postcard captured a scene at the historic Oak Grove Cemetery, established *c.* 1788, in St. Marys Historic District. In this peaceful setting, the men and women whose lives contributed to the richness of Camden's past rest amidst moss-draped live oaks, wrought-iron fencing, and charming funerary art. Within the walled "tomb of the Acadians" cemetery visitors find the resting spot of early Camden settlers with surnames such as Desclaux, Cormie, Vocelle, Carbon, and Comeau. The plight of James Vocelle's paternal great-great grandmother Marguerite Carbon Comeau suggests a tale of the French-speaking Acadians' banishment from Nova Scotia in July 1755. Separated from her parents, Marguerite wandered to Santo Domingo where she fled a bloody rebellion to Charleston, South Carolina and eventually to the seaport town of St. Marys. (Courtesy of Eloise Bailey Thompson.)

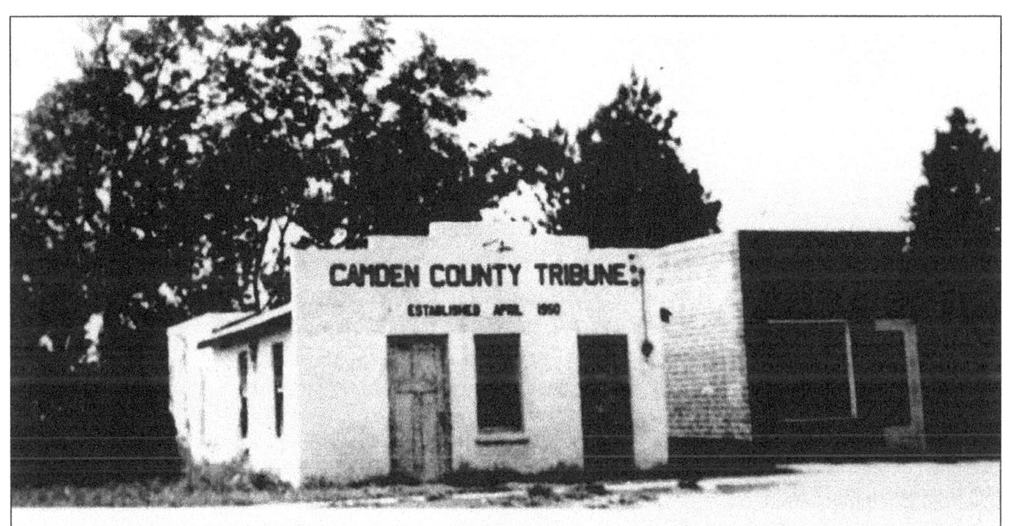

The *Camden County Tribune* began in St. Marys as a weekly newspaper when the April 14, 1950 edition rolled off the press. Published by R. Ward Harrison Sr. and his son Kenneth L. Harrison, the paper competed with Camden's oldest established newspaper, *The Southeast Georgian*. The *Tribune* was sold in December 1977. Today a merged weekly paper—*Camden County Tribune & The Southeast Georgian*—is owned by Community Newspapers, Inc. of Spartanburg, South Carolina. Carrying forth the old *Tribune's* motto "Newspapers get things done!" the newspaper's staff is "dedicated to truth, integrity, loyalty, quality and hard work." (Courtesy of St. Marys Woman's Club.)

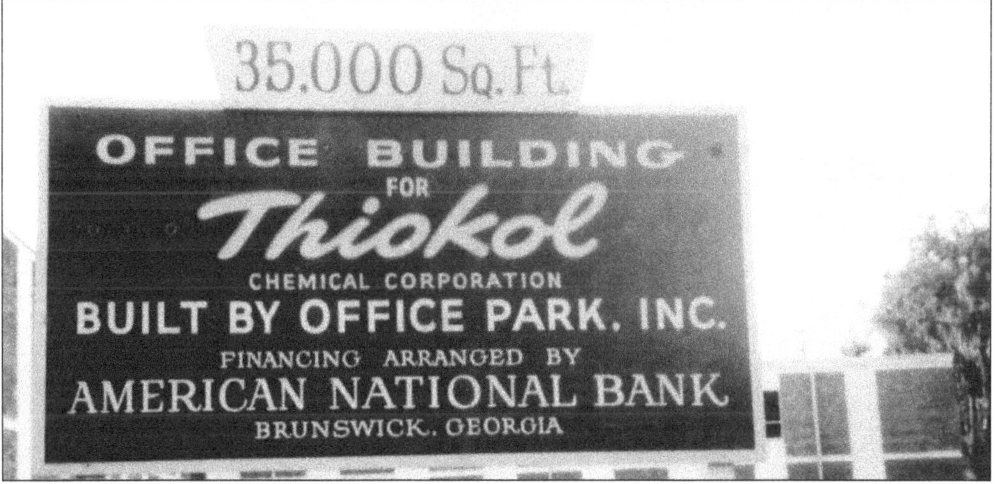

In the mid-1960s, Thiokol Chemical Corporation tantalized coastal Georgians with prospects for a share in NASA's space program. Headquartered in Brunswick-Glynn County at the Office Park Building constructed for the firm at 1803 Gloucester Street, the Camden County division purchased approximately 7,000 acres at Floyd's Neck. Deep in Camden woods, Thiokol Chemical Corporation produced solid propellant rocket motors, an innovation for the period. In January 1965 the company suffered cutbacks due to President Lyndon B. Johnson's "tight-money" policy, and this foreshadowed the future. On February 3, 1971 one of the greatest tragedies to occur in coastal Georgia history happened. A magnesium flare assembly building exploded, killing 29 dedicated employees of the plant and irretrievably embedding the name "Thiokol" in the memory of coastal Georgians. (Courtesy of Hugh K. Tollison.)

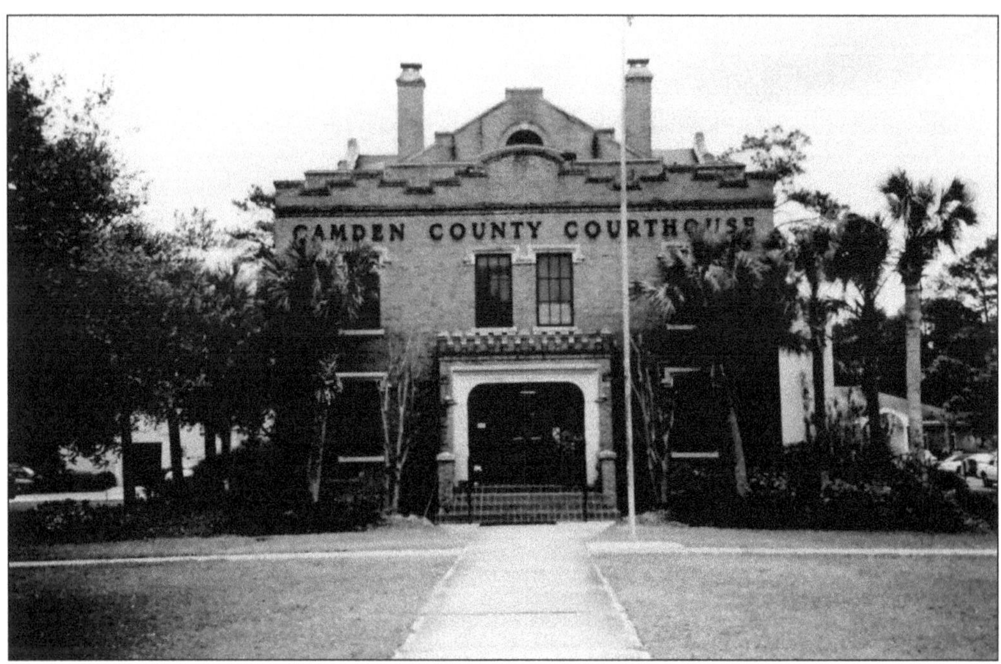

Laid out in 1908 on a grid pattern encompassing 15 blocks, Woodbine's 20th-century plan conforms to a "railroad strip community" type. The railroad, now gone, bisected the center of the community plan and a main road (Bedell Avenue) ran parallel to the railroad tracks. Within this context, a community landmark building was constructed in response to moving the county seat in 1923 from St. Marys to Woodbine. Previously undeveloped land east of Bedell Avenue was platted for a courthouse square with four streets intersecting the square. The historic Camden County Courthouse was designed by Julian de Bruyn Kops (1862–1942) and completed in 1928. This imposing structure represents the Late Gothic Revival style of architecture, featuring shaped parapets with battlements, drip-mold window crowns, and a front portico with castellations. When the imposing, grand and new Camden County Courthouse opens in 2004, this old historic courthouse will continue serving the needs of county government. (Courtesy of Bryan-Lang Historical Library.)

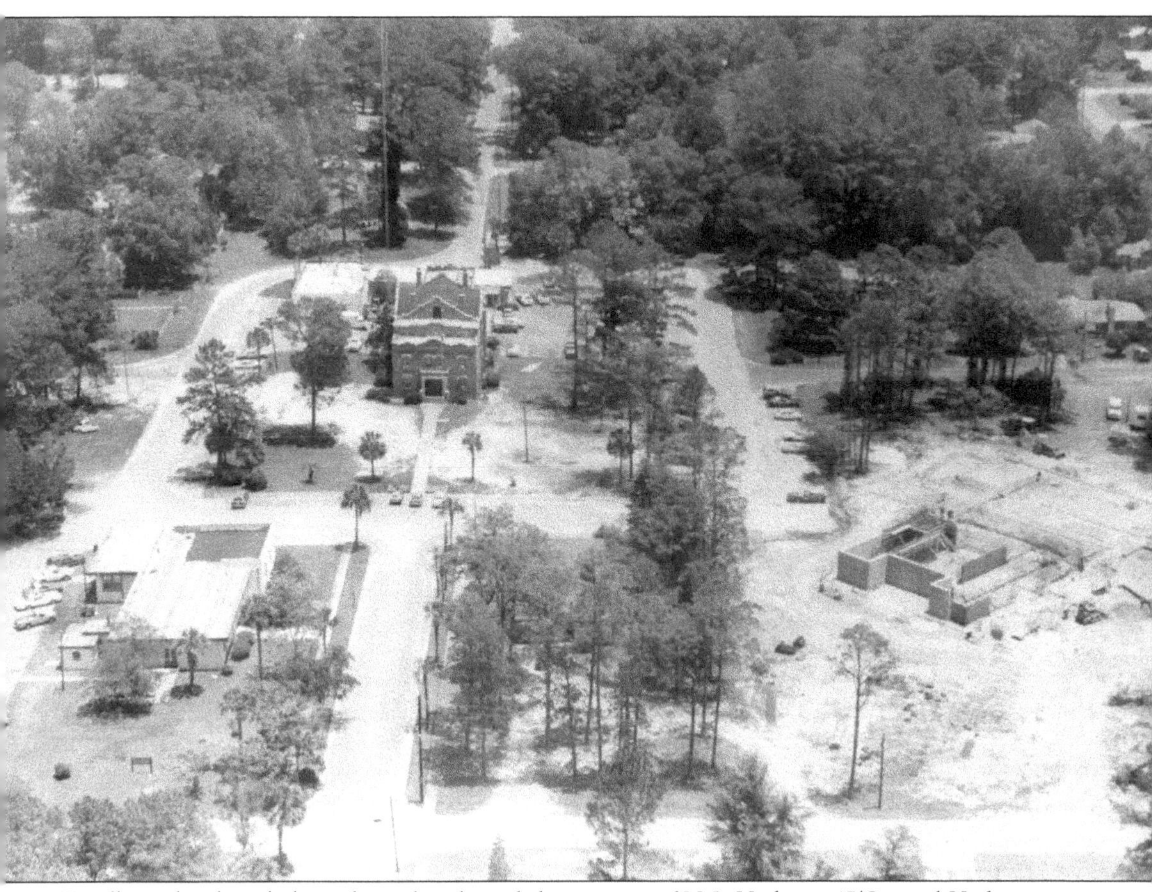

Woodbine developed along the railroad until the coming of U.S. Highway 17/Coastal Highway. With the relocation of the county seat from St. Marys in 1923, previously undeveloped land east of Bedell Avenue was platted to function as a courthouse square to which the grid pattern was extended. All roads lead to the historic Camden County Courthouse seen in the center of a 1987 image. At bottom left, a sign indicates the future Bryan-Lang Historical Library, the vision of Miss Bebe Lang, and whose construction was made possible through county support and a grassroots effort from coastal Georgia's preservation community. On the right, the Camden County Public Safety Complex was under construction. (Courtesy of *Camden County Tribune & The Southeast Georgian.*)

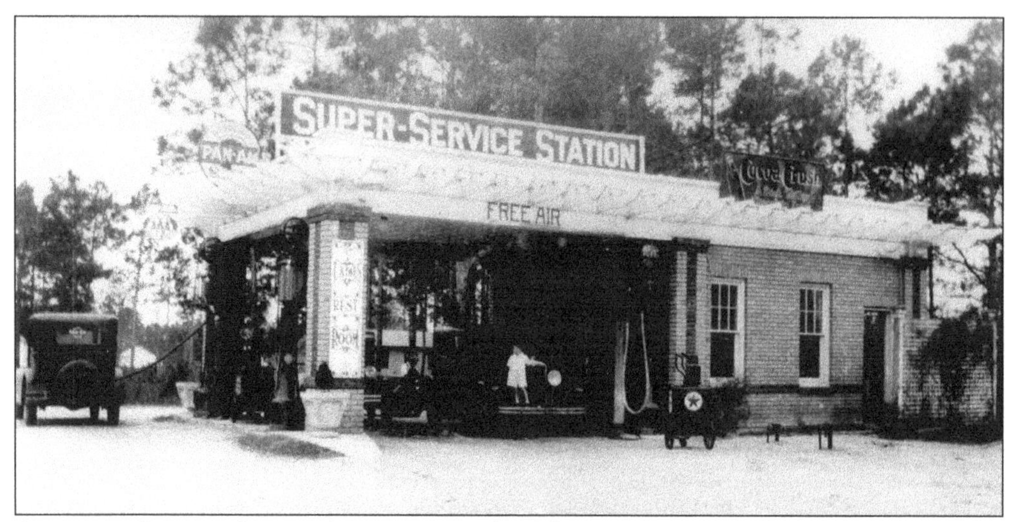

A woman of many talents, Bebe Lang opened a full-service station built on a large corner lot located at Bedell Avenue and Fourth Street in the late 1920s to capture tourist dollars. After completing the Satilla River Bridge in 1927, U.S. Highway 17 came through Woodbine and the time was ripe for enterprising businessmen and women with a vision toward opportunity and prosperity. In the center of the image is Bebe Lang's dear, devoted namesake and niece Bebe Colson (Williams) whose rural route postal carrier father, Joel Edward Colson (1895–1929), can be seen at far left. Lang arranged boxing matches for entertainment and built a ring on her downtown property where tickets for admission were sold for 25¢ each. (Courtesy of Bryan-Lang Historical Library.)

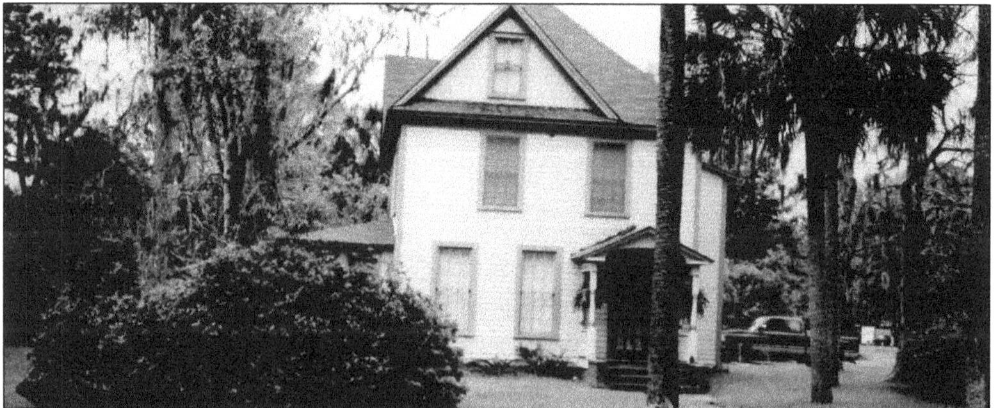

Within the Woodbine Historic District, architectural types include Gable Ell cottage, Queen Anne cottage, Side Hallway, Georgian cottage, and bungalow; architectural styles represented include Queen Anne, Folk Victorian, Colonial Revival, and Craftsman. Located at 307 East Oak Avenue, the historic Swift-Bryant House represents the Queen Anne style and stands today as a two-story, wood frame, Gable Ell–type dwelling. Its character defining elements include decorative shingle patterning in the front gables and a cutaway bay window. This architectural style remained popular throughout Georgia from the 1880s to about 1910. This home was built by Dr. Addison Knox Swift (1872–1956) who served as surgeon for the Florida Central and Peninsular Railroad's successor, the Seaboard Railroad; was president and part owner of the Satilla Telephone Co.; was a member of the Camden Board of Education and the County Commission; and served as mayor of Woodbine for many years. (Courtesy of Bryan-Lang Historical Library.)

An unidentified man poses in front of the Masonic Lodge beside the FC&P tracks. Dating from 1895, this community landmark building clearly stands on Oak Street within a few feet of the railroad tracks. Brick and wood frame buildings for commercial enterprises were constructed along the railroad corridor, but this changed in the 1920s with the construction of Highway 17 and a new emphasis on automobile transportation. (Courtesy of Bryan-Lang Historical Library.)

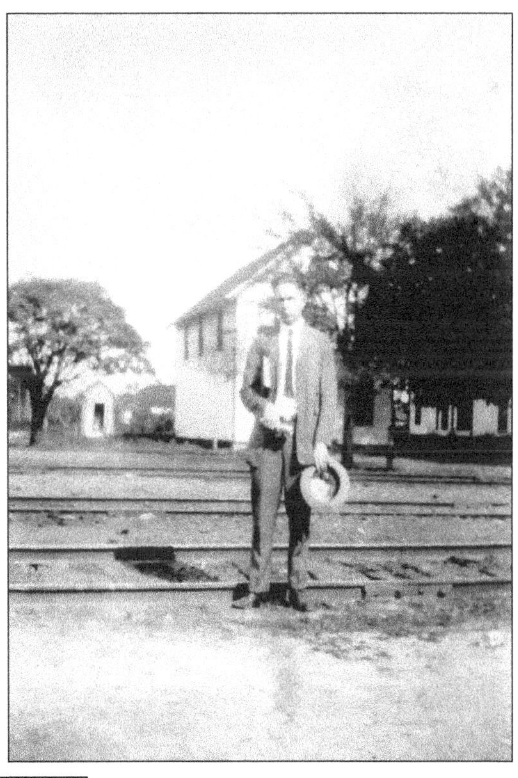

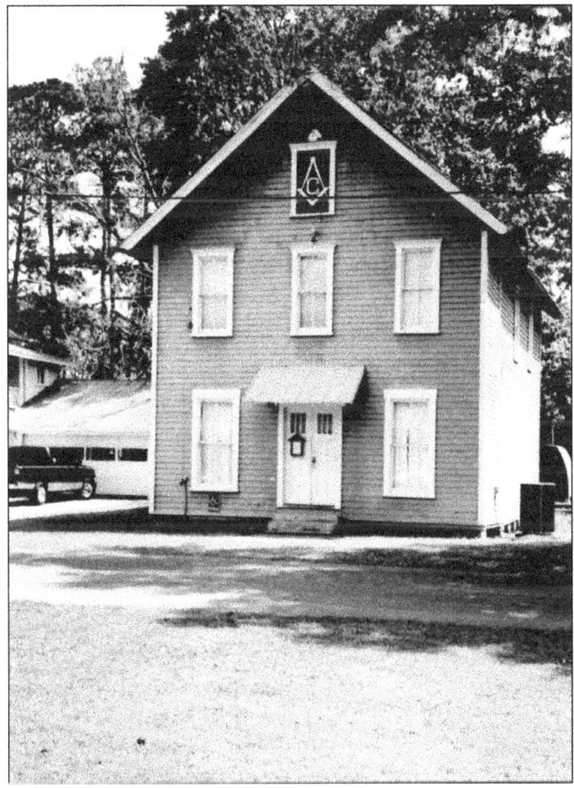

Today, a restored Woodbine Masonic Lodge located at 305 East Oak Street features a two-story, wood frame, gable-front vernacular building with symmetrical front facade. Notice the removal of the railroad tracks, which occurred during 1990, and the grassed area fronting the lodge's entrance in the contemporary image. As an active fraternal organization, the Woodbine Masonic Lodge 326 meets at the Lodge building on the second and fourth Tuesdays each month. (Courtesy of Bryan-Lang Historical Library.)

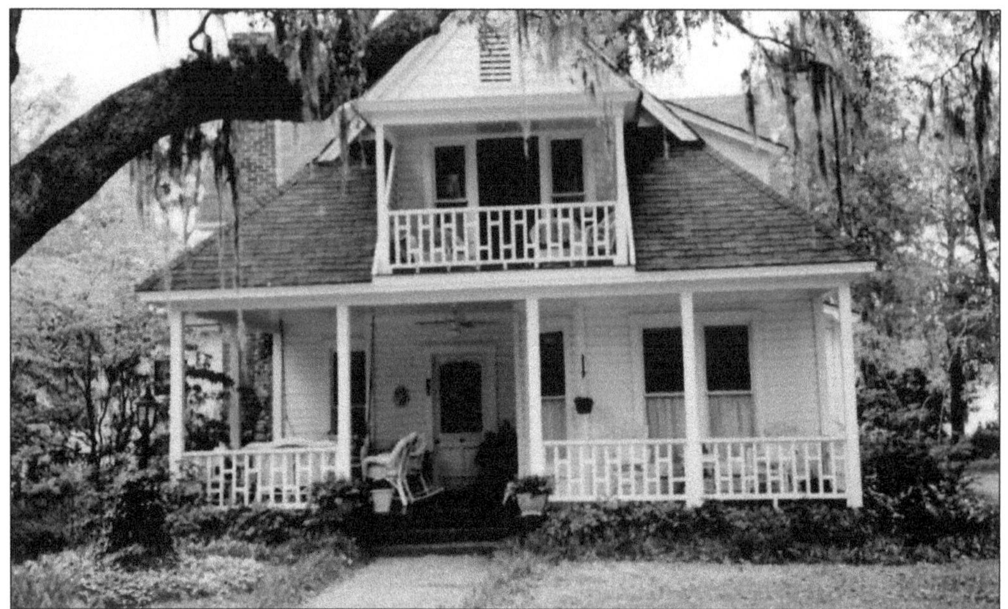

Situated in a lovely oak-shaded setting at 309 East Oak Street, the Davis-Colson House represents a Queen Anne–type dwelling. Built by J.S.N. Davis, this home dates from 1906 and its character-defining features include a square mass with projecting gables on the front and side elevations, a hipped roof, and interior chimneys. Whether housing a fraternal organization or a family, both of the structures in the previous images align with a railroad right-of-way and share a similar neighborhood with this historic home. (Courtesy of Bryan-Lang Historical Library.)

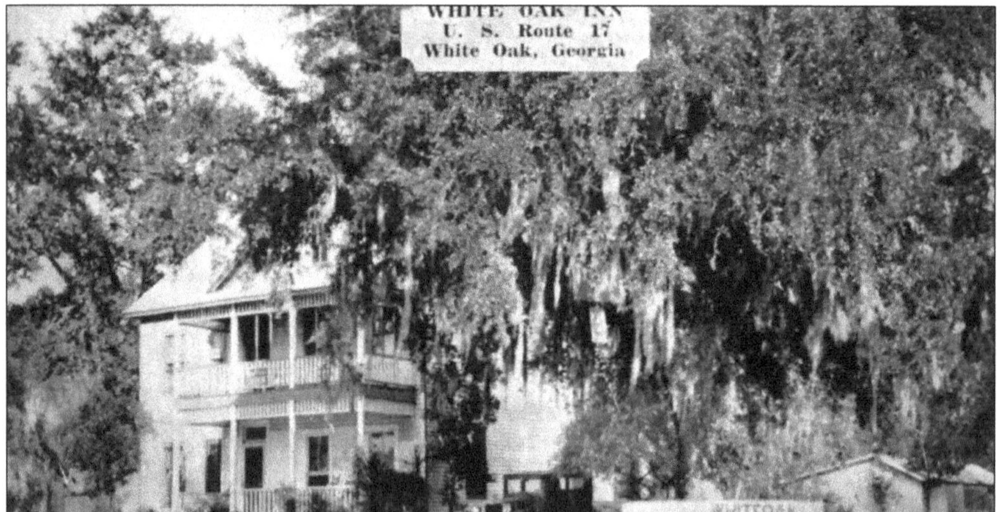

Dexter Post Card Corporation produced this image of the White Oak Inn that stands today along Highway 17 and serves as reminder of late innkeeper Mrs. George Varnadoe Baker, who chronicled her good neighbors' presence. A Shaker colony from Union Village, Ohio purchased 716 acres of land from L.T. McKinnon in 1899, and the hardworking, thrifty group built a three-story house of pine timbers, engaged in truck farming, and made beautiful furniture. Failure to gain converts led to a short-lived White Oak residency, and the Shakers' property was sold in October 1902 by business manager Richard T. Clark. (Courtesy of Bryan-Lang Historical Library.)

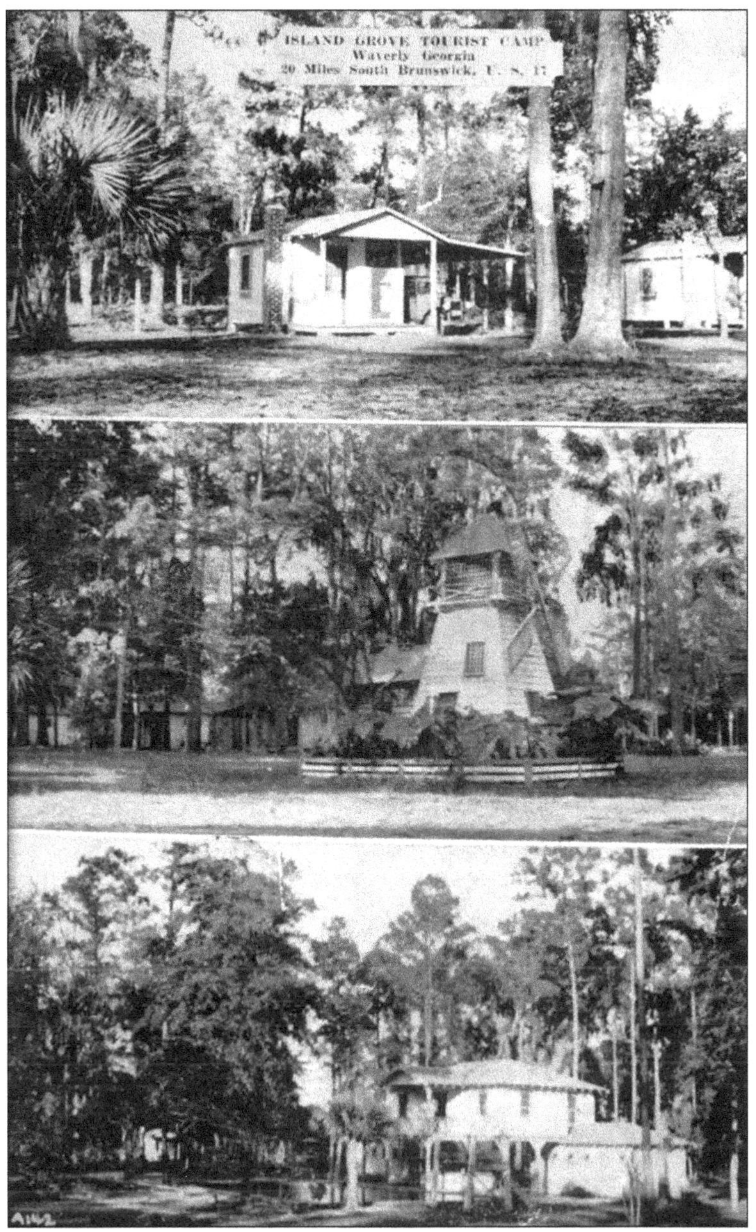

With the coming of a paved Atlantic Coastal Highway, a portion of Clark's Island was developed in 1929 as a tourist court—the Island Grove Tourist Camp—seen here in a period postcard. Following World War I, Burwell Atkinson returned to Waverly, expanded his timber business, and saw an opportunity in the tourist business. Covering 200 miles of "rolling business—U.S. Route 17," the *Highway Herald* in March 1937 advertised the Island Grove Tourist Camp as the "Gem of the Coastal Highway." Its sub-tropical setting appealed to those seeking a taste of the wild. Palm trees and alligators were the backdrop for this sprawling tourist court, where an ice-cold artesian well was put to work flooding the roadside swimming pool. Aiming to please travelers headed from Maine to Miami, this popular business was managed by Miss Charlotte Liles and offered trailer accommodations, cabins, showers, a large pool, home-cooked food, and wonderful memories. (Courtesy of Eloise Bailey Thompson.)

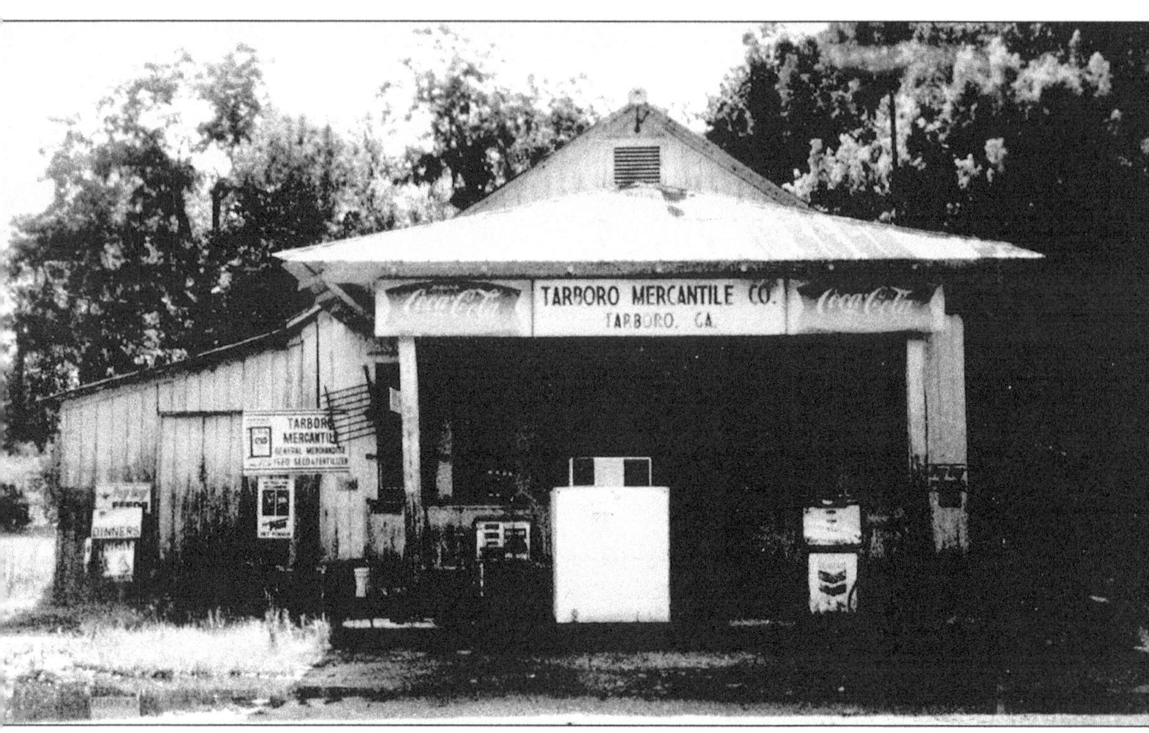

Named for a North Carolina town east of Rocky Mount where relocated turpentiners formerly lived, Tarboro remains an important spot on the rural Camden County landscape. When Tarheels in search of work came south with Leonidas T. McKinnon Sr. (1850–1921), they brought with them not only a community's name, but also substantial skills for working with resinous pine trees. Clyde L. McCarthy Sr. (1882–1970), seen in an image on page 73, allied himself with L.T. McKinnon in mercantile interests. In 1927, Clyde's brother Edgar Allen Poe (E.A.P.) McCarthy (1885–1960) bought out his brother and Clyde's business partner. Shortly thereafter, E.A.P. McCarthy built the Tarboro Mercantile Company store, seen above, a prominent feature on Highway 252 leading to Folkston and Charlton County and operated today as the Tarboro Country Store. In 1966, the McCarthy family placed a bronze monument next to the flowing artesian well in loving memory of E.A.P. McCarthy and the Biblical scripture, "I was thirsty and Ye gave me Drink." Until recent times, the free-flowing artesian well fountain offered passersby thirst-quenching respite. "The old landmarks are still standing, but the pilgrims have all moved on." (Courtesy of Hazel McCarthy White.)

At the junction of the Owen's Ferry, Refuge, and Burnt Fort Roads, near the present and second Tarboro, a settlement sprang up in response to prosperous times. The Stafford brothers drilled an artesian well powering a large water wheel for the operation of a grist mill, and Marion Clayborn "Stub" Joiner (1894–1962) worked the mill and served the community as a skilled blacksmith. In time the settlements of Forkville and Tarboro merged into one—Tarboro—and the McCarthy family became prominent in turpentining, naval stores production, and timbering activities.(Courtesy of Eloise Bailey Thompson.)

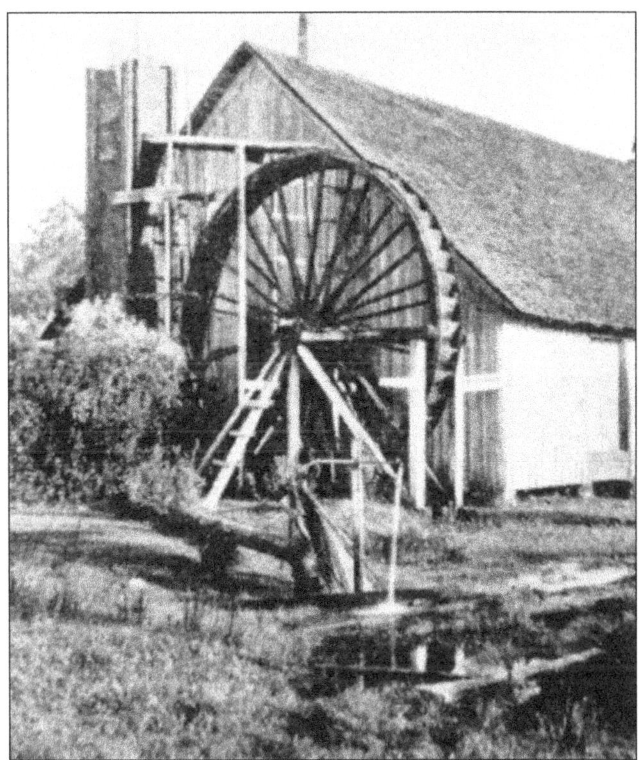

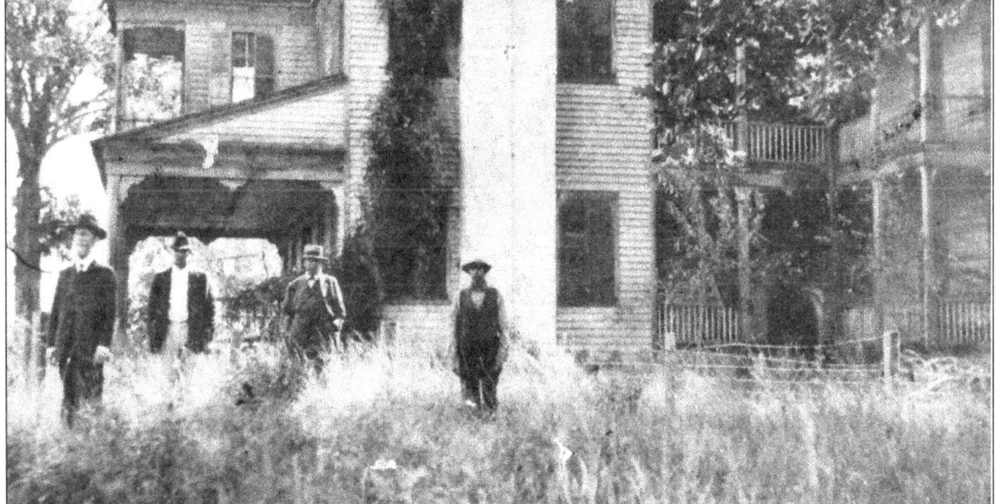

Dating from the colonial period and Donald MacKay's construction in the 1760s of a sawmill near the banks of the Satilla River, timber activities have driven Camden's economy. Brothers John and James S. "Jim" Bailey established sawmills on the Satilla in the 1870s, and when their partnership broke up, John moved farther up the Satilla. At Bailey's Mill he built a thriving business, including not only the sawmill, but also a post office, commissary, and a hotel. Encroached upon by its wooded setting and in decline with the exhaustion of timber, the once prosperous settlement is just a memory but the Bailey's Mill name remains on the landscape. In this image are, from left to right, ? Bailey, John Clark Buie, ? Bailey, and unidentified at the Jim Bailey home near the Satilla River. (Courtesy of Shirley Joiner Thompson.)

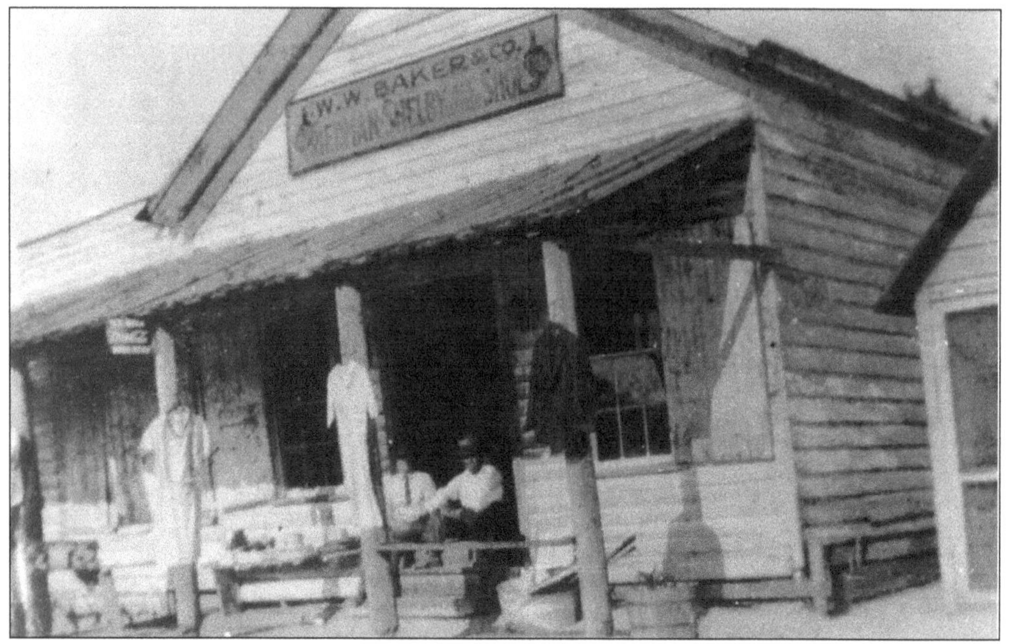

Located in the vicinity of Edmund Gray's platted town of New Hanover dating to the 1750s, a river settlement derived its name from the 1790s destruction of a blockhouse and earthenworks; hence, a burnt fort. By the 1830s, enterprising sawmillers arrived at Burnt Fort to exploit virgin stands of long-leaf yellow pine, and after the Civil War, William Lang continued cutting the extensive stands of forest. Later, L.M. Bedell engaged in timber buying for the Hilton and Dodge Lumber Company, and Bedell sold his interests to John Clark Buie, who operated a store at Burnt Fort. (Courtesy of Eloise Bailey Thompson.)

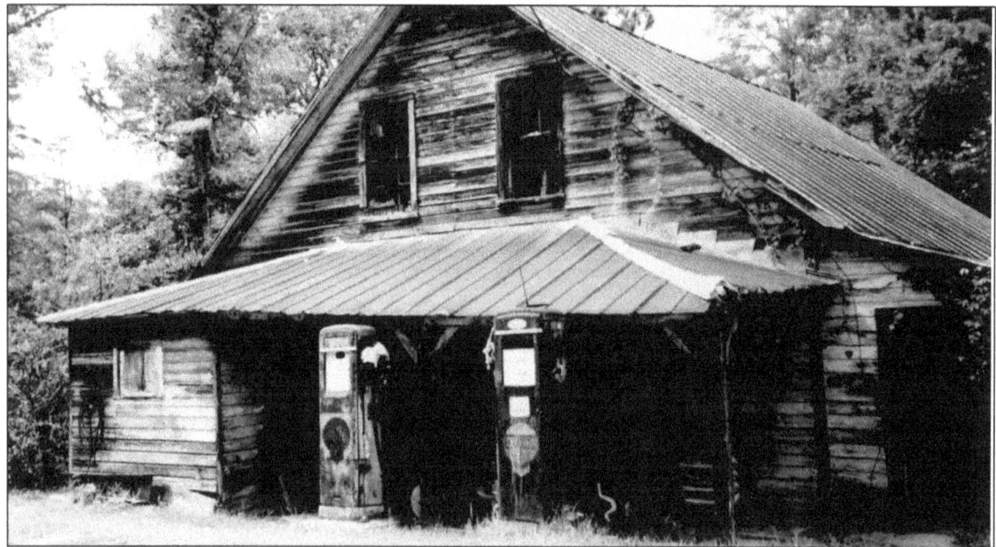

By 1907, John Clark Buie enlarged the commissary at Burnt Fort. As his enterprises expanded so did his workforce. He employed family and friends such as J.C. Littlefield, who joined Buie in the turpentine business in 1914. In the early 1930s, his nephew Archie Buie returned to Burnt Fort as general manager. After the elder Buie's death in 1933, the business was operated as A.A. Buie, and later as Buie and Wright until the death of the owners. (Courtesy of the Author.)

Four

PEOPLE OF CAMDEN

Life was often hard for early settlers in the wilds of southeast Georgia. Self-reliance, fortitude, perseverance, and crafty ingenious ways proved great virtues, as did a knack for survival. Acknowledged here are some of the men, women, and children whose lives have dictated the rich history of Camden, who have created proud legacies on the landscape and a goodly heritage for their descendants. Newlyweds, formidable businessmen, editors and publishers, Victorian-era ladies and nurse midwives, surveyors, bookkeepers, hunting guides and historians, law enforcement men and judges, sawyers, turpentine workers, and civil engineers all step across these pages. Writing in The Woodbine Twineth, *Shirley J. Thompson said, "The times were rough and the wilderness mocked and they said their prayers with their shotguns cocked."*

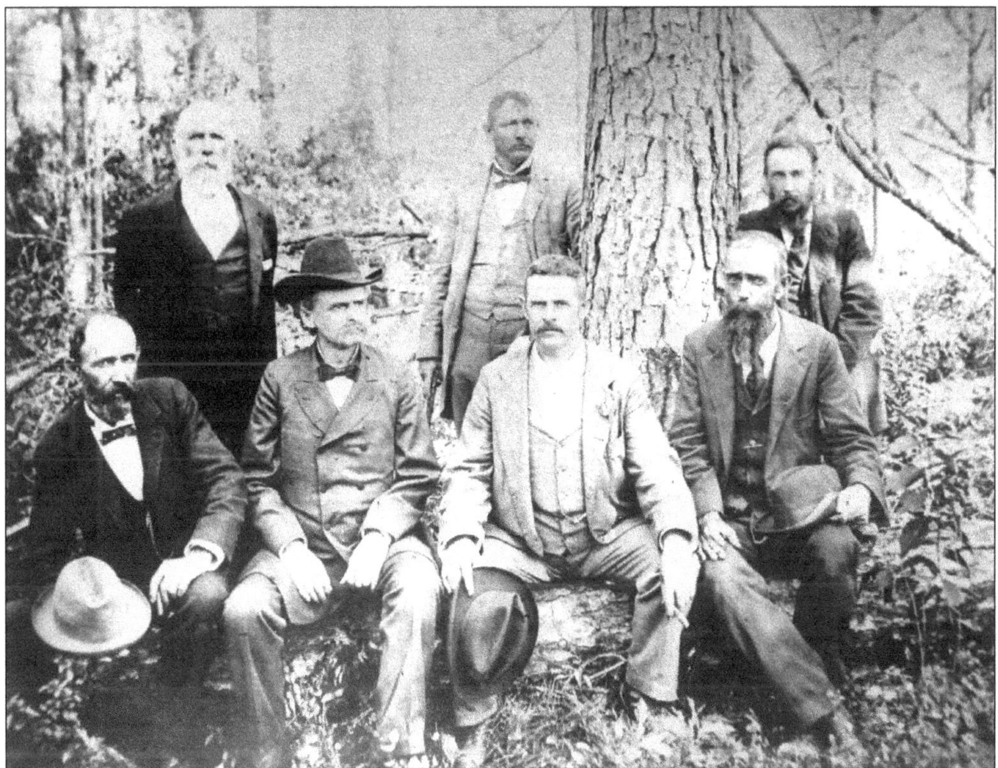

In this group of illustrious men posing in a woodland setting are, from left to right, (front row) John Foster, associated with the Ceylon Community's Hilton-Dodge mill; William Yates Atkinson (1854–1899), the 37th governor of Georgia (1894–1898); Rufus S. Lang Sr., a timber broker and storekeeper at Satilla Bluff; and James King Bedell (1849–1915) of Woodbine Plantation; (back row) Barney James Gowen (1840–1919); merchant David P. Rose; and Walter Wyatt, editor and owner (1897–1900) of *The Southeast Georgian*. (Courtesy of Bryan-Lang Historical Library.)

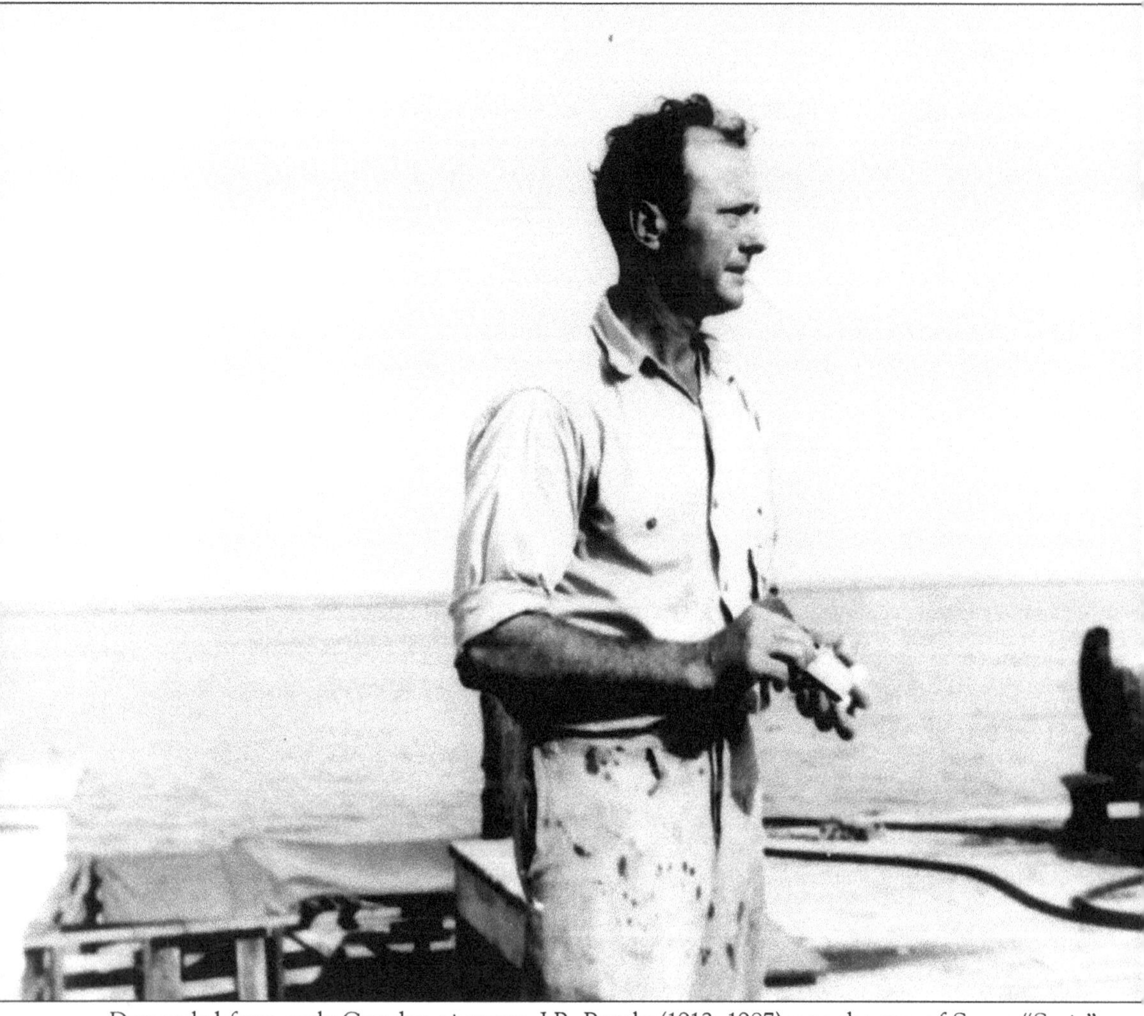

Descended from early Camden pioneers, J.B. Peeples(1912–1987) was the son of Susan "Susie" Adelaide Joiner (1887–1949) and William Escott Peeples (1884–1957). Raised on the edge of the St. Mary's River swamp, where at one time the Peeples family owned over 1,200 acres, Peeples roamed the fields and forests and honed his knowledge of animals, tasty concoctions, and the use of wild plants for healing and food. Although characterization of this great woodsman defies words, two come to mind: crafty and ingenious. Peeples farmed a portion of the old family homeplace until his death; raised cows, hogs, and chickens; and was surrounded by his family and loving wife, "Miss Lillian." Many Camden Countians recall his lifetime work with members of the Cumberland Carnegie family. Peeples's reputation as a supreme outdoorsman who possessed a great love for nature's bounty looms large on the Camden landscape. (Courtesy of Georgia Department of Archives and History, Lucy Coleman and Thomas Morrison Carnegie Family Papers, AC 94-003.)

The oldest son of Donald Tompkins Peeples (1861–1919) and Olive Brazell Peeples (1862–1941), sawyer Donald Joseph "D.J." Peeples supported his large family of 11 children through farming and timbering activities. His demanding lifestyle kept Peeples busy from sun up to sun down. In this image, Peeples stands near his "push hard lumber company," once located on Peeples Road near Clark's Bluff where his ancestors and descendants have lived for six generations. (Courtesy of Daniel Peeples.)

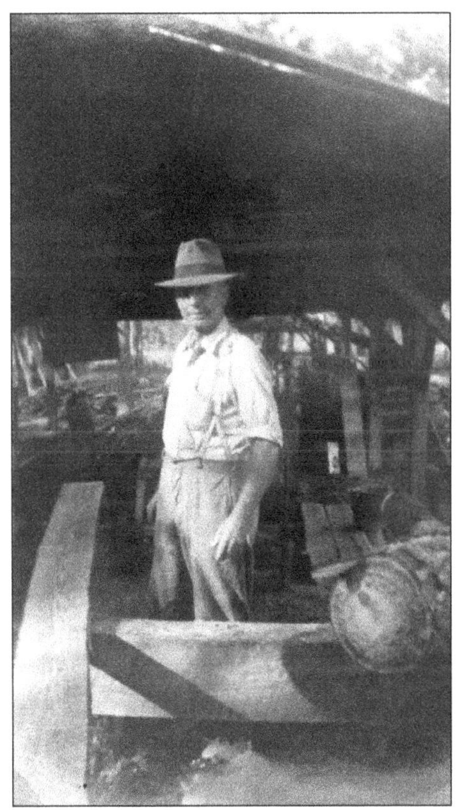

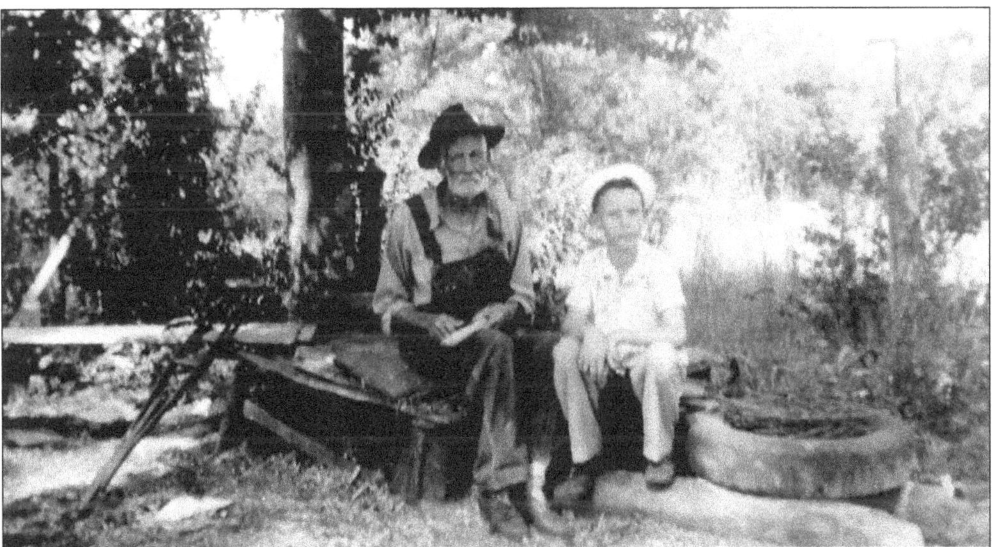

The son of William and Mary Ann Cribbs Brazell, Richard "Dick" Brazell (1866–1951) and his grandson Leonard take a break from their conversation and pause for the camera. Photographed at the old Brazell homeplace located on Scrubby Bluff Road, the elder Brazell could often be seen sitting in his yard whittling as a favored pastime. His older sister Olive B. Peeples appears in two images on page 94. (Courtesy of Daniel Peeples.)

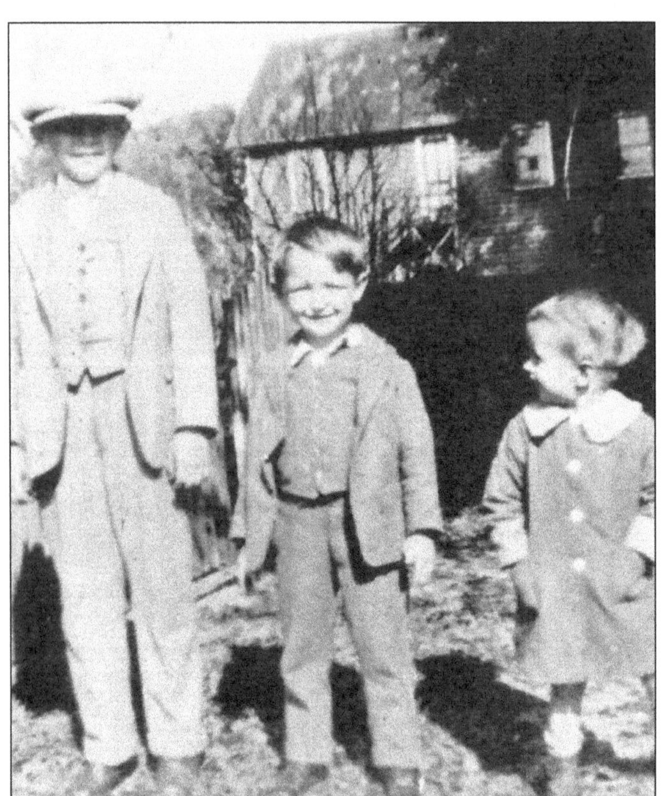

The three young Sheffield brothers posing for the camera in 1928 are, from left to right, a nattily dressed Carl, Wilbur, and baby Arnold. The image provides not only one of several portraits of a well-to-do family but also a view of Sheffield's Store in the background. This business is also seen in an image on page 50. In 1894, Kingsland's first hotel, the Blue Diamond Hotel, was added onto Sheffield's Store, a landmark until its demolition in the 1960s. (Courtesy of Rodney Sheffield.)

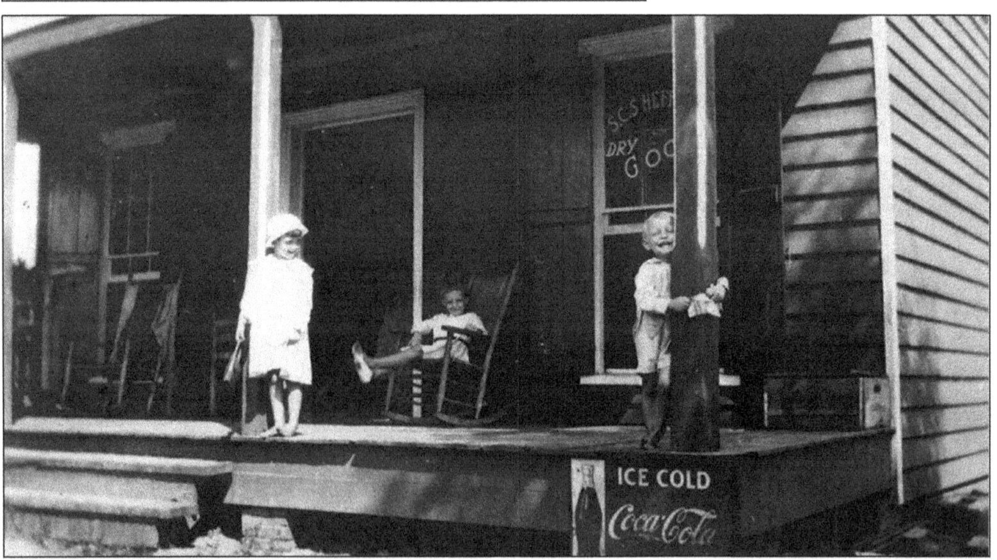

S.C. Sheffield's Dry Goods sign can be seen in the window of his store, where comfortable rocking chairs offer pastime conversations. The now collectible Coca-Cola sign advertised a tasty soda that offered respite from the heat of south Georgia's summers. The image was taken after the Blue Diamond Hotel had been detached from Sheffield's Store. Shown on the porch are the barefoot children of S.C. Sheffield (1889–1972) and Shirley P. Sheffield (1893–1993): Ida West Sheffield (left), an unidentified child in the rocking chair (center), and Ida's brother Wilbur. (Courtesy of Rodney Sheffield.)

Newlyweds Louise McElroy Sheffield (1920–1999) and her husband, Wilbur H. Sheffield, pose for the camera in 1943 in Kingsland at the old S.C. Sheffield homeplace, visible in the background. Built from the recycled materials of the Blue Diamond Hotel, this 1911 structure was moved in 1998 to St. Marys and stands near historic Oak Grove Cemetery. Serving as a private residence, the home now belongs to owners who have allowed its inclusion in a celebration of St. Marys Tour of Homes. (Courtesy of Rodney Sheffield.)

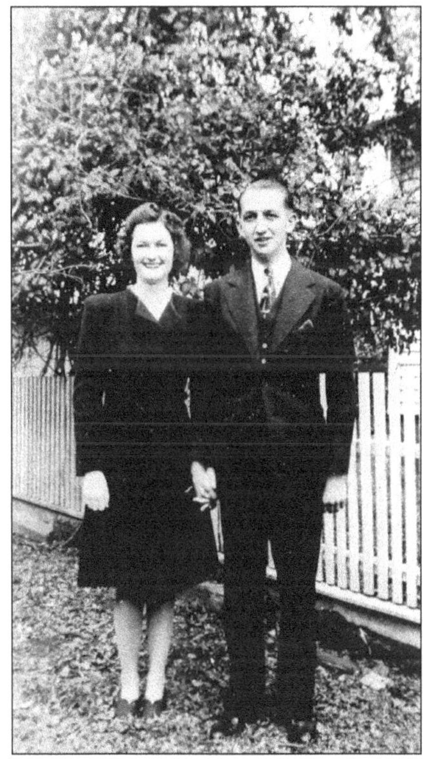

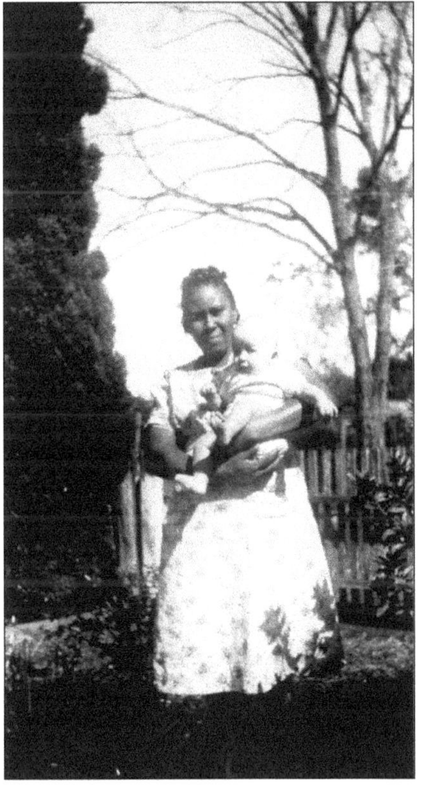

Domestic helper Ruby Cody served generations the Sheffield family and appears in this image with baby Rodney Sheffield, part of the sixth generation of this old Camden family. Miss Cody's parents owned a confectionary business in north Kingsland. In this *c.* 1945 image, Ruby and Rodney stand in the backyard of his paternal grandmother Shirley P. Sheffield. The yard was formerly land belonging to Camden Sheffield at Beauvoir Plantation that he inherited from his father, John. Today, Rodney serves the Camden community on the board of an important repository at Woodbine's Bryan-Lang Historical Library and as president of a growing Guale Historical Society. (Courtesy of Rodney Sheffield.)

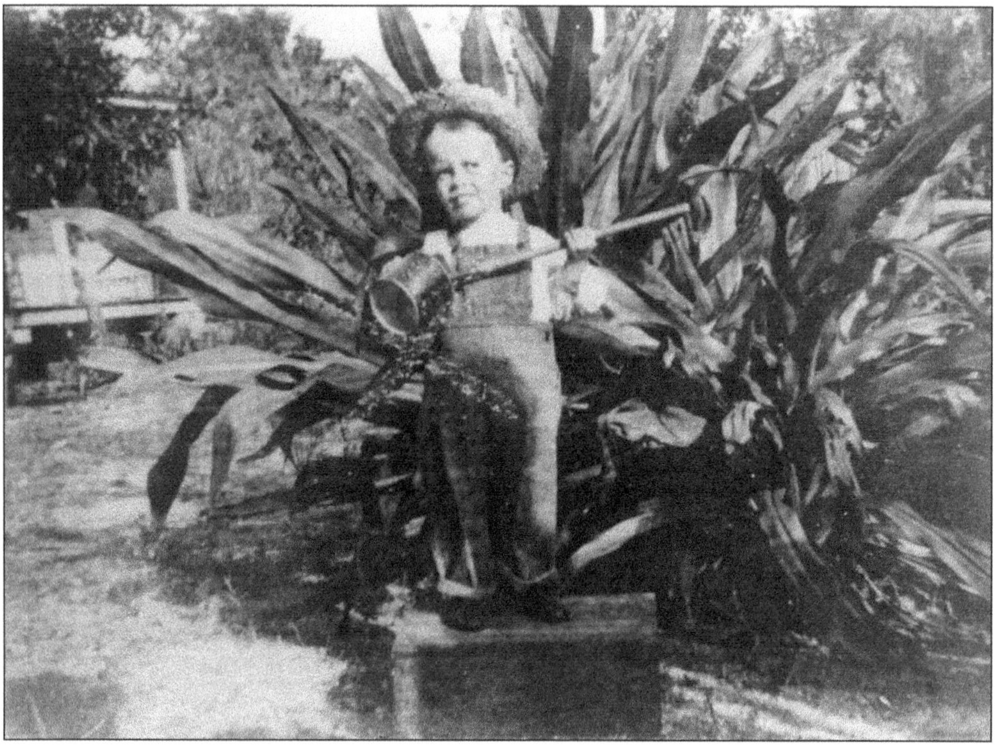

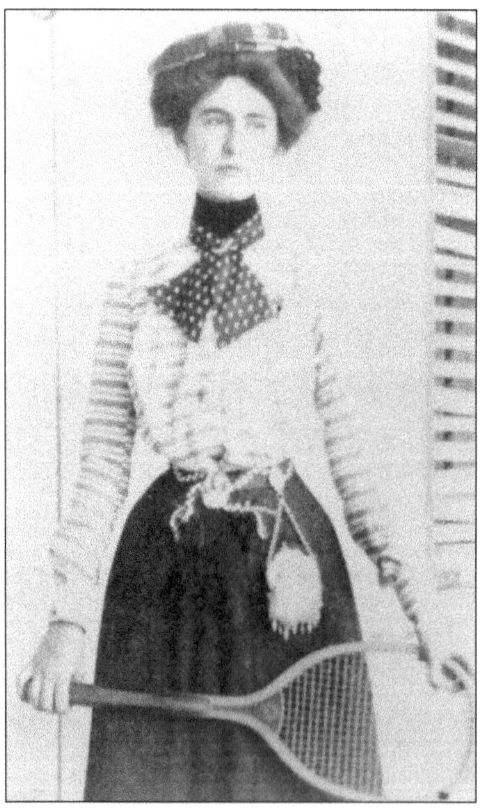

In this image, three-year-old John Richardson MacDonell (1904–1989) poses for the camera with the backdrop of a very large crinum, a fragrant, summer-blooming plant with lily-like flowers often used in Victorian-era landscaping. Later MacDonell worked as a marine contractor and civil engineer. He served his country as a U.S. Army captain in World War II and Camden County as county engineer and mayor of St. Marys. (Courtesy of Eloise Bailey Thompson.)

Decked to the nines, a lovely Maria Elizabeth "Ria" Richardson MacDonell (1882–1974) poses for the camera holding her tennis racket. Through her maternal line, Ria was a descendant of John Bessent Sr. (1765–1844), a prominent St. Marys merchant. In 1903, Ria Richardson married Alexander Henry MacDonell (1879–1954). The couple's son John is seen in the image at the top of this page. A talented musician, Ria MacDonell attended the Red Springs Seminary in Red Springs, North Carolina where she received a certificate in music and art. She served local churches as an organist, performing for 50 years. (Courtesy of Eloise Bailey Thompson.)

A descendant of Lucy Thomas Stafford Spalding (*c.* 1766–1836) and Thomas Stafford, Susan Tompkins King (1867–1915) was born to John and Mary S. Tompkins. The Tompkins family lived on the mainland at St. Marys, and their daughter married well when she wed Julius King (1854–1937) in October 1894. Early in the first year of their marriage, King and his business associate Newton Stafford established *The Southeast Georgian*, and King served as editor until the paper was sold to Walter Wyatt (pictured on page 65). Dressed in the finery afforded by a privileged life, Susan T. King appears pensive as a Savannah cameraman captures her image. (Courtesy of Eloise Bailey Thompson.)

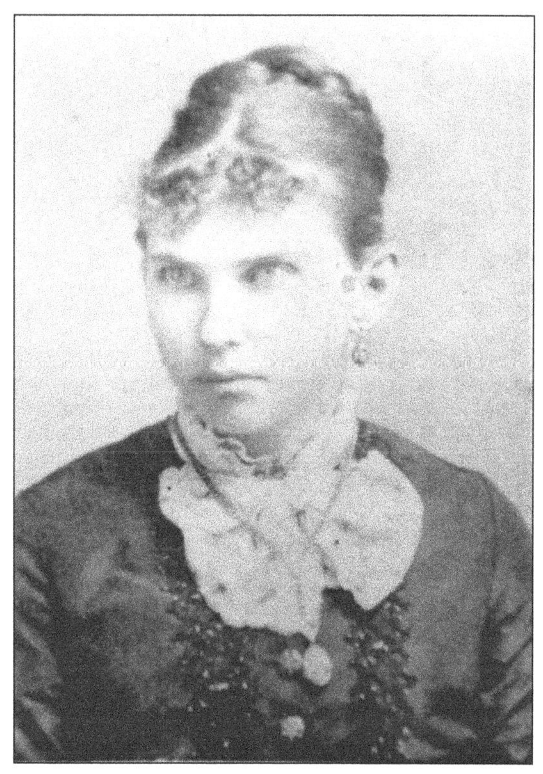

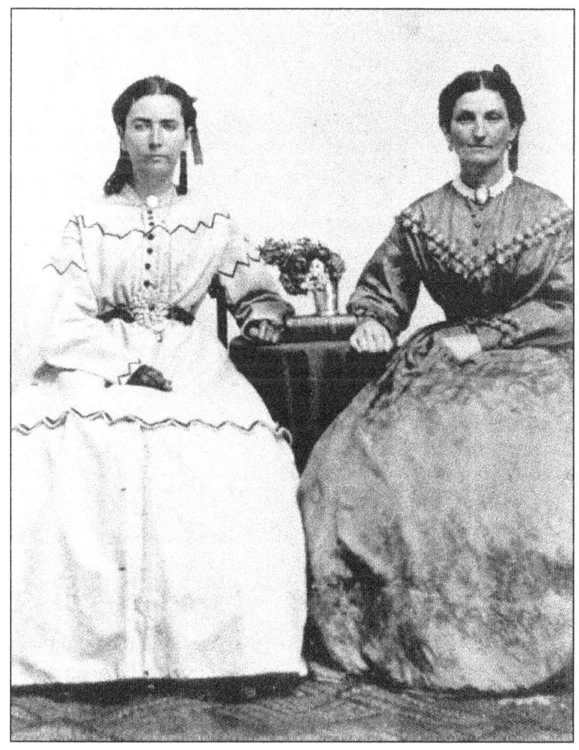

Dressed in their Victorian-era finery, sisters-in-law Emily Lang Tompkins, daughter of George Lang, and Amanda Tompkins Peeples pose for the camera. Amanda was the daughter of John Tompkins and descended from Revolutionary War soldier John King. The two ladies appear in their day clothes—a fashion statement that covered women from head to toe in cloth and was greatly influenced by Queen Victoria, who gave her name to the styles of the era. Notice Emily's stylish fingerless mittens and Amanda's heirloom cameo broach. Thirteen years his junior, Emily married Robert Tompkins, and Amanda was the wife of planter A.M. Peeples Sr. (Courtesy of Eloise Bailey Thompson.)

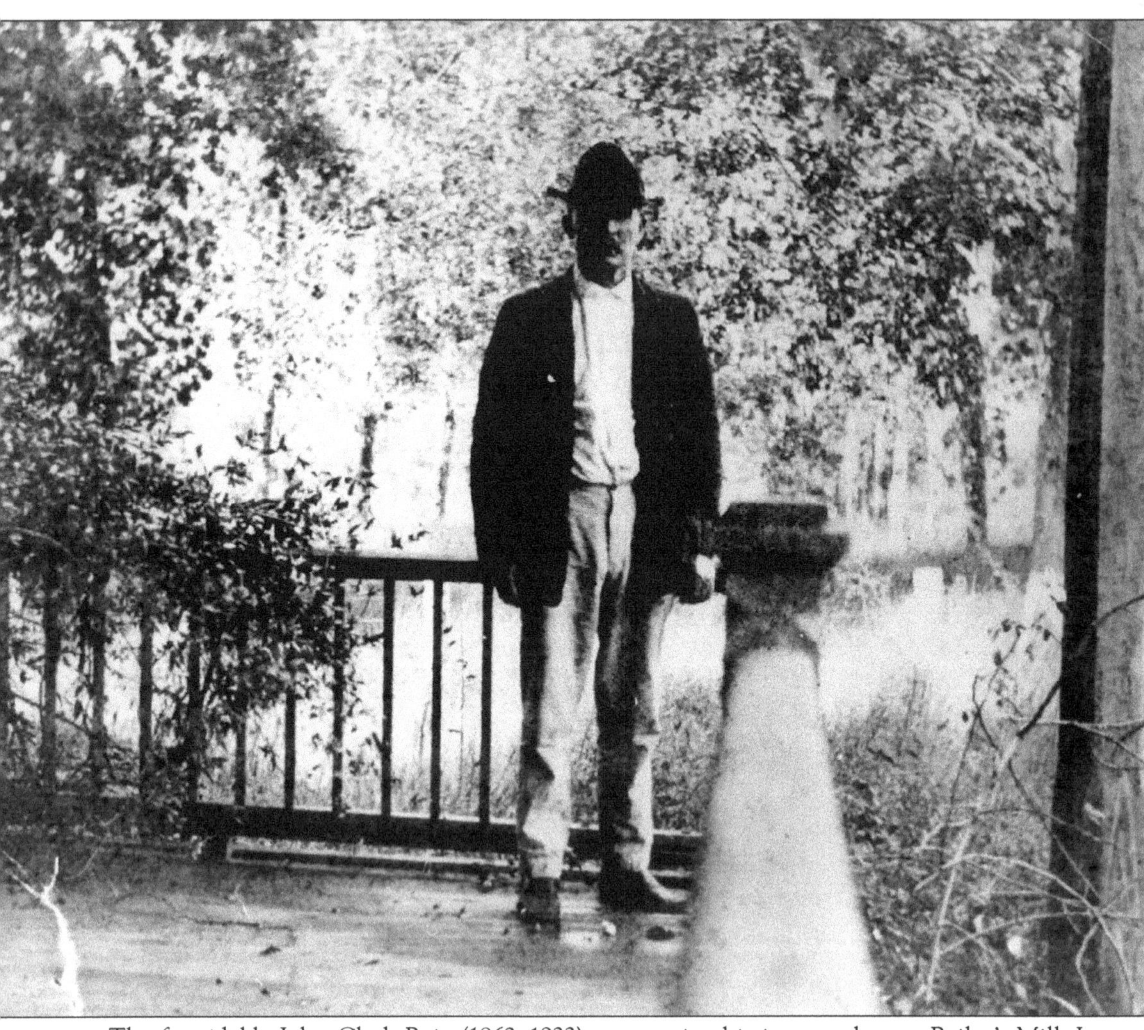

The formidable John Clark Buie (1862–1933) appears in this image taken at Bailey's Mill. In 1889, he came to Camden from Fayetteville, North Carolina, seeking a cure for ill health. Because of his prior education and an insatiable curiosity about the dictionary, he taught school in rural settings. An uncanny foresight served Buie well when he deduced that the timber-rich, old growth stands deep in Camden swamplands could be exploited. Some people assumed Buie was a "North Carolina sucker," but he parlayed an initial investment into large tracts of lowlands in Camden and Charlton Counties. When the upland timber was exhausted, Buie's intuition proved profitable. As a land baron he employed thousands of workers throughout his lifetime, amassed a great fortune, and was credited as "the wealthiest man in Camden County." (Courtesy of Neil Buie McClurd.)

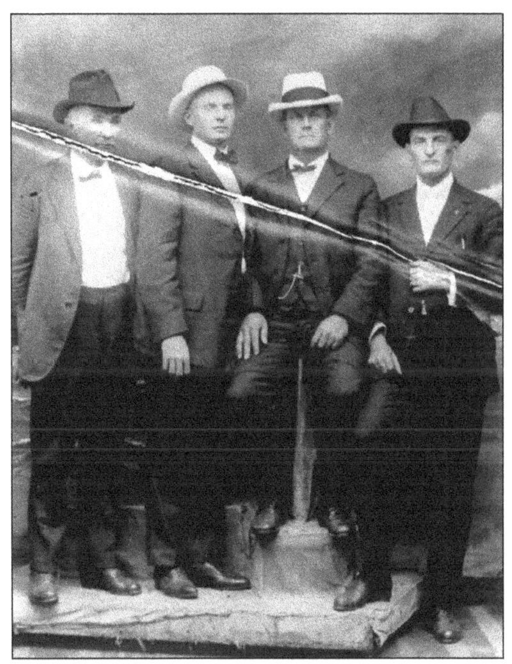

Four handsome men pose for a Coney Island photographer in this souvenir portrait. In the image are, from left to right, John Clark Buie, E.A.P. McCarthy, an unidentified man, and Clyde Lawrence McCarthy Sr. (1882–1970). Befriended by Buie and another transplanted North Carolinian and powerhouse in his own right, Leonidas T. McKinnon, both McCarthy brothers prospered. E.A.P. McCarthy operated the Tarboro Mercantile Store and administered justice in a rural, remote setting while his brother Clyde engaged in timbering activities and naval stores production, amassing his own fortune and joining the ranks of Camden's land barons. (Courtesy of Neil Buie McClurd.)

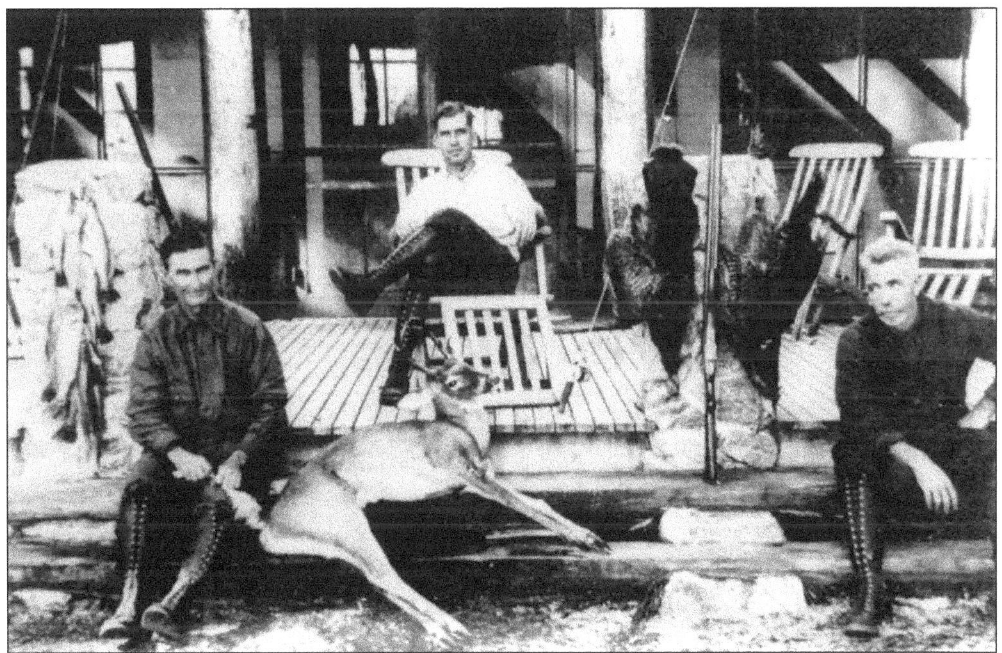

In November 1927 developer Howard Coffin purchased over 50,000 acres at Cabin Bluff, where a hunting preserve was developed for the delight of his Sea Island guests. Camden County's wild lands and estuaries abounded with white tail deer and a large variety of finfish. Offering employment for Camden natives during hard times, Coffin enlarged his private preserve, with the property remaining in the ownership of Sea Island Company until 1942. In recent years, some of the property was re-acquired by Sea Island Company and A.W. Jones III. Shown here, from left to right, are a few of the Cabin Bluff hunting guides: Zack Colson, Nub Colson, and Jim McKinney. (Courtesy of Camden County Historical Commission.)

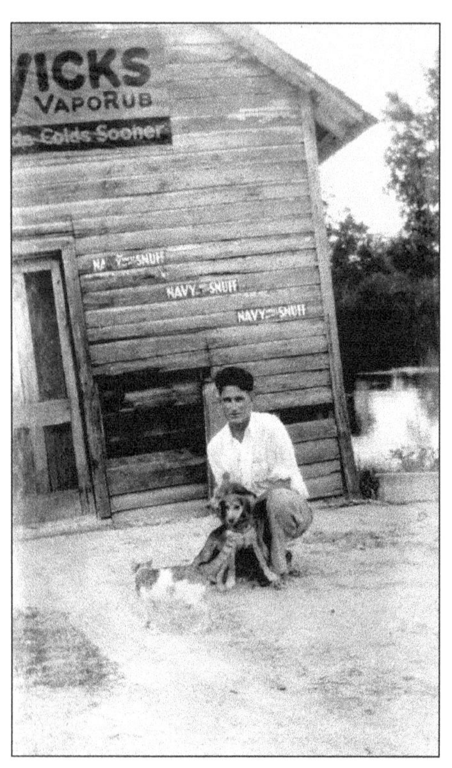

A favored nephew of John Clark Buie, the legendary Archie Alexander Buie (1897–1976) kneels to pet his dogs. Educated in the public schools of Camden County and Duval County, Florida, Buie returned to his family holdings at Burnt Fort where he made his home and, in 1933, married Sara Cornelia Davis Buie, formerly of Folkston. Beginning in 1930, Buie worked with his paternal uncle's business, the J.C. Buie Company, and engaged in pulpwood and timber production. He also raised prize-winning hogs and, in September 1938, won the championship of the Coastal Empire Ton-Litter and Fat Barrow Show at the Savannah Stockyards. The Buies raised their two girls along the banks of the great Satilla River amidst pastureland and farm animals. (Courtesy of Neil Buie McClurd.)

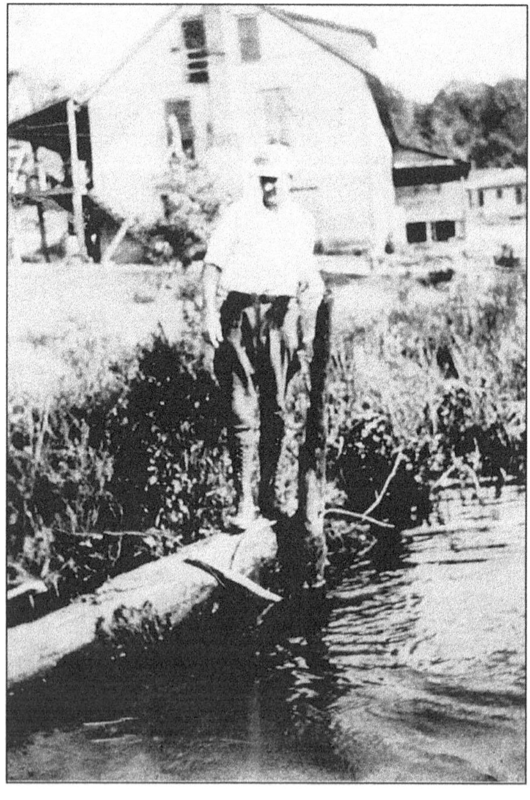

Wearing protective leather boots, Archie Buie stands behind the Burnt Fort Store, near the sunken 95-ton steamer *Atlantic*. When the vessel caught on fire about 1928 near John Clark Buie's Store and turpentine still, clerk Newt Boring Sr. cut the lines, and the vessel drifted across the Satilla where it burned. The charred timbers sank into the white sands of the great Satilla River, becoming an underwater archaeological treasure and a reminder of those days when steamers plied Camden's waters. They made regular trips hauling passengers and supplies far up the Satilla River to settlers in remote village settlements who were dependent upon basic supplies transported on the river corridors. (Courtesy of Neil Buie McClurd.)

Only 14 years after the Emancipation Proclamation of January 1, 1863, a number of freedmen were recorded in the Camden County tax digests. In the 30th District at Baileys Mill, Fly Walker was among those enumerated. According to Camden's 1870 census, the 46-year-old Walker was the head of a household of eight that included his 40-year-old wife, Eva, and their children, who ranged in age from 20 to 4 years old. The Walkers' 10-year-old son was dubbed "Little Fly" and is the Fly Walker seen in the image on the Archie Buie homeplace where he worked. (Courtesy of Neil Buie McClurd.)

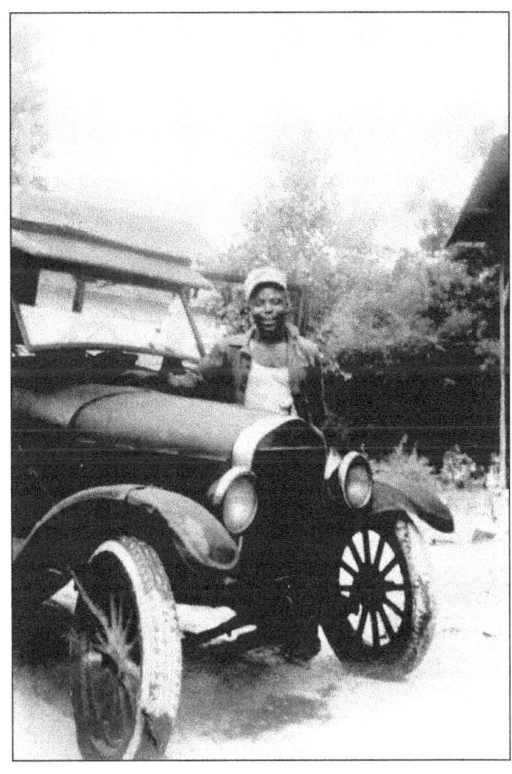

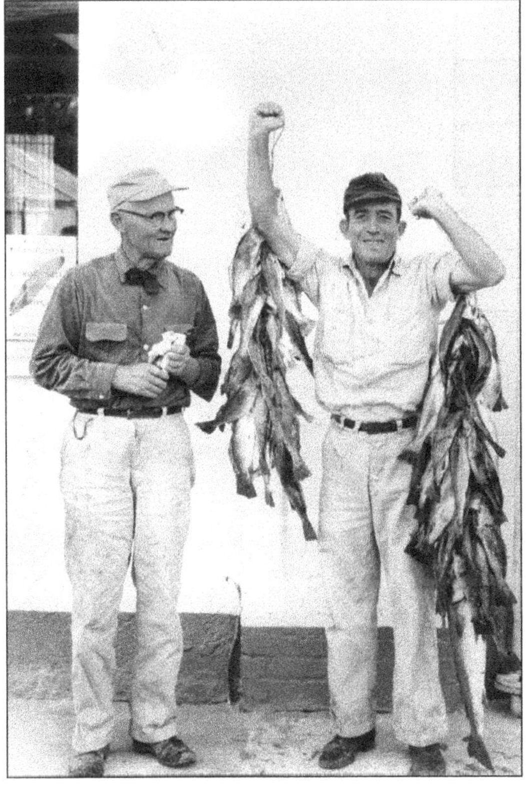

Expressing glee over his unidentified friend's large fish catch at Burnt Fort, Burwell Atkinson (1892–1973) was captured in this image. Born at Incachee Plantation to Dr. Burwell Atkinson and Julia Boston Atkinson, son Burwell was educated in Camden County schools, attended the University of Georgia, and received a law degree through the University of Virginia. He served his country in World War I and remained active in community affairs after returning home to Camden County and gaining accreditation as a registered land surveyor. In the late 1920s, Atkinson saw opportunity and developed the Island Grove Motel and Tourist Camp on Clark's Island and, in doing so, contributed to the rich memories of coastal Georgians. (Courtesy of Neil Buie McClurd.)

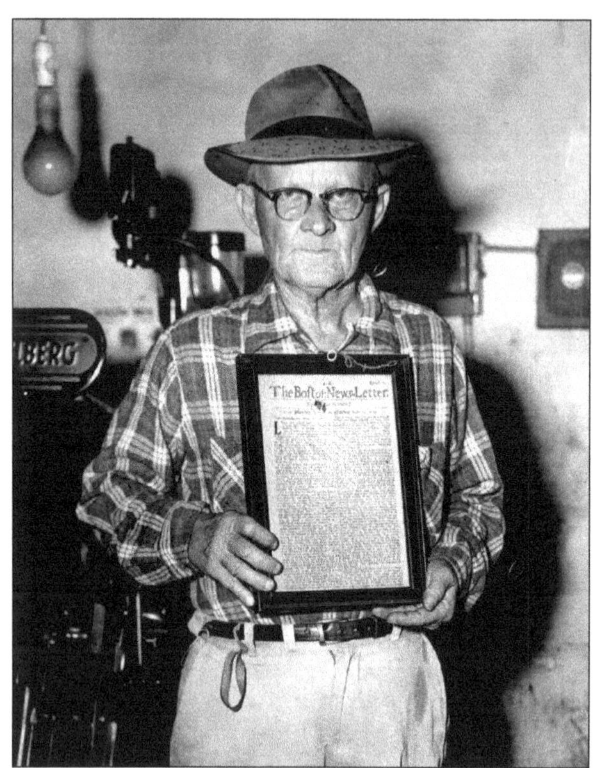

Burwell Atkinson poses for the cameraman while holding an historic framed copy of the *Boston News-Letter* dated April 24, 1704. He possessed a great reverence for the past and for the preservation of historic sites, many of which he had seen deep in the Camden woods during the course of his land surveying activities. This public-spirited man devoted countless hours toward the preservation and expansion of the historic Homeward Cemetery. He rests there today in company with his revered ancestors. Atkinson's sense of community obligation extended to working with the Civilian Conservation Corps Camp (CCC), for which he served as engineer, and in getting CCC roads built in Camden County. (Courtesy of Neil Buie McClurd.)

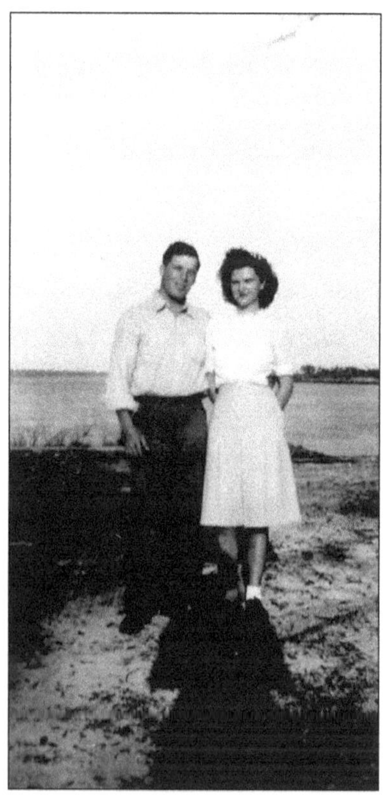

In 1944, newlyweds Joseph Donald "J.D." Peeples and his bride, the former Helen Ray Readdick, pose for the camera at the Crooked River Club, which was managed by Helen's mother. Peeples' law enforcement career spanned over 20 years of service; he was a deputy for the Camden County Sheriff's Department and for the Kingsland Police Department and also served as chief for many years. Between 1968 and 1983, the Peeples raised white leghorn chickens—24,000 of them—on their farm and, with their sons' help, gathered eggs three times per day for shipping to the Dixie Egg Company in Jacksonville, Florida. (Courtesy of Daniel Peeples.)

In the following two images, logger Burwell Atkinson Brown Jr. (1849–1922) and his wife, Isabella Hardy Harrell Brown, pause for the camera. Descended from two of Camden's oldest families—the Atkinsons and the Harrells—this couple married in December 1870 and were the parents of seven children: Joseph Emerson Brown, James Augusta Brown, Emma Brown Drury, Annie Norah Brown Clark, Fannie Lee Brown Manning, Isabella Hardy Brown Liles, and Maggie Gertrude Brown Taylor. Burwell Brown's grandparents were Elizabeth Atkinson Brown (1795–1878) and David Brown (1790–1869), who married in 1815. They lived on 150 acres of former Hardy land bordering the Little Satilla River that was given to the newlyweds by Elizabeth's father, Burwell Atkinson (1767–1854), and at Boggy Swamp prior to selling their property to Alexander Atkinson (1795–1840) and moving to White Oak in 1837. Today, their descendants live throughout the coastal community. (Courtesy of Wilbert Taylor and Miriam Cate Manning Davis.)

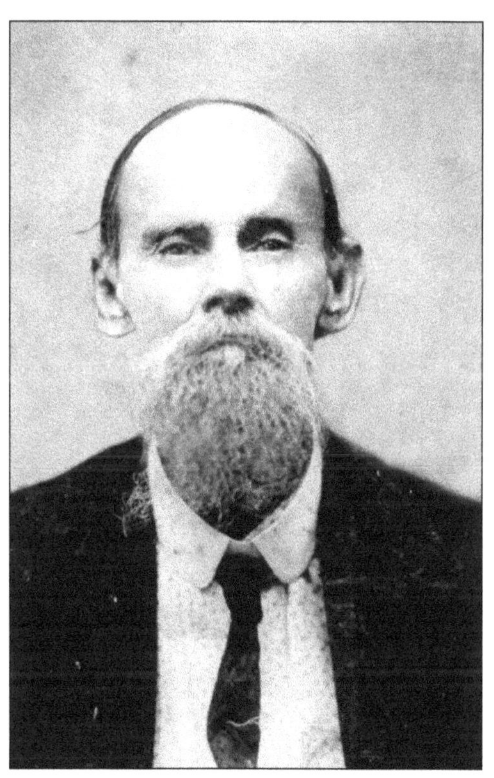

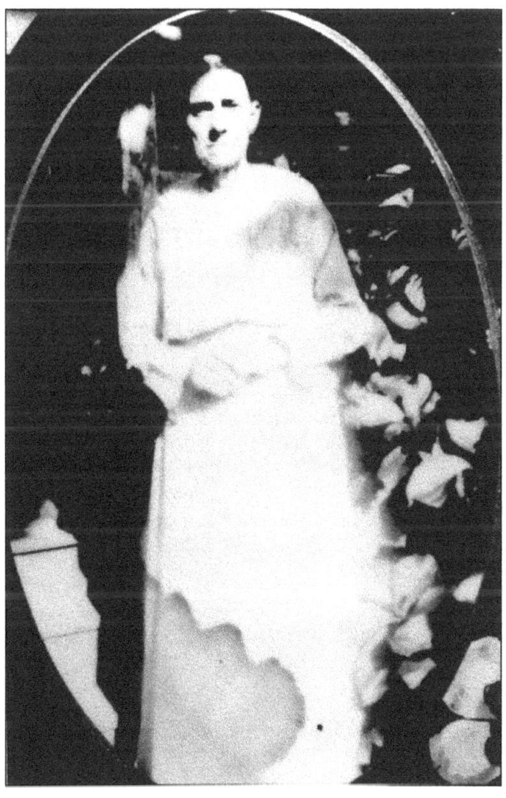

Isabella Hardy Harrell (1855–1928) grew up in the sandhill section of Camden County and was the daughter of Abner Harrell Jr. and his second wife, Elizabeth Highsley of Wayne County, whom he married on January 16, 1853. By his first wife, Harrell fathered eight children, including Isabella's step-brother Claborn Wright Harrell (pictured on page 12), but he re-married when his first wife died and, by Elizabeth, had three more children: Isabella, Henrietta, and Augusta. Isabella's expert instructions in the domestic arts proved a saving grace for her daughter Fannie Lee when this young mother was faced, in depressed times, with supporting her small children. A gifted seamstress, Fannie Lee Brown Manning served in Brunswick as the supervisor for a Glynn County Works Projects Administration (WPA) Sewing Room. (Courtesy of Wilbert Taylor and Miriam Cate Manning Davis.)

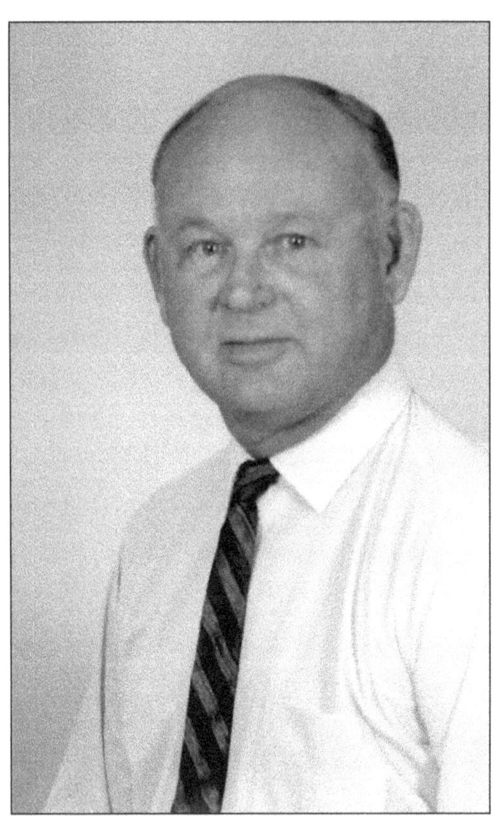

Burwell A. Russell, pictured here in 1964, was born at Incachee Plantation where he made his home surrounded by family and his wife, Martha Couper Murphy Russell. Influenced by his grandfather Dr. Burwell Atkinson whom he recalled as a benevolent, magnanimous, outstanding man, Russell followed the vision outlined for him in forestry management. After graduating from secondary school in 1937, he attended and graduated from the University of Georgia in 1941. Subsequently, Russell served his country during World War II in the Southwest Pacific Theatre as Maj. Burwell Russell, 5th Air Force, and as a pilot, he participated in 137 missions from 1943 to 1945. He received the Distinguished Flying Cross for his service and remained active in the military reserves until 1953. Since the early 1950s, Russell has practiced forest land management, conserving a climax, hardwood forest. As a tree farmer he cultivates slash and loblolly pines on his large estate where generations of the Atkinson and Russell families have lived. (Courtesy of the Burwell A. Russell family.)

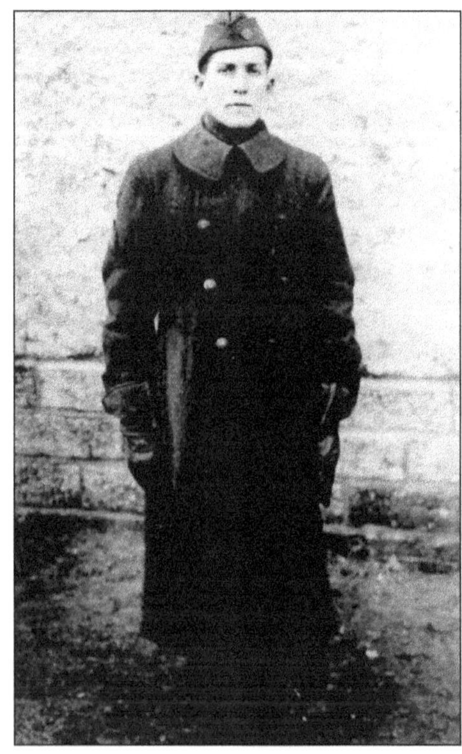

In this image a long-lived Luther Wesley Readdick (1889–1989) was dressed in his warm World War I uniform. He served his country as a corporal, 1st Georgia Infantry. Afterwards, he returned home and worked for various timber businesses as a bookkeeper and retired from St. Marys Pulp and Paper Company. He and his educator wife, Myrtle Ann Godley Readdick (1900–1960), resided in Kingsland where they reared their family of three children and were active members of the Kingsland Methodist Church. Readdick was a longtime county resident and the great-grandson of Peter Readdick. (Courtesy of Eloise Bailey Thompson.)

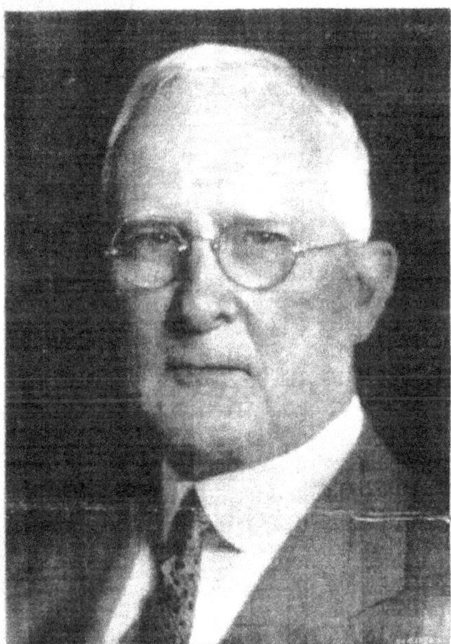

Born in Scottsboro, Baldwin County, Judge Samuel Carter Atkinson (1864–1942) was the ninth child of Alexander Smith Atkinson and his bride, Mary Ann McDonald, whose father, Charles J. McDonald, served as Georgia governor (1839–1843). Son of legendary, distinguished families, the future judge received his education through the University of Georgia, graduating in 1884, after which he was admitted to the bar and returned to Camden to practice law. Judge Atkinson holds the distinction of serving as the first judge of the City Court of Brunswick, later re-named State Court, over which he presided from 1896 to 1900. Subsequently, he was appointed to the Georgia Supreme Court where he spent 36 years on the bench, the longest tenure to date and one that spanned from 1906, when Justice John S. Candler resigned, until Judge Atkinson's death. Notably, he upheld the doctrine of *stare decisis* (to abide by or adhere to decided cases) and remained adamant about construing the law so that a law-abiding citizen held no doubt about the correct path in life. Characterized as fair-minded, generous, thoughtful, and a true gentleman, the Judge maintained high ideals. According to A.B. Estes, Judge Atkinson's secretary of 22 years, "He was a grace to the profession and an honor to the bench." (Courtesy of Charles Russell and the Burwell A. Russell family.)

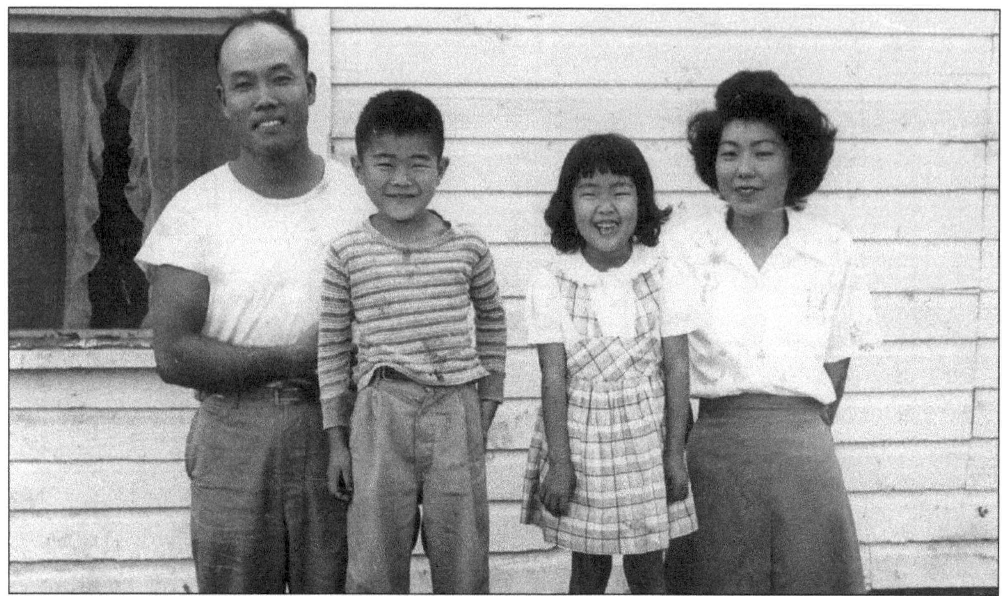

Mrs. Hana Shirokawa Ozaki, shown in this May 1949 image (fourth from right), received a treasured plaque in March 2001 honoring her 50 years of service to the Woodbine Woman's Club. It reads, "You forgot *not* to be kind and *Have* touched the great human heart of us all." When the children, Roger (left) and Donna (right), were ages four and two years, Bill Ozaki (far left) and his family moved to southeast Georgia from Cleveland, Ohio. After their move from the city to the small town of Woodbine, this brave couple faced many challenges. Setting up housekeeping at the remote Maryfield Plantation, the Ozakis lived for ten years in a lap-sided frame home lacking amenities such as indoor toilets, electricity, and running water, and engaged in truck farming on Maryfield's former rice fields. (Courtesy of Hana Ozaki.)

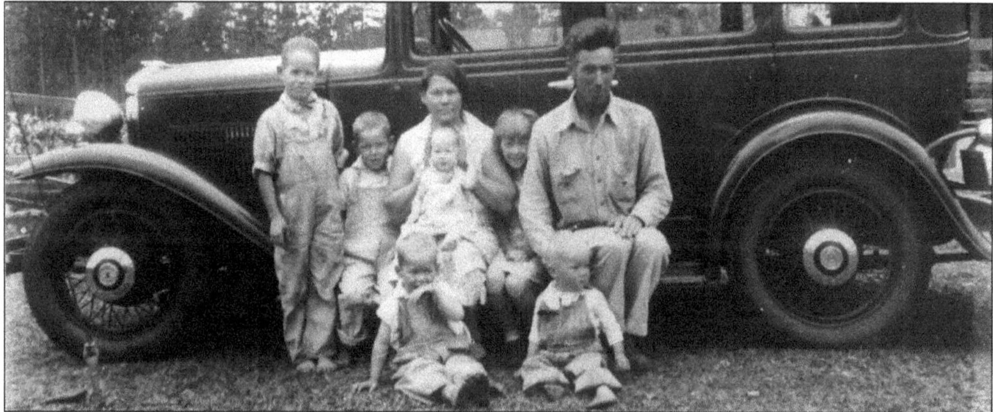

Allen O'Berry "Jim" Miller (1899–1984) and wife, Ada Lorain Head Miller (1903–1971) pose with their family beside a 1930s vehicle. Gazing in wonder at the camera are, from left to right, (front row) David and Elmer; (back row) Jimmy, Albert, baby Betty, and Lois. This image was taken about 1933 at Satilla Bluff where the Millers lived in the old St. Clements Episcopal Church—one of the oldest churches in North Camden and where some of their descendants currently live. Formerly attended by those who lived and worked at the Satilla Bluff sawmill, this 100-year-old structure was purchased in 1927 by Jim's father William. Jim Miller worked as a shrimper and toiled long hours in dangerous waters near Jekyll Island to support his growing family. (Courtesy of Shirley Joiner Thompson.)

Justine Lattany (1877–1964) served north Camden County as a rural midwife often accepting farm products or "country pay" such as a side of bacon for her services. Similar to many other Camden County midwives, Lattany birthed both white and black children. Another former nurse practitioner, Viola D. Hummings recalled that in the early years of midwifery, whenever they received money, the fee was $3. When her woodsrider husband, William Lattany (1851–1924), died, she bore the brunt of rearing four of twelve children in the sandhill community of "Red Cap," where Lattany family members live today. (Courtesy of Abra Lattany Reed and Phorestine Appling.)

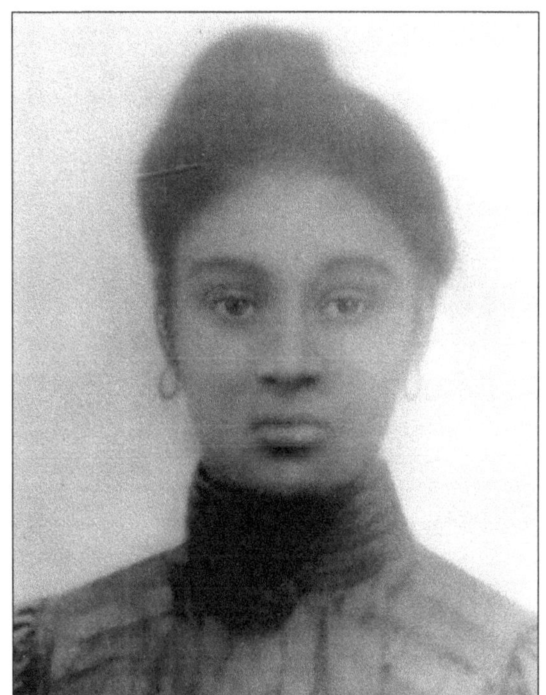

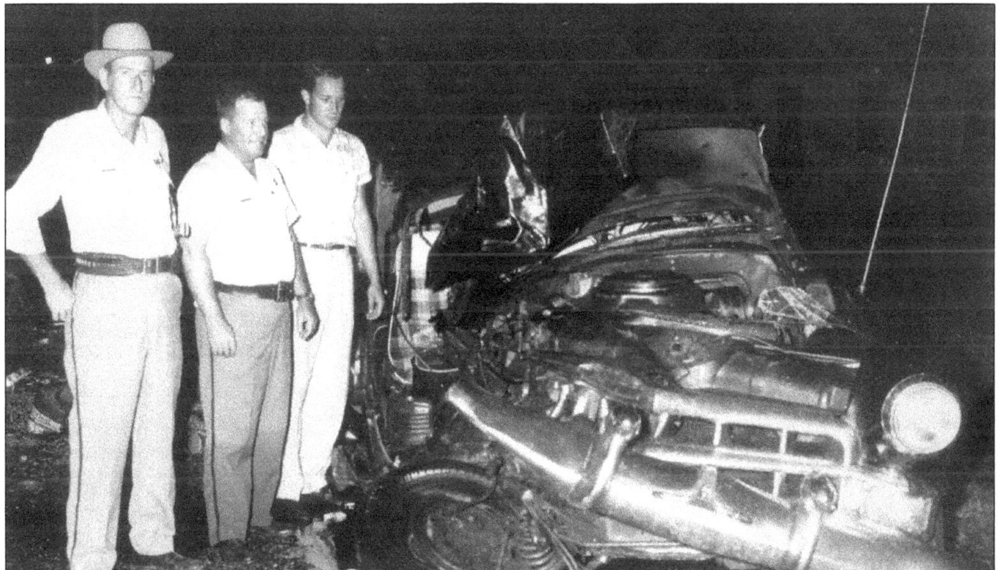

While Camden County accommodated tourists on Highway 17, heavy traffic posed challenges for law enforcement. Pictured in the 1950s, from left to right, Deputies John Hazelton, J.D. Peeples (1918–1998), and Jimmy Middleton survey the mangled wreckage of a vehicle. A well-liked officer, Hazelton was killed tragically in a fiery 1964 wreck near the Atkinson community. In May 2001 Camden County sheriff Bill Smith announced an endowment for eligible students at three south Georgia universities or the Camden Center, affiliated with the Coastal Georgia Community College. This stellar program honors four deputies who died in service with the Camden County Sheriff's Department: Dennis Ray Herring, Walter Nathan Coleman, Sgt. Dan Jenkins, and John Hazelton. (Courtesy of Don Peeples.)

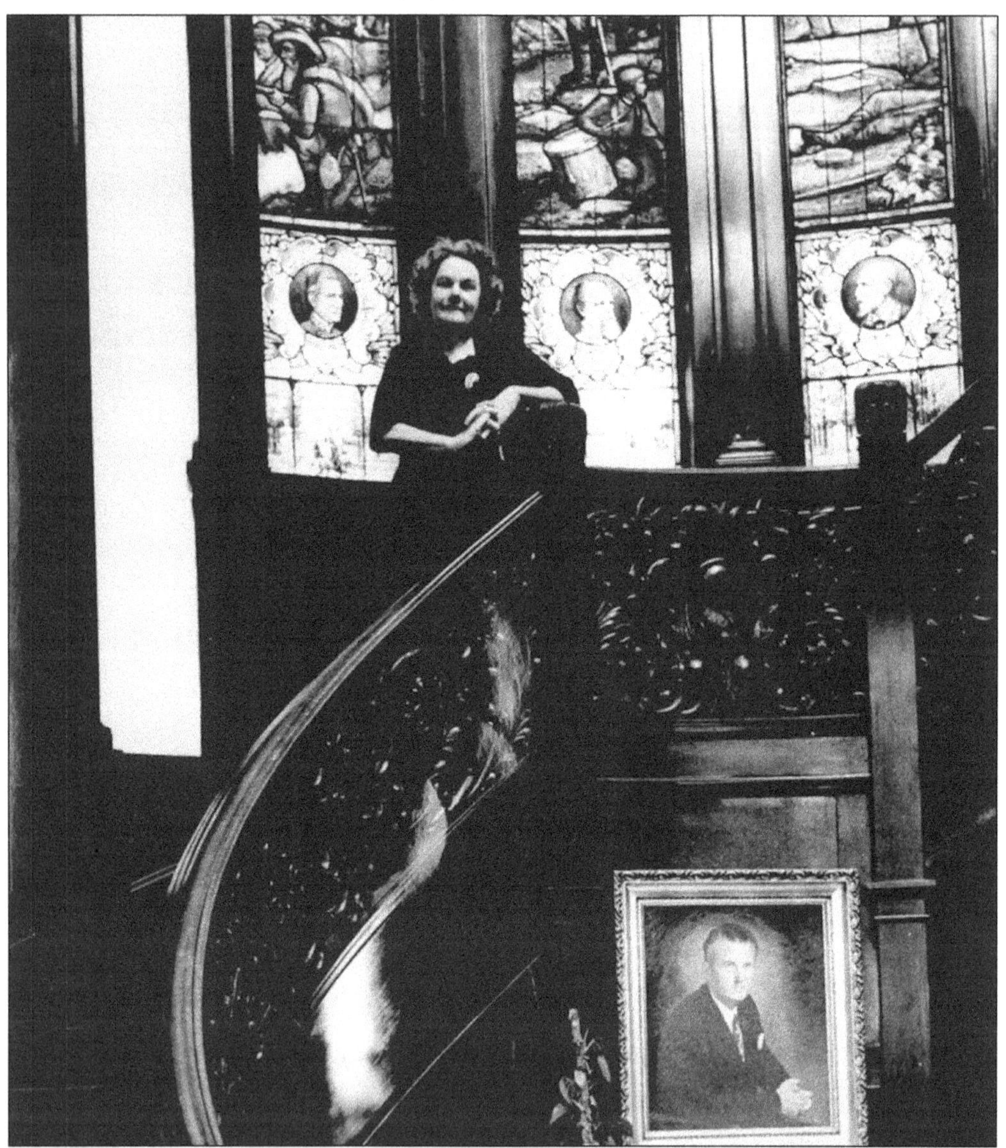

Born in LaGrange, Mary Givens Bryan (1910–1964) earned the title of "Georgia's Miss Mary" through her lifetime of work with the Georgia Department of Archives and History. Educated in Decatur public schools, Bryan and her quest for knowledge were fostered by family and teachers, and she completed professional training in archives administration and records management. In 1933, she began an archival career as a clerk with Georgia Archives and worked her way through the ranks to a 1950 appointment as acting director. In 1951, Bryan was named director and state archivist and served Georgians in this position until her untimely death. When Bryan took office in 1951, Rhodes Hall, the repository for Georgia's past where this image was taken, needed substantial restoration; a $6-million appropriation at Bryan's urging resulted in a new Archives Building. An ambitious and zealous professional, Bryan was elected president of the Society of American Archivists in 1959. She worked tirelessly to save Georgia's historic records and befriended Bebe Lang with whom she collaborated. Camden County honors this professional with its naming of the Bryan-Lang Historical Library. (Courtesy of Bryan-Lang Historical Library; photograph by Kirk Wooster.)

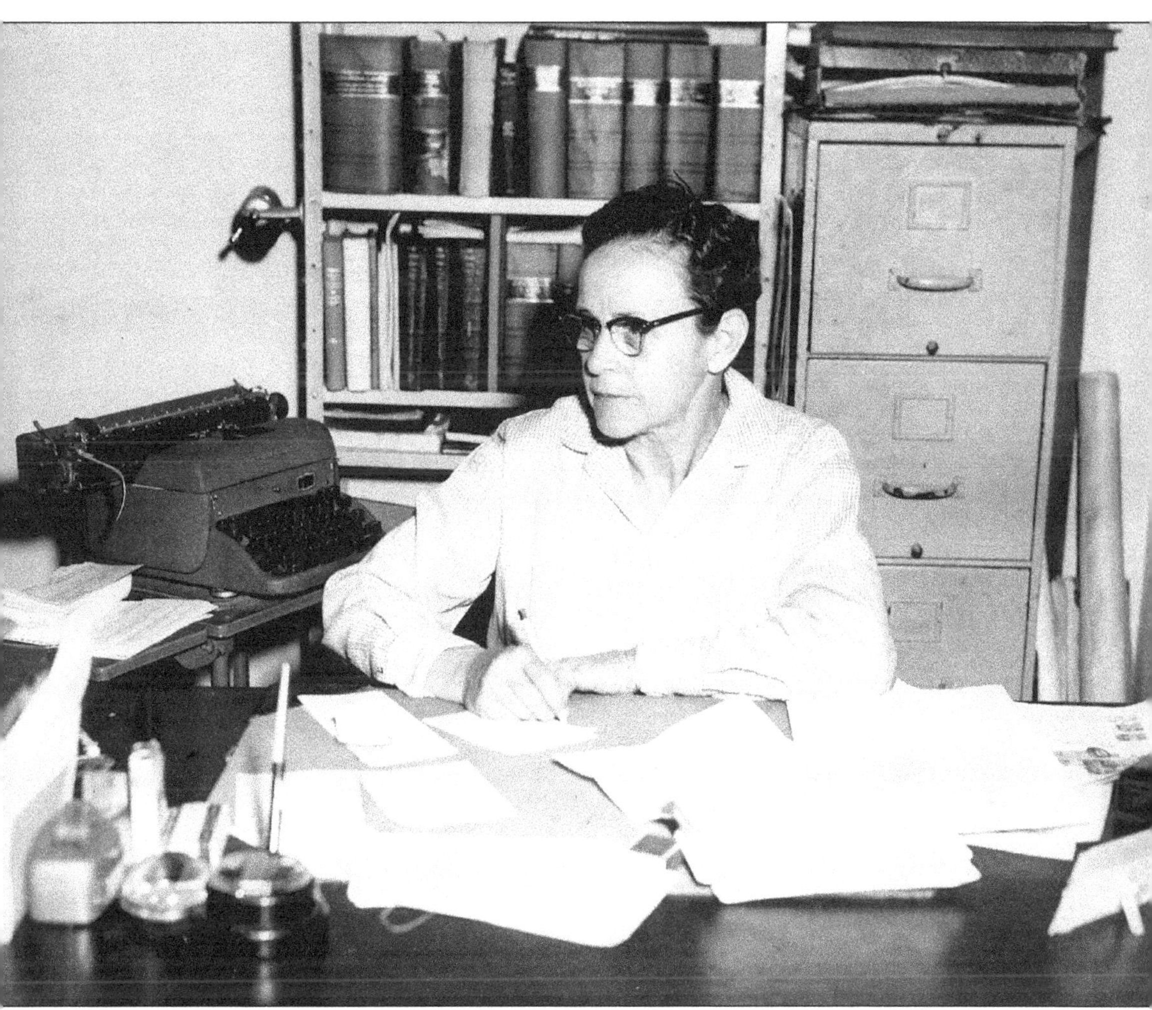

Shown at her Georgia Archives desk where she worked for over 20 years, "Miss Bebe" Lang (1903–1989) was born at Satilla Bluff, the daughter of Rufus Sumner Lang (1858–1913) and Beatrice Dufour Lang (1870–1949). A descendant of Isaac Lang Sr., Beatrice Fairchild "Bebe" Lang claimed one of Camden's oldest families as her own. Her father brokered timber and operated a store at the river mill village of Satilla Bluff. While living at Satilla Bluff, Bebe Lang learned about the business world; later, spotting an opportunity when the Coastal Highway opened, Lang opened a full-service gas station on the corner of Fourth Street and Bedell Avenue in Woodbine. An outdoorswoman, she enjoyed riding horses and hunting, as well as arranging boxing matches for neighbors. She received her formal education at the Georgia State Woman's College and, during World War II, worked at Cecil Field in Jacksonville in support of the war effort. She returned to Woodbine in 1947 to care for her invalid mother. After returning home, she served as registrar and justice of the peace, and a serendipitous meeting with Mary Givens Bryan in 1952 changed her life's work. Hired as a county archivist to collect, microfilm, and preserve the musty documents of Georgia's original eight counties: Wilkes, Richmond, Burke, Effingham, Chatham, Liberty, Glynn, and Camden Counties, Lang traveled the state; in 1956, she was selected as director of Georgia's county archives section. After retirement, Lang focused on creating an archival library in her native Camden County and realized this ambition after four years of grassroots fund-raising to build the Bryan-Lang Historical Library in Woodbine. (Courtesy of Bryan-Lang Historical Library.)

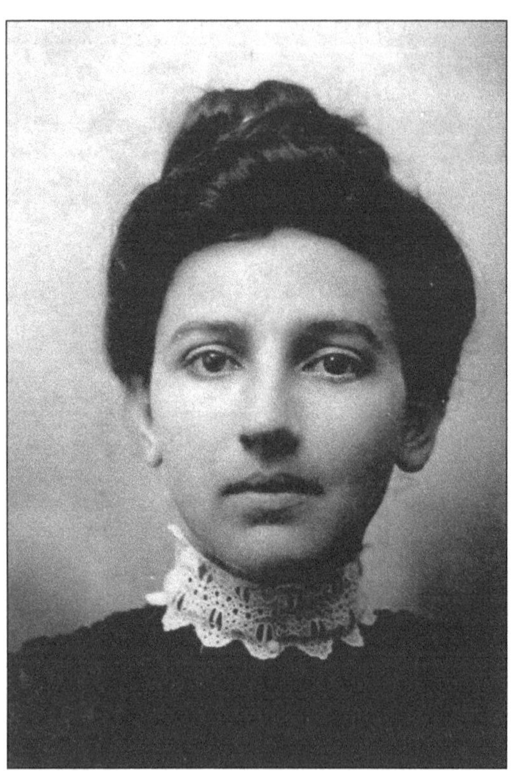

Sisters Gertrude and Addie Timmons were descended from a family that came to North Camden shortly after the American Revolution. Gertrude Armstead Timmons (1884–1960) was a daughter of Henry Crum Timmons (1847–1893) and Martha Brockington Littlefield (1858–1891); all are buried at Quarterman Cemetery. She married Eugene Everett Berrie, a son of Efford Jones Berrie and Mary Sileta Holtzendorf. This marriage joined a number of old Camden families who owned large tracts of land through wedded ties: Berrie, Brockington, Crum, Holtzendorf, Littlefield, and Timmons. From this exercise it is simple to determine how through extended family, many Camden Countians claim ancestral ties! (Courtesy of Beth Berrie Williams.)

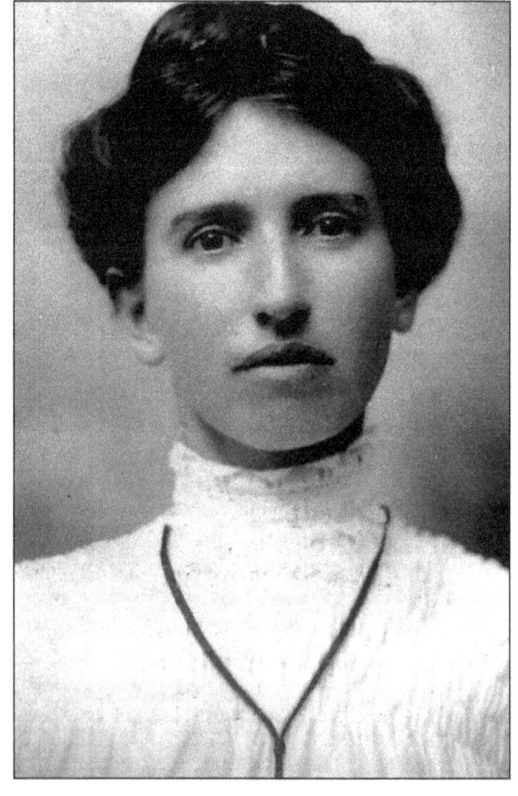

The soft features of this beautiful woman belie her prowess as an outdoorswoman and a sharp shooter. Yet, Mary Adaline "Addie" Timmons (1880–1963) was celebrated in an October 1947 *Atlanta Journal-Constitution* feature article in which a play on words suggested a hit Broadway show. Titled "Addie Get Your Gun," the story told of the Waverly resident's penchant for deer hunting and the large collection of antlers that adorned the old Timmons place where she lived all her life. She taught the Berrie boys how to hunt, and through time, family and friends contributed to the back porch mélange. At her death the count was 300 antler racks! Involved in missionary society work, Miss Timmons was one of the founders of Horse Stamp (pronounced Horse Stomp) Church in North Camden. (Courtesy of Beth Berrie Williams.)

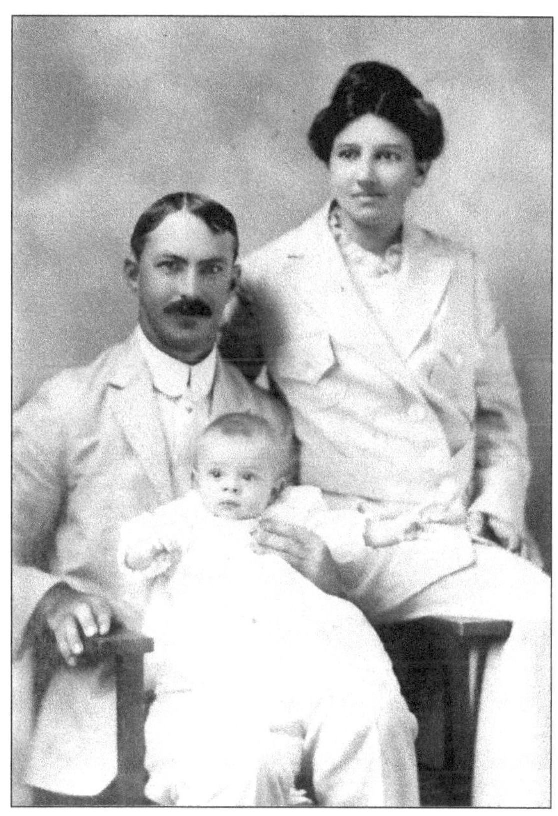

Eugene Everett Berrie Sr. (1885–1941), his wife, Gertrude, and their first-born son, Eugene Everett Berrie Jr., who was tragically killed in a 1940s automobile wreck, pose for a family photograph. Members of the Berrie family claim descent from William Berrie (1777–1841) of East Florida who bought Hickory Bluff Plantation from the William Scott estate at an 1823 sheriff's sale. Recognized as a prominent Camden County citizen, William Berrie served his community on the Camden County Militia and as justice of Inferior Court from 1817 to 1821. Although he made his home at Hickory Bluff, Berrie accumulated other large tracts of land in the Hazzard's Neck section of North Camden, including a 600-acre tract at Pernambuco (pronounced Piney Buckam) and a 150-acre tract at Hozier's Bluff, later devised to his heirs. (Courtesy of Beth Berrie Williams.)

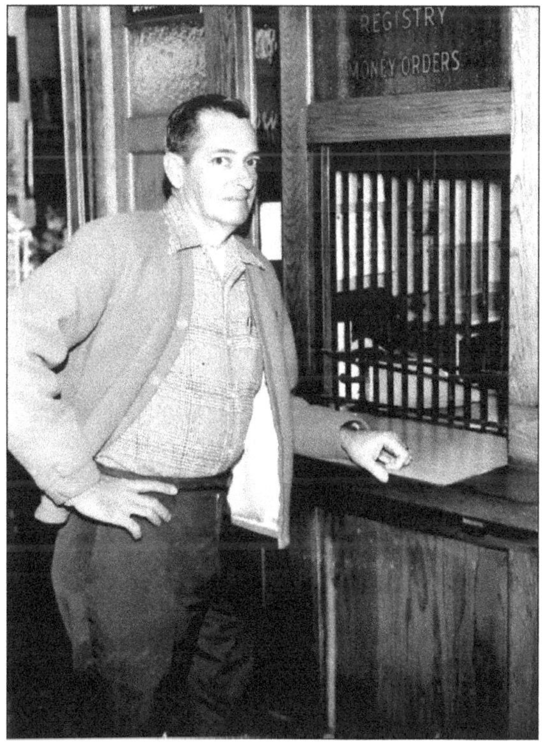

Heir to Berrie properties, the incomparable Elmer Ingerville Berrie (1928–1994) made his home at Hickory Bluff where his descendants live today on Maiden Creek, a tributary of the Little Satilla River. One of 16 graduates of North Camden County High School in June 1945, Berrie had an upbeat class motto, which was "May our difficulties be stepping stones to success." Following in his father Eugene's footsteps, Berrie was a businessman; he cruised timber, operated the Ocean Breeze Campground on the Dover Bluff Road, and served as a Camden County tax assessor. In this image, Berrie stands near the window of the old post office, once located in G.C. Harrell's General Store at Waverly, where the well-liked Berrie served a one-year stint as postman. (Courtesy of Beth Berrie Williams.)

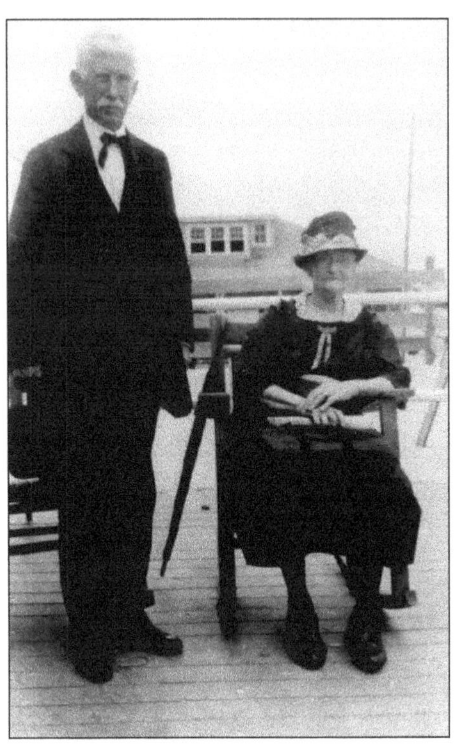

Taken on the Cumberland Dungeness dock, John Dilworth Ross and his wife, Caroline Mehrtens Ross, pose for posterity. Descended through his paternity from North Camden families and Andrew Miller Ross, John Ross relocated from Camden to Brunswick-Glynn County where he was employed as a bookkeeper. The couple parented seven children, the most famous of whom was Camden-born Mary Letitia "Mamie" Ross (1885–1971), a lifelong student of the Anglo-Hispanic struggle for empire. In 1925, she and Spanish Borderlands scholar Professor Herbert Eugene Bolton of Berkeley published a controversial book titled *The Debatable Land*. Their scholarly work examined in a new way the claims of Spain to the American Southeast and the borderlands of which Camden was an integral part. (Courtesy of Georgia Department of Archives and History, Mary L. Ross Papers, AC 73-163.)

Growing up on a remote St. Simons Island, Carl Olaff Svendsen Jr. (1909–2000), the lightkeeper's son, romped on southend beaches, sailed in a small sailboat, and fished for trout, bass, whiting, and sheepshead out of a 14-foot rowboat. Through the colonnades of live oaks and on the marshes' edge, he hunted squirrels, dove, and rabbits and anticipated the fall arrival of migratory waterfowl, such as the handsome mallard ducks. He combed the island beaches between the lighthouse and East Beach and assembled a large collection of Southeastern Indian artifacts. Proud of his Norwegian ancestry, Svendsen passed along to his children, Carl, Harold, Stanley, Sonja, and Mary, stories of his family's Old World ties. Although fishing and hunting proved his avocation, Svendsen supported his family through his work as captain of the St. Simons Island Fire Department. Unwilling to accept the vast changes affecting his island landscape, Svendsen moved to Camden County and lived at Harriett's Bluff in a home overlooking the Crooked River for over 25 years. (Courtesy of C.O. Svendsen Jr.)

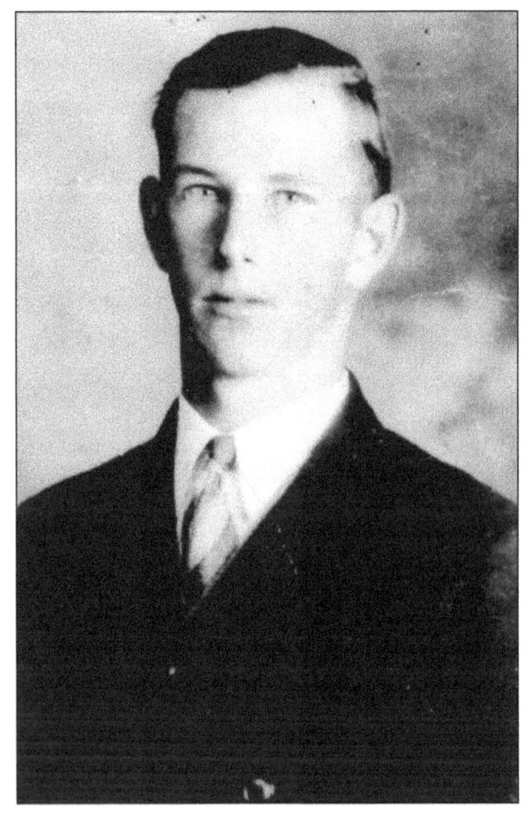

Alex L. Chaney (1905–2001) was born at the White Oak community to Joseph Bradford Chaney (1878–1957) and Nora Elizabeth Brogdon Chaney (1887–1973). Between 1924 and 1928, he worked as a Camden County deputy sheriff under his father, High Sheriff Joseph B. Chaney. Later, Chaney commuted from his Woodbine home to Tarboro where he worked with the E.A.P. McCarthy family at the Tarboro Mercantile Company from 1931 to 1939. As store manager, he was responsible for daily reports and bookkeeping and clerked six days per week with fellow employees Johnny Sarman, Theodore Bruce, and John Buie. During World War II, Chaney accepted a position with the Naval Air Station at Jacksonville, Florida. His sharp memories have contributed toward the richness of Camden's past in recollecting the heyday of the old Tarboro Mercantile Store. Merchants from Spring Bluff, Waverly, White Oak, Woodbine, Colesburg, Seals, Scotchville, Kingsland, and Brunswick purchased there. Grits and meal arrived in boxcar load shipments, in addition to timothy hay, and rice arrived 100 bags at a time. Horse, mule, and cow feed arrived at White Oak by the railroad boxcar load. (Courtesy of the Author.)

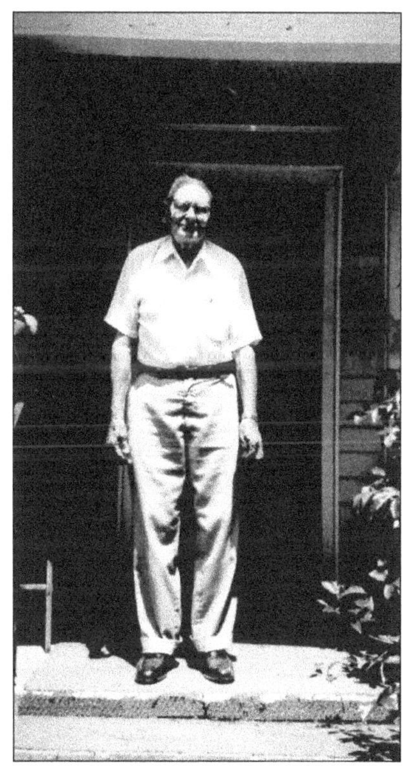

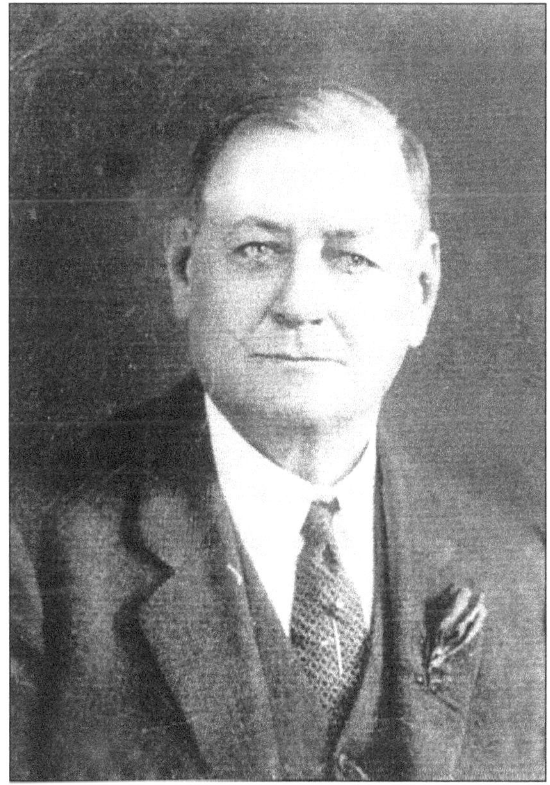

Descended from Isham Peeples Sr. and the son of George Henry "G.H." Peeples and Julia Ann Cooner Peeples, W.H. Peeples Sr. left his mark on the landscape. His father served as the executor of Isham Peeples' estate, and was wounded in the American Civil War in service to Clinch's 4th Georgia Cavalry. G.H. Peeples owned a store and brick kiln and operated a post office at Oakwell, located on Clark's Bluff. His son W.H. inherited the sawmill from his father where in later times, he sawed the timber to build the First Baptist Church of Kingsland. Hebron Church, Ruhamah Church, and Kingsland Baptist Church also bear his mark. W.H. Peeples' wife, Mary Ida Wingate Peeples (Crow), can be seen on page 95 with the couple's grandson Wilbur H. Sheffield, and the W.H. Peeples' Store on Kingsland's Railroad Avenue can be seen in other images on pages 35 and 47. (Courtesy of Rodney Sheffield.)

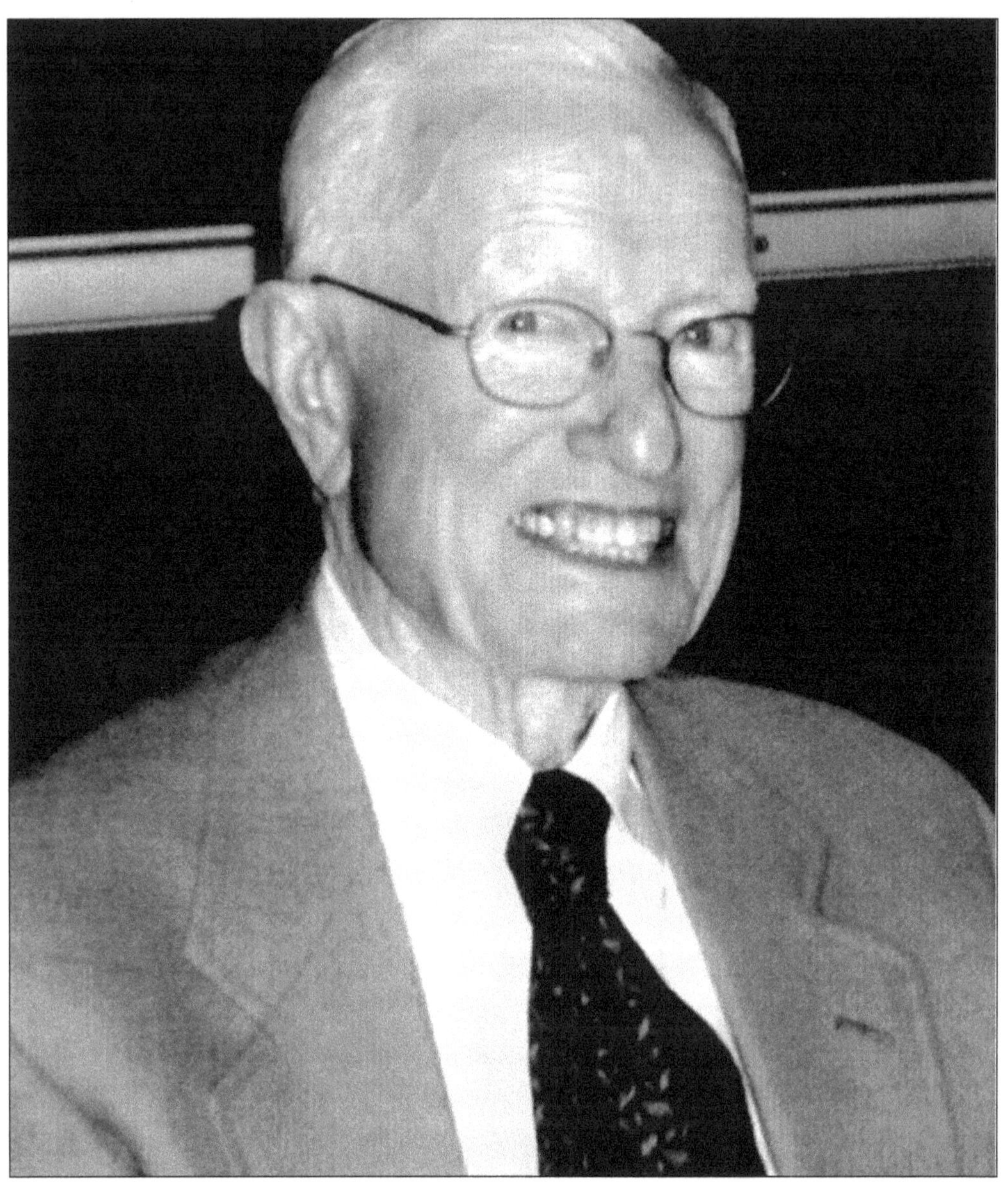

Born on February 8, 1915 and reared in Hortense, Judge James Causey "Joe" Strickland grew up during the Great Depression. His father, Jim Strickland, owned a turpentine still, and when scarcely 21 years old, the future judge worked as a woodsrider, "riding the crop," monitoring hundreds of piney woods acres and supervising turpentine workers chipping and dipping. Later, Strickland spent 35 years working in the signals maintenance branch of the Seaboard Coastline Railroad and moved to Woodbine with his family after World War II. Hired by Camden County in 1975, Strickland served as the first county building inspector and zoning officer, held an elected position as justice of the peace for an eight-year stint, and in 1983 was appointed Camden's first chief magistrate judge. Subsequently, Judge Strickland was elected to the position three times and served until his retirement in December 2000. Judge Strickland also made time for active membership in the Woodbine Methodist Church and was a charter member of the Woodbine Lion's Club. In retirement, the Judge will have more time to check on his tree farm in Brantley County. (Courtesy of the Strickland family.)

Five

Gatherings and Special Events

History demonstrates that reunions and family gatherings create a greater sense of family and well being for those who participate, connecting them with their mutual past. Wander through these images and learn about those people whose lives were enriched by family gatherings, get-togethers, and reunions. In a spirit of celebration, remember those people who can point to the present as well as to the past, recalling advocates for progress and the prominent men and women who color Camden's pages, some of whom may be seen here. Read about high-water marks for history making, building roads and bridges, facing adversity with fortitude, groundbreaking, a 50th anniversary event, patriotic service, and those colorful characters whose rascal ways spice our lives.

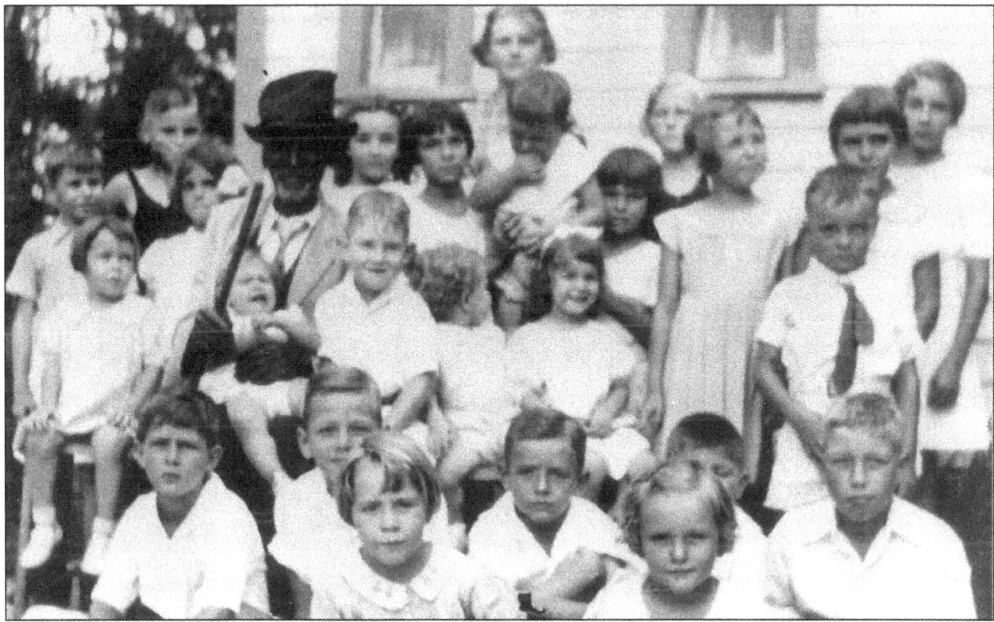

A group of 25 children have gathered around "Uncle London" Jackson for storytelling at "Cousins' Day," c. 1936. Held at Island Grove, this event evolved into a "Lang Family Reunion" held annually on the second Sunday of each June at Crooked River State Park. Family members convene from all over the country to share memories and time with one another. In this image are, from left to right, (front row) Mary Lang (Morris) and Charlotte Gale (Miller); (second row) Jasper Lang, Dave Gale, Neal Gale, Jack Lang, and Hubert Lang Jr. Uncle London holds the baby Margaret Lang (Mitchell) and just to the right of Uncle London is Pete Lang. Other identified cousins include, standing fourth from right, Lillian Lang (Meyers), followed by, from left to right, Phillip Cason, Virginia Lang (Barnes,) and Helen Cason. (Courtesy of the Lang family and Virginia Lang Barnes.)

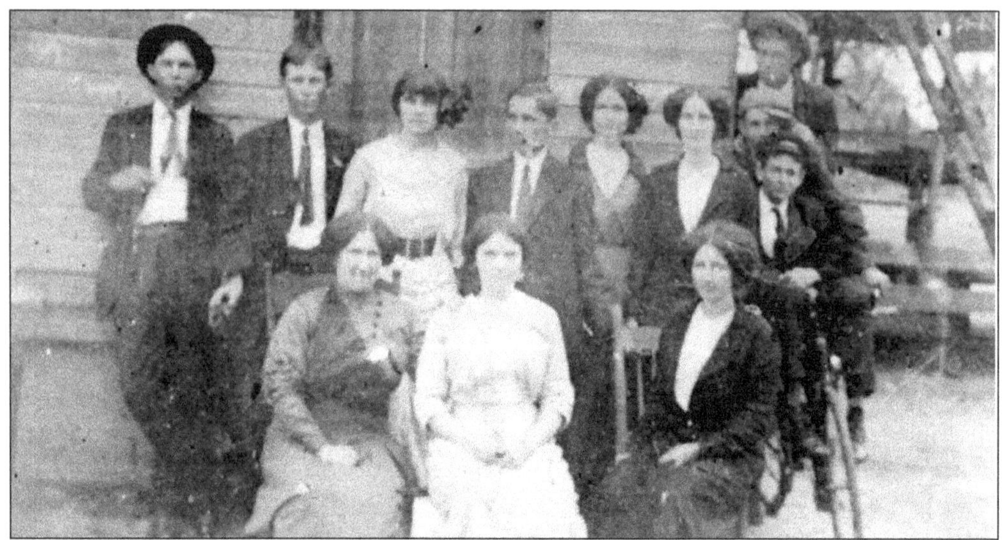

Seen in a 1910 image, from left to right, (front row) Mary Riley Buie, Susan Joiner (Peeples), Flo Buie (Gray); (back row) Joe Brown, Farris Brown, Sadie Joiner (Jackson), David Nevill Drury, Annie Buie, Kate Buie (Harrell), Sinclair Ribron, Lonnie Drury, and Archie Buie have gathered at the Joseph Lemuel Drury homeplace known as the Lang Post Office—the first post office located north of the Satilla River. Associated with an early Camden settler, Isaac Lang, Jr. (1800-1870) and his wife, Caroline Atkinson Lang (1809-1889), the site served as the ancestral home for this family at Langsbury Plantation until it was abandoned. (Courtesy of Shirley Joiner Thompson.)

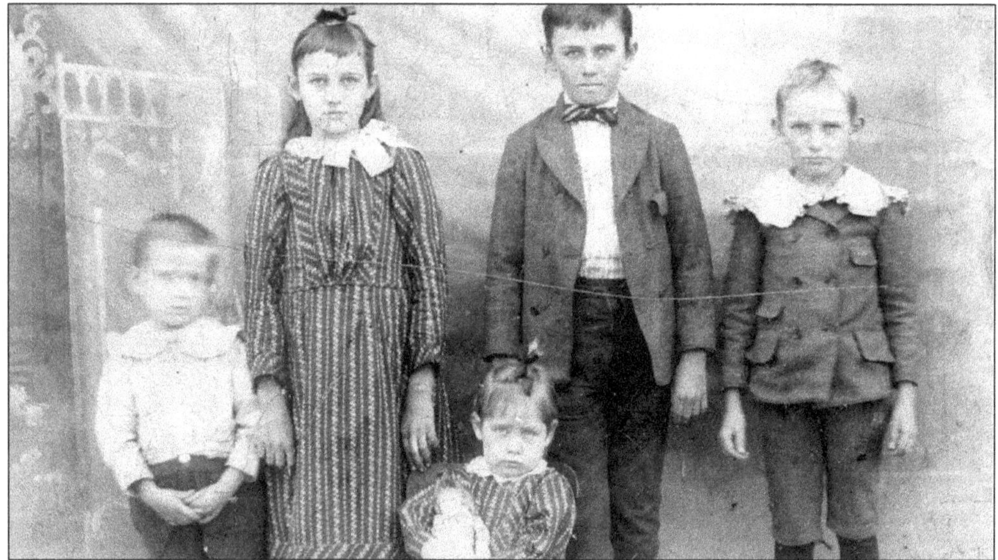

Five of Joseph Lemuel Drury and Elsie Minchew Drury's children gathered for this photograph, including, from left to right, (front) the baby Pearl, who died young; (back row) David Nevill Drury, Mamie Drury, Oliver Cleveland Drury, and Joseph Mills Drury. Their father was the son of Joseph Mills Drury, born ca. 1818 to Charles Nevill Drury and Rachel E. Mills. An indenture documents C.N. Drury's sale in July 1839 of 202 acres land to Peter Readdick who later sold to C.W. Harrell. Hence, for 150 years about thirty acres of this property has remained in the Drury-Readdick-Harrell and related families. (Courtesy of Shirley Joiner Thompson.)

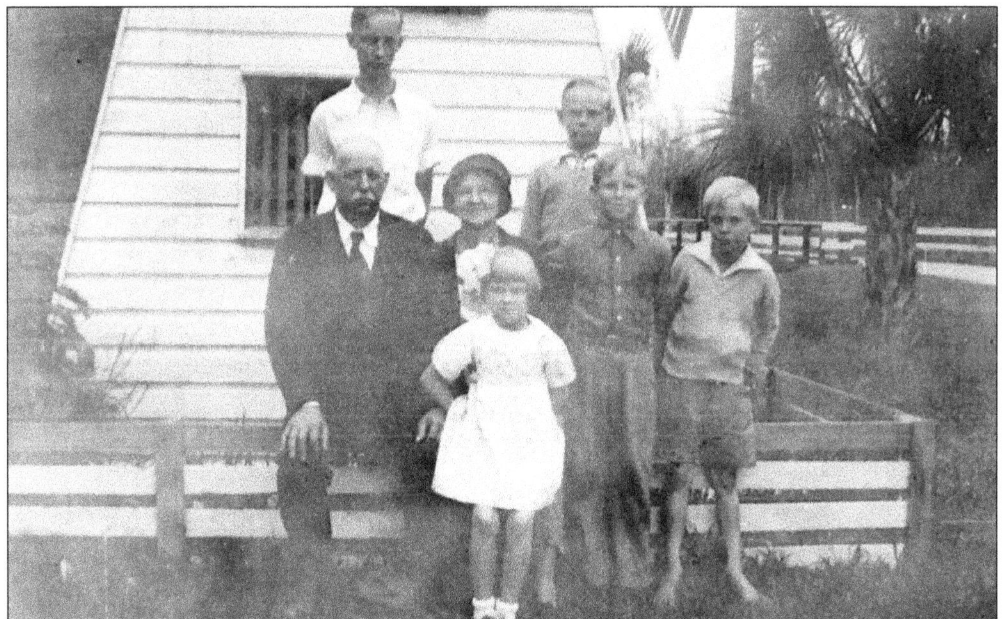

This image was taken of the Russell family in the early 1930s at a family reunion picnic held at Island Grove. On Clark's Island, a cold artesian well furnished more than ample water to the sheer delight of children who swam and played in the spacious concrete swimming pool. The very large Atkinson-Russell family has assembled for this important family gathering. Seen in the image are (front row) a young Julia Camilla Boston Russell Green; (middle row), Henry Clement Russell and Mary Cleveland Atkinson Russell, Charles Russell and Jim Russell; (back row) Henry Clement "Harry" Russell, Jr. and Burwell Russell. (Courtesy of the Burwell A. Russell Family.)

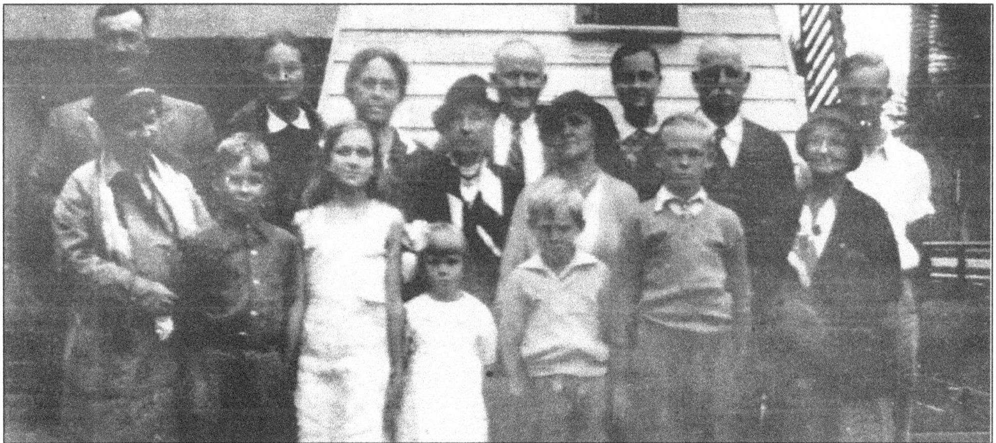

Taken in the early 1930s, possibly 1933, members of the Atkinson-Russell family pause for the cameraman, reputedly Paul Lovejoy. From left to right are (front row) Elizabeth Atkinson Lovejoy, Charles McDonald Russell, Catherine Atkinson Adams, Julia Russell, Jim Russell, Burwell Russell, and Mary Cleveland Atkinson; (back row) John Atkinson, Estelle Atkinson Quarterman, Catherine Foster Atkinson, Rosa Lee King Atkinson, Burwell Alexander Atkinson, Marian Atkinson Nolan, Rosa Lee Atkinson, Henry Clement Russell, and Henry Clement "Harry" Russell Jr. In the background are the paddles of a large windmill at Island Grove Tourist Court, seen in the image. (Courtesy of the Burwell A. Russell family.)

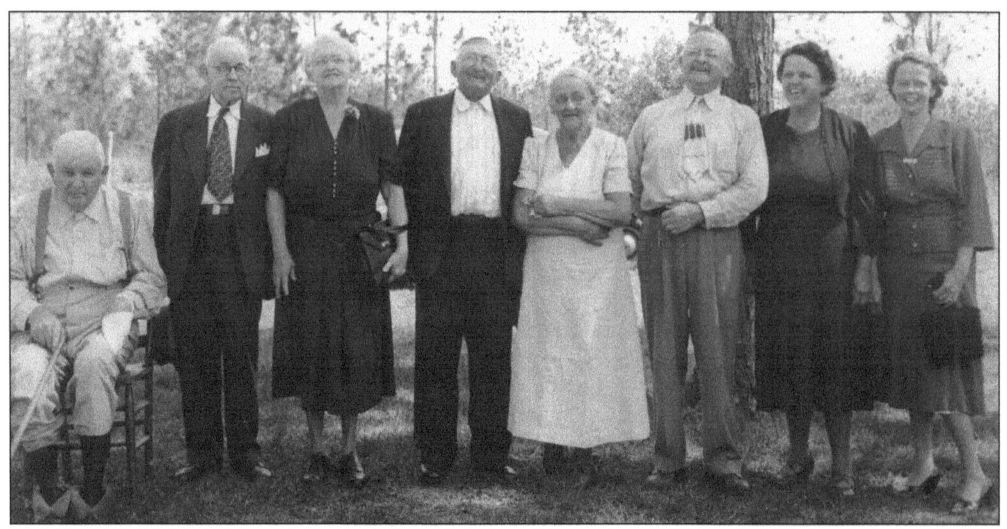

Revolutionary War veteran West Sheffield and his second wife, Elizabeth Randall, were the parents of two sons, Randall and John (1804–1883), the latter being the ancestor of all Camden County Sheffields. John received five separate land grants from the state of Georgia, totaling 1,484 acres. When the American Civil War ended, Sheffield owned over 20,000 acres of land, including North Kingsland to the Coleraine Road. Later, he deeded to his nine daughter's husbands and an unmarried daughter. Camden Mason Sheffield (1841–1912) was the son of John and his wife, Sarah Ann Cook (1806–1895), and eight of his children have gathered for this family portrait. From left to right are Herbert Sheffield (seated), Lee Sheffield, Mamie Stafford Pickren, Downey Sheffield, Lila S. Blount, Sherard C. Sheffield, Lucille S. Wells, and Lillian S. Stover. (Courtesy of Rodney Sheffield.)

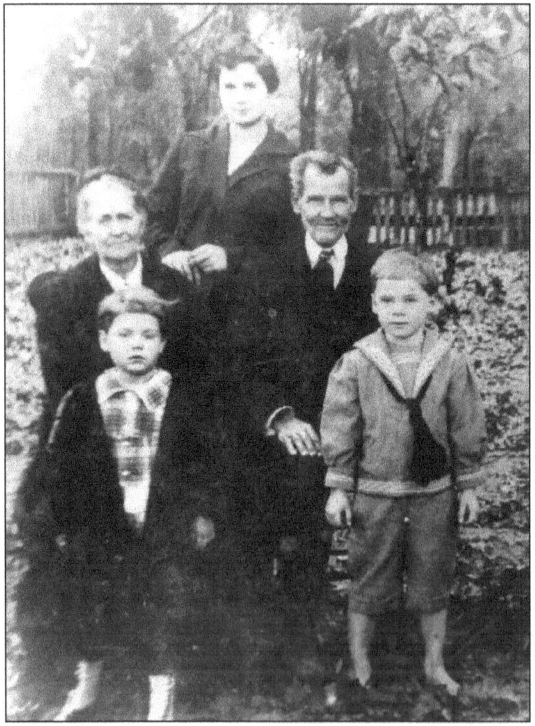

Seen here, from left to right, are (front row) Hazel Gowen and William Mann Bryant; (second row) Maybelle (Mabel) Pope Godley Dean (1855–1930) and Emory Franklin Dean (1853–1946); (back row) Ruth Dean. Born in Haralson County to Marquis Lafayette Dean and Martha Watson Andrews Dean, Rev. Emory Franklin Dean received his calling *c.* 1871 at a Bethel Camp Meeting. He converted to Methodism and served as a circuit-riding preacher for the 72 years he was licensed to preach as a minister of the Methodist Episcopal Church (North). His studies at Grant University/East Tennessee University in Athens, Tennessee prepared him for his life's work, which carried him from the mountains of north Georgia to the Okefenokee in south Georgia. In Camden County, he taught, preached, and built buggies. (Courtesy of Hazel Dean Overstreet and Bessie Dean Dent.)

The son of Rev. E.F. Dean and his wife, Emory Fuller Dean (1880–1968) was born at Burnt Fort and was one of seven children. He married Lillie Gibson (1891–1971) at Folkston, Georgia on February 5, 1911, and they were the parents of seven children: Henry, Roscoe, Lillie, Hazel, Harry, Bessie, and Mildred. Throughout his life, Dean was involved in turpentine and naval stores production and timber activities. In earlier days, he managed turpentine camps when rosin was sold to the Downing Company in Brunswick; he worked with woodsriders, set up turpentine stills, leased timber, and was a successful businessman and large landowner. The Deans lived in Camden County between 1926 and 1927 at Lampadosia and the younger children recalled attending school at Waverly. (Courtesy of Hazel Dean Overstreet and Bessie Dean Dent.)

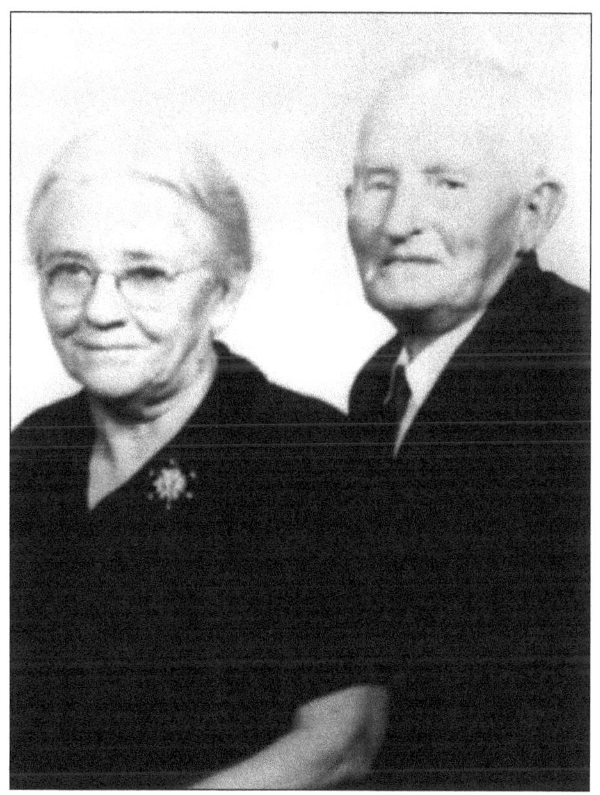

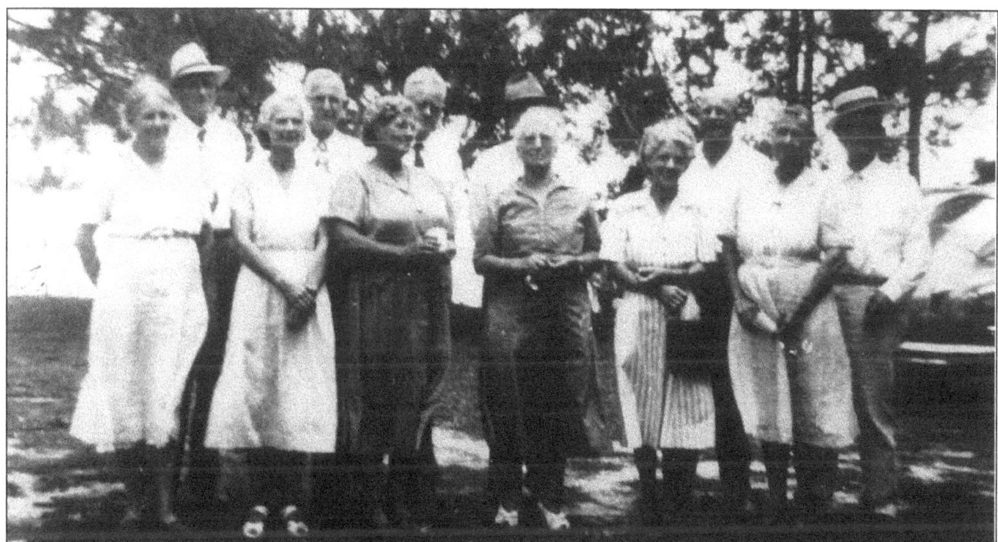

At a 1955 Dean family reunion, the children of Rev. and Mrs. Emory Franklin Dean gathered with their spouses at the Dean Cottage, located on the bluff of the private Dover Bluff Hunting Club. Seen in this image are, from left to right, (front row) Lillie Gibson Dean, Ruth Dean Gibson, Anna Dean Jacobs, Annie Mizell Dean, Emma Casey Dean, and Agnes Dean Gowen; (back row) Emory F. Dean, Madison Gibson, Charlie Jacobs, Thomas LaFayette Dean, Guy Albert Dean, and James V. "Jim" Gowen. (Courtesy of Hazel Dean Overstreet and Bessie Dean Dent.)

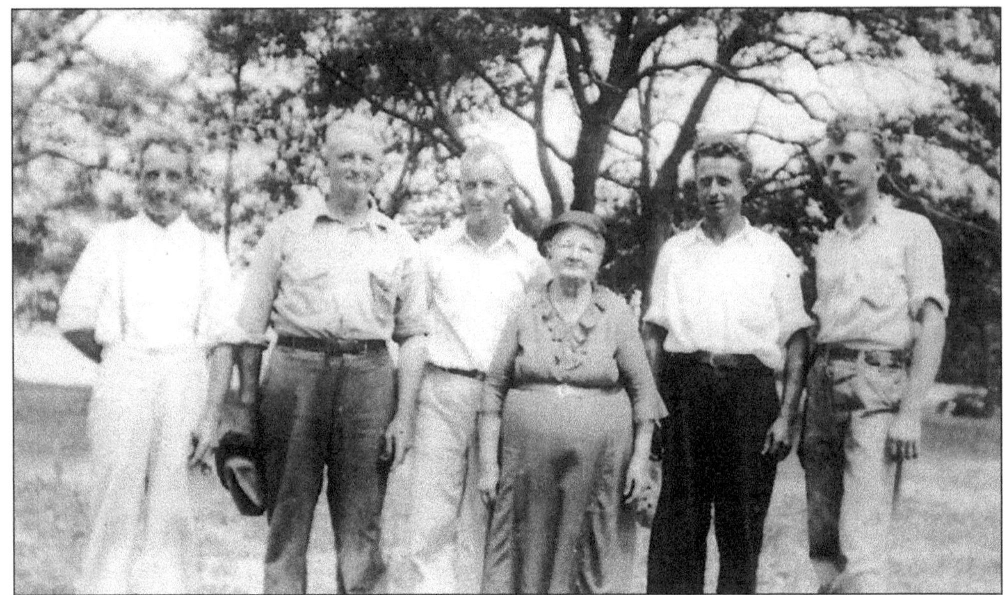

In these images, members of the Donald Tompkins Peeples family pose for the camera. When he wed Olive Brazell in 1881, Peeples joined the two families in eternity. Today, they rest beside one another in the Brazell Cemetery, just south of Kingsland. Shown above are Olive and her five sons, from left to right: Donald Joseph "D.J." (1882–1963), William Escott, Richard Donald (1897–1917), Alton Parker, and John. Their ancestor Isham Peeples Sr. moved from Carolina to Camden with his two older brothers and parents in the early 1800s, married in Camden County, and settled west of the present Ruhamah Church. In July 1849 he was awarded a contract as a rural mail carrier and rode his horse from his home to St. Marys for mail collection, then on to Nassau County at Woodstock Mills, located between Bolougne and King's Ferry, and back to St. Marys for mail delivery. (Courtesy of Daniel Peeples.)

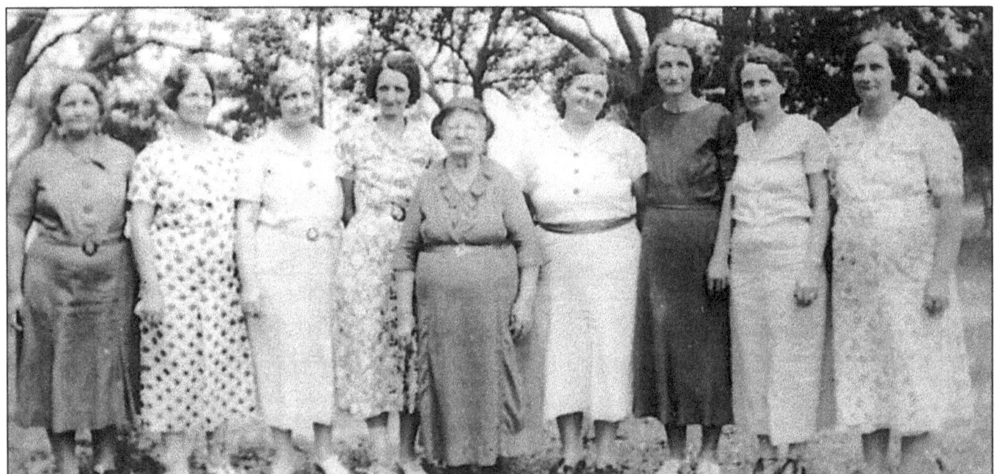

Olive B. Peeples (center) is surrounded by her eight daughters, from left to right: Fostina P. Brewton (1885–1980), Eleanor P. Cooner, Irene P. Wright (1887–1971), Olive Geneva P. Anderson (1889–1950), Maude P. Joiner, Doolie P. Lewis, Ruby P. Readdick, and Emma P. Lewis (1895–1973). In a far less transient period of the rural American South, families who lived near one another often inter-married. In this instance, two sisters, Emma and Doolie, married two brothers, Horace and Raymond Clarence Lewis. (Courtesy of Daniel Peeples.)

Accompanied by his maternal grandmother, Mary Ida Wingate Peeples Crow, young Wilbur H. Sheffield stands on a pine stump at Kingsland's City Park, which was formerly owned by W.H. King. The image was taken in 1927 when Kingsland celebrated the opening of U.S. Highway 17 and the Georgia-Florida Bridge at the St. Marys River crossing. Herbert Forsyth Sheffield (1874–1951) hosted a festive barbeque in the park, offering finger-licking good pork and beef for all celebrants. Sheffield served the Camden community as first mayor of Kingsland after incorporation and as county surveyor for 30 years prior to his retirement. (Courtesy of Rodney Sheffield.)

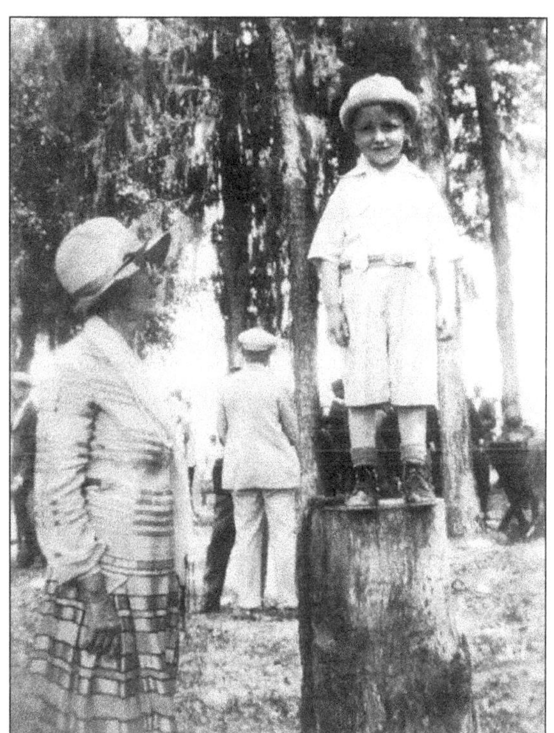

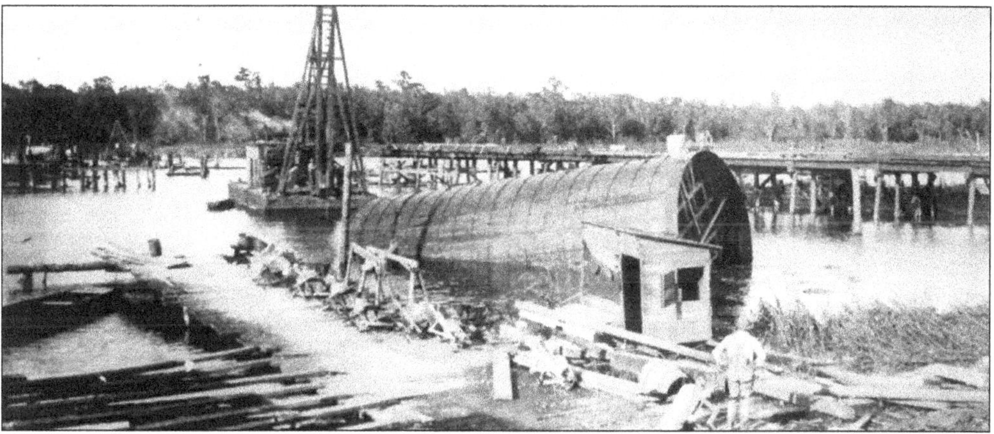

An April 1927 report informed the public of a major highway construction project funded by state and federal authorities. Work progressed on the new road that served as the Atlantic Coastal Highway, or Highway 17, and linked Chatham to Camden County and the Florida line. The new highway deviated from the old Dixie Highway, c. 1912 route, and beginning at the small community of Waverly in Camden paralleled the Seaboard Air Line Railway tracks through White Oak, Woodbine, Kingsland, and on to the St. Marys River. Completed in summer 1927, the new Satilla River Bridge (seen here under construction) replaced a toll bridge. The completed north/south route placed new demands upon coastal law enforcement. Businesses catering to the needs of Florida-bound tourists seeking sun and fun flourished. One of the more unusual traffic-stoppers, Charles "Ches" McCartney, known as "The Goatman," made an annual trek during the mid-20th century through Camden to the delight of young children. This folksy eccentric, who was a proponent of simple truths, died in 1998. (Courtesy of Bryan-Lang Historical Library.)

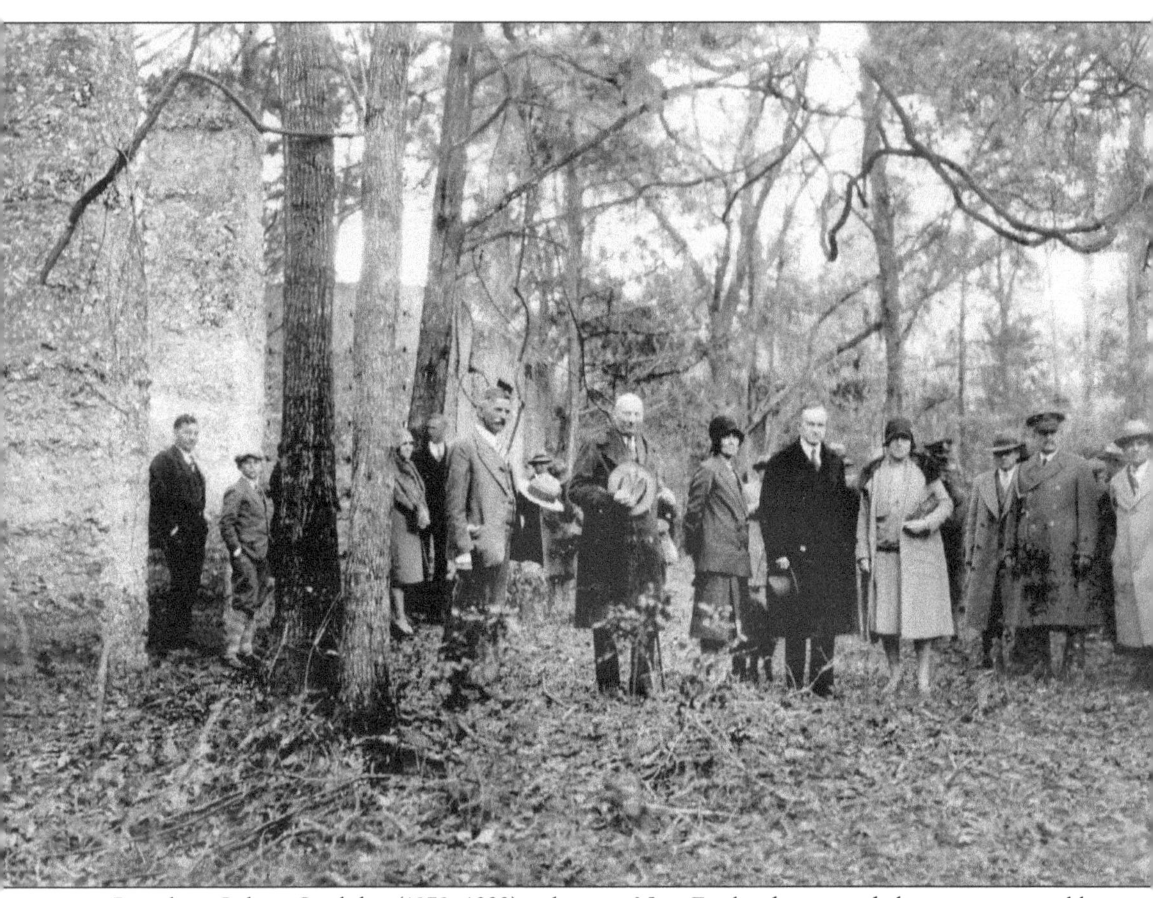

President Calvin Coolidge (1872–1933), a laconic New Englander, visited the impressive tabby ruins at the McIntosh sugar works in 1928 with his friend Howard Coffin (with hat held to his heart). A Detroit automobile magnate, Coffin came South and invested in the mystique of the coast and southeast Georgia at Sapelo Island, Long Island/Glynn Isle (Sea Island), and at Cabin Bluff located in the Floyd's Neck section of Camden County. Coffin shared game preserves and historic sites, Southern-style hospitality and plantation-era entertainment with influential and prominent friends. In the late 1920s, these limey ruins were recognized as the remains of a 17th-century Santa Maria Mission site. Subsequently, in the late 1930s historians determined that ruins in Camden, Glynn, and McIntosh Counties dated from the 18th-century Oglethorpe era, or were antebellum period structures. A young and future managing editor of *The Southeast Georgian*, Howard H. Davis stands (second from the left) near the ruins. His mother, Beulah Mizell Davis King, escorts President Coolidge and stands to his immediate left. (Courtesy of Camden County Historical Commission.)

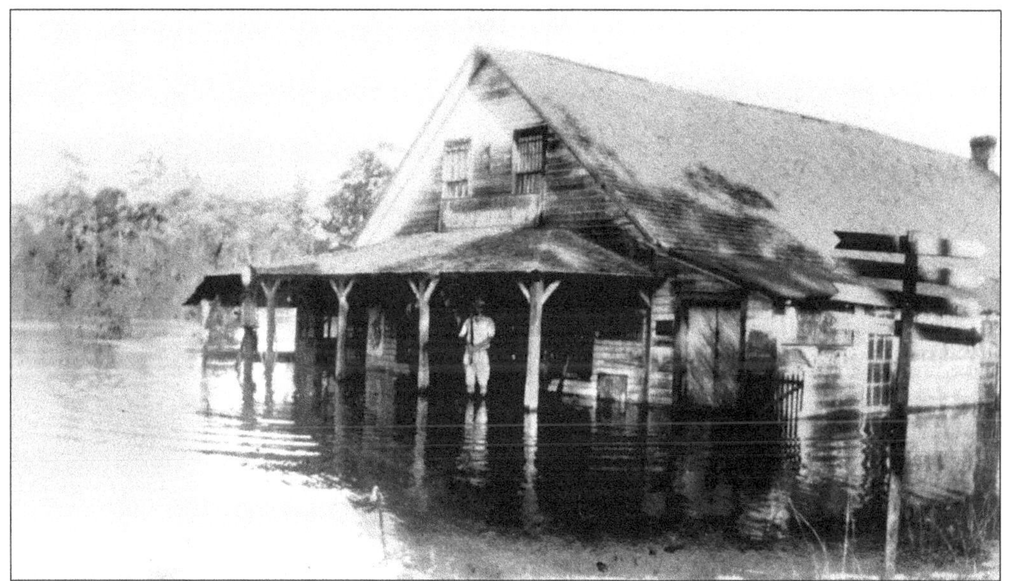

In the early 20th century, a number of men served as bookkeepers or clerks in John Clark Buie's store at Burnt Fort. They included Jim Brown, Holland Brown, John A. Buie, Newt Boring Sr., Buster Godley, Barney Gowen, Paul Proctor, and Furman Clark. When the floodwaters of a great freshet in 1928 enveloped Burnt Fort, Newt Boring Sr. worked as a clerk for Buie's commissary. Dramatic, plunging bluffs elevating the land 30 to 40 feet above the river's edge were swallowed up by the swirling freshet, and 18 inches of water stood in the store. In this image, an unidentified man stands ready with a shotgun at the Burnt Fort Store. Whether he was wary of looters or the ubiquitous water moccasins and alligators is unknown. (Courtesy of Eloise Bailey Thompson.)

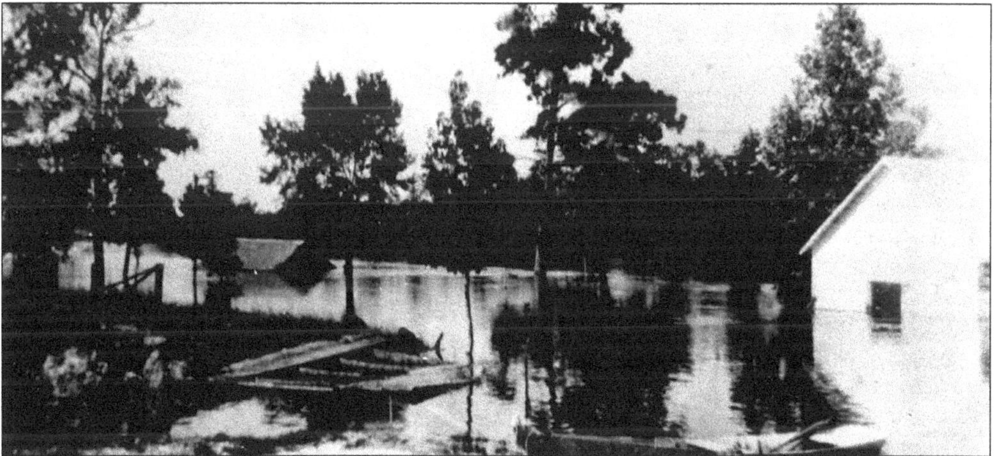

While none of the Burnt Fort residents were stranded due to the freshet, many were inconvenienced; bridges and paved roadways did not exist. Clerk Newt Boring Sr. boated out to the hill and brought commissary customers into the store where merchandise had been elevated for safekeeping and to prevent spoilage. In this manner, basic staple commodities were sold under extreme cataclysmic weather conditions, and community residents cooperated with one another for survival. High water from the freshet lasted about one week, and in this image, an unidentified child stands on the dry ground; Madena Arnow Proctor preserved this photograph for posterity. (Courtesy of Eloise Bailey Thompson.)

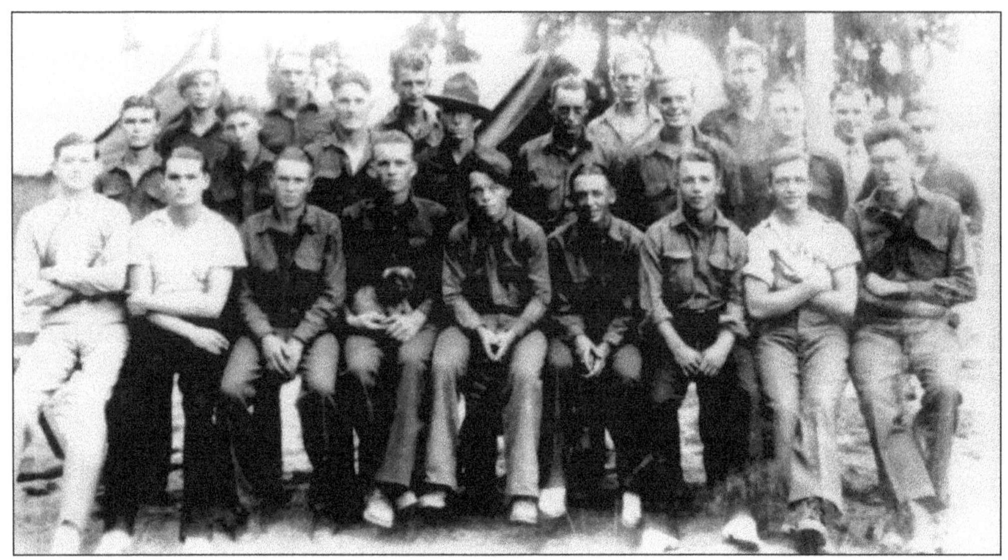

During the Great Depression, a program targeted the training and education of youth, beginning in 1932 with the Civilian Conservation Corps (CCC). Employed by the federal government to plant trees, combat fires and tree diseases, young men were put to work in Camden where forestry related activities and industries offered economic livelihood. Initially, a CCC Camp was located at Colesburg but was relocated to Satilla Bluff, where this image was taken. A regimented lifestyle followed U.S. Army rules and regulations enforced by Capt. F.C. Buckley, the commanding officer of the CCC Camp #452 in Camden County; Elmer E. Dyal, head of the forestry division, supervised the men in field with the able assistance of Burwell Atkinson, who served as engineer. (Courtesy of Eloise Bailey Thompson.)

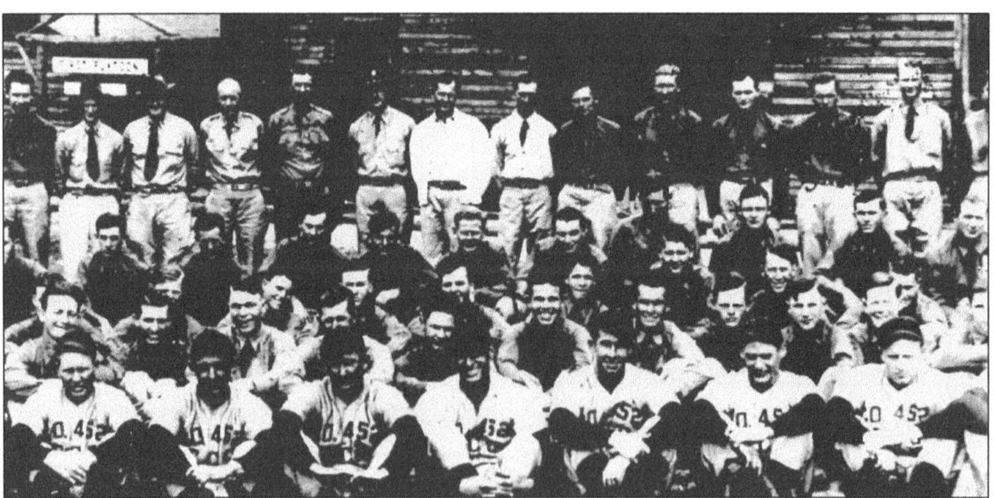

These young men received classroom instruction as well as practical work in the field, preparing them for future employment with useful job skills. CCC youths constructed 16-foot-wide, single-lane roads, or "truck trails," which served as firebreaks for Camden's several hundred thousands of acres set aside as forestry lands. Culverts and bridges, fire suppression and the construction of the Colesburg ranger station were among the contributions of the CCC youth in Camden prior to disbanding in 1938. But life was not all hard work, as this image attests; ballplayers paused from their play and gathered for this group photograph. (Courtesy of Eloise Bailey Thompson.)

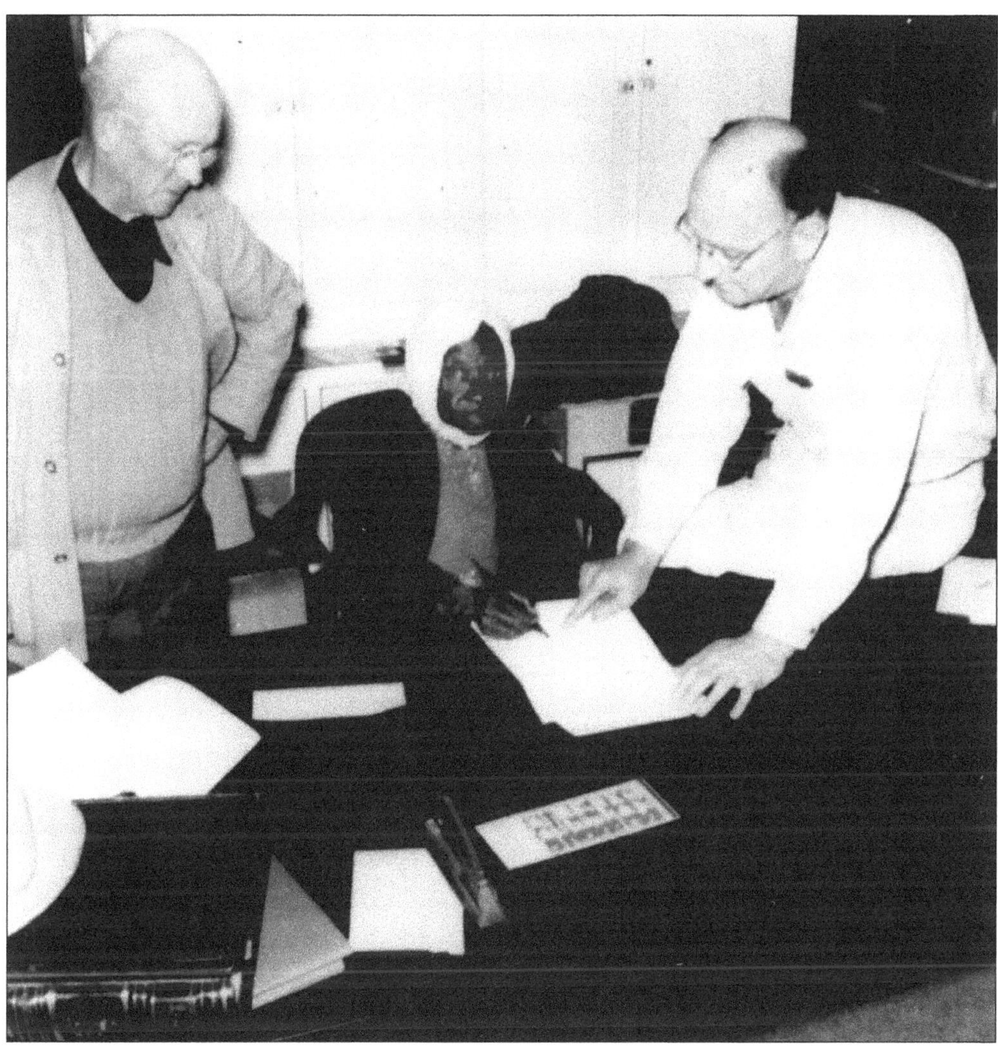

Prior to 1953, motorists traveling south of the Satilla River crossed a wooden bridge southbound onto a two-lane Highway 17 through the county seat of Woodbine. After years of planning, the Georgia Department of Transportation faced a mammoth project with new bridge construction crossing the Satilla, as well as road widening through town. Captured for posterity is property owner Lizzie Hicks flanked by Karl W. Brittain (left), a Georgia DOT employee and J.E. Godley (right), clerk of Camden County Superior Court as Hicks signs a deed of right-of-way to the State Highway Department for 47 feet of her property necessary for the widening of Highway 17 through Woodbine. (Courtesy of Bryan-Lang Historical Library.)

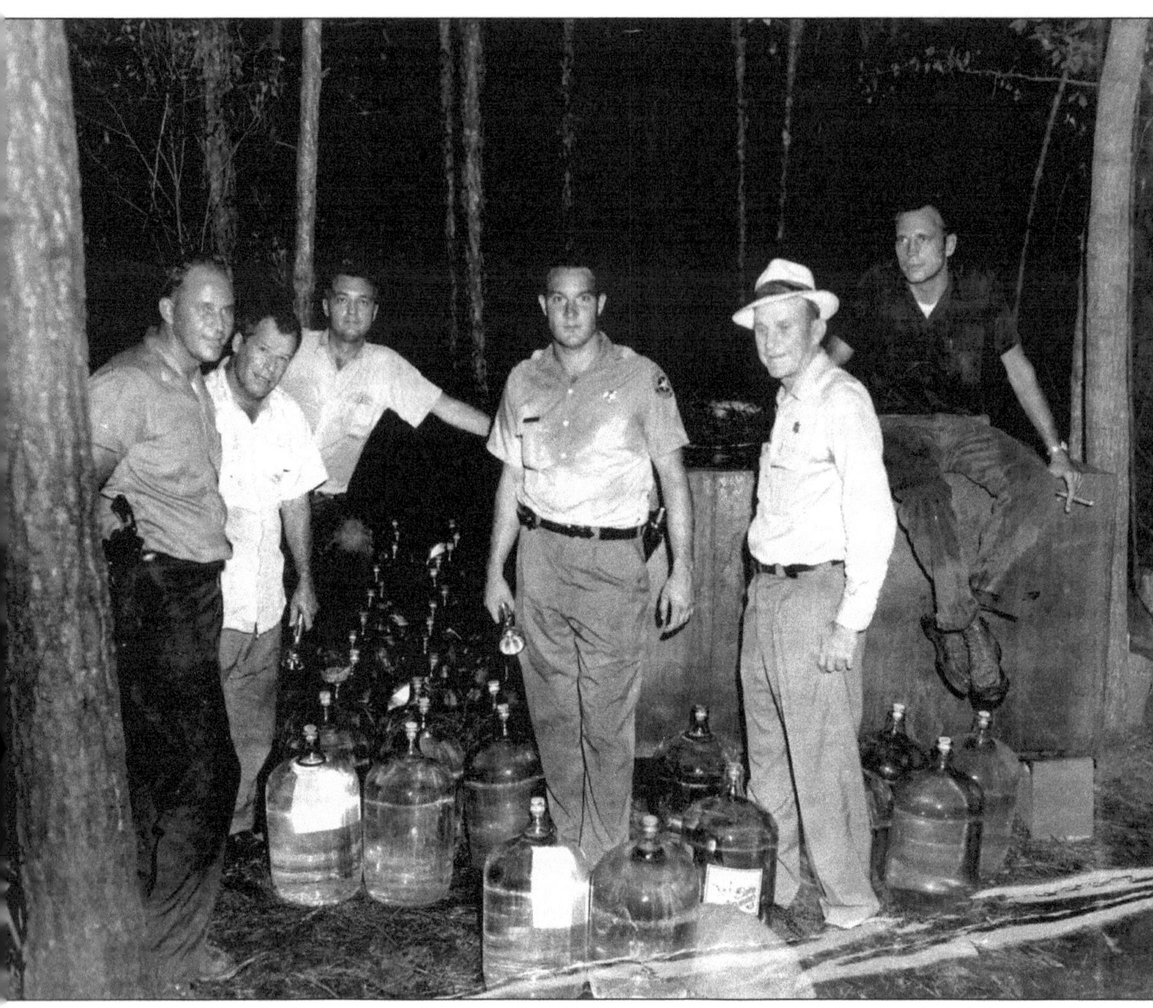

On a muggy 1950s evening, three unidentified revenue agents were accompanied by Camden County Deputy Sheriff J.D. Peeples (second from left), Deputy Sheriff Jimmy Middleton (fourth from left), and Sheriff W.E. "Willie" Smith (fifth from left). Sheriff Smith succeeded his father, Gordon Blake Smith, at his death in 1942 and served as Camden County sheriff for 34 years until his retirement in 1976. Middleton was elected sheriff in 1976 and served two four-year terms, from 1976 to 1984. Although an upside-down label on one of the 42 demijohns reads "Orange Cup Water," the fiery concoction was old-fashioned moonshine, likely brewed from the waters of the St. Marys River swamp. These law enforcement men have made quite a haul. Frowned upon by conservatives and its brewing illegal according to Georgia law, the longstanding Scot-Irish tradition of making fine whiskey was passed from father to son. Families jealously guarded their home receipts. (Courtesy of Don Peeples.)

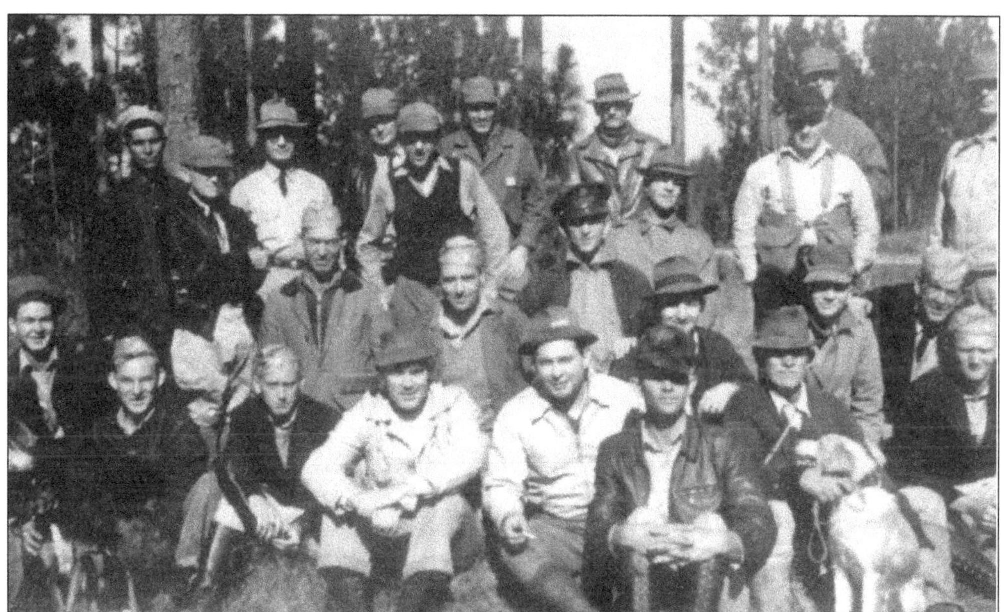

Reflecting the Southern traditions associated with the hunt and an outdoor lifestyle, this group of men pause for the camera. Taken in 1942, the image captures men of the Georgia Guard Unit #25, Woodbine Home Guard. Their piney woods setting was at Middleton Neck in north Camden County near historic Homeward Cemetery. District commanders John Kaufman and Jim Gould of Brunswick regularly met with the Camden County Home Guard for practice drills held near the Woodbine Community House. From left to right are (front row) Jasper Lang, James B.F. Russell, Harvey Bruce, County Agent Carnell, Dr. J.O. Simmons, Riley L. Harrell, Ben C. Lang, and J.T. Brewer; (middle row) Matthew Williams, T.J. McCullough, three unidentified, and "Jerry" William Lang; (back row) Roy Miller, Cecil Mizell, Barney A. Gowen, Oscar Raynor, Franklyn Dyal, Willie E. Smith, two unidentified, ? Sessions, Henry T. Berrie Sr., and Capt. Clayton Perry. (Courtesy of Jasper N. Lang.)

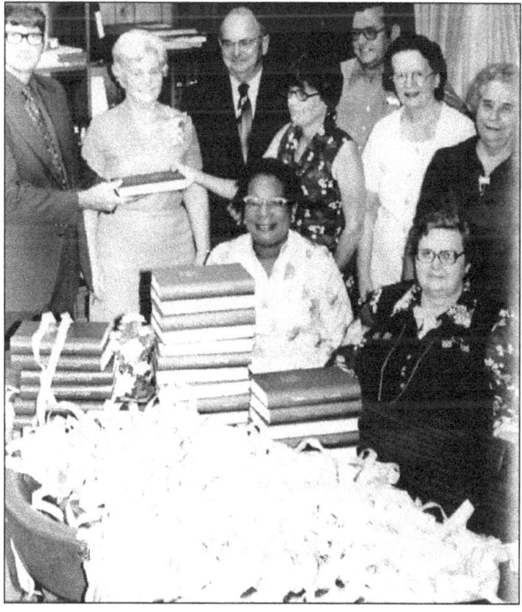

Having created the first county history since James T. Vocelle's 1914 book *History of Camden County*, the Camden County Historical Commission (CCHC) celebrated and gathered to present a first copy to Chairman George L. Hannaford (top, far left) of the Camden County Commission. Compiled by Marguerite Reddick (top, far right) and a labor of great love, this bicentennial history book was edited by Virginia Proctor (top, second from left) and Eloise Bailey Thompson (top, fourth from left) who presented the book to Hannaford. CCHC members, from left to right, are (front row) Edna Armstrong, Matilda Lang Bridges; (back row) Howard Davis, G.C. Harrell, and Mignon Sterling. (Courtesy of Eloise Bailey Thompson.)

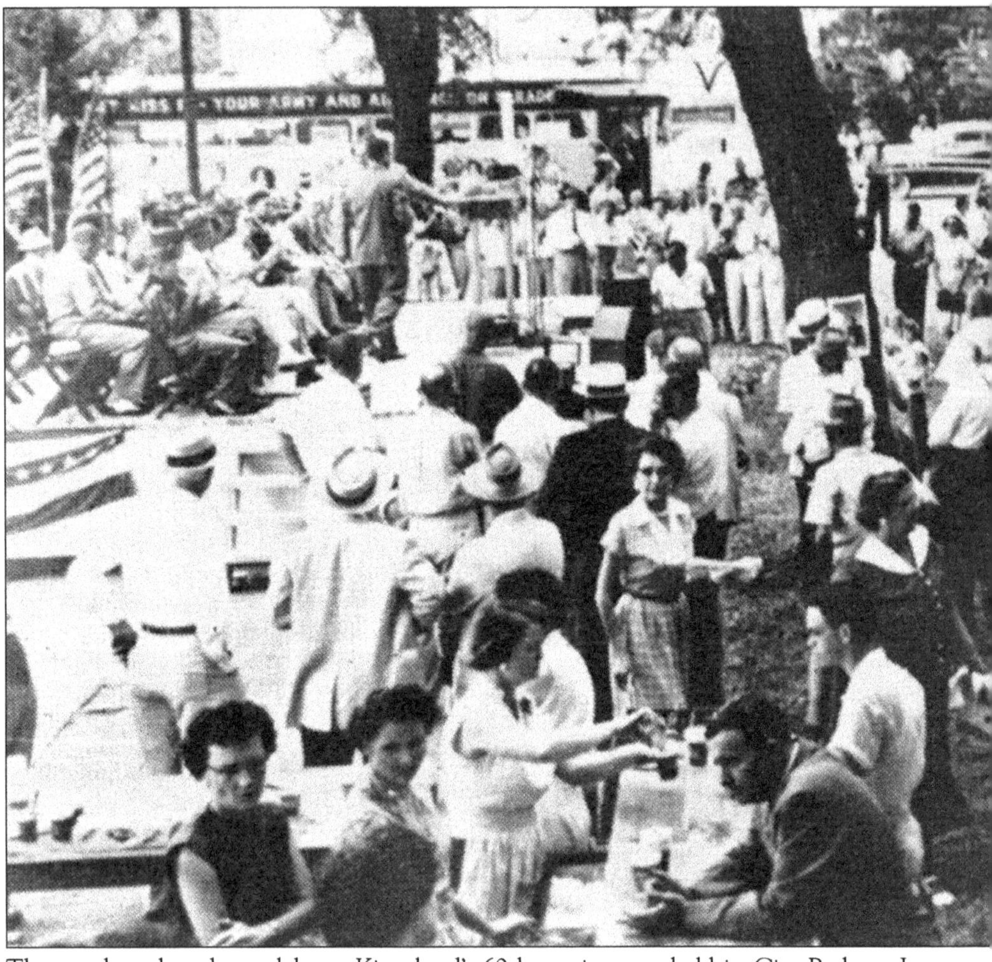

Thousands gathered to celebrate Kingsland's 60th anniversary held in City Park on June 17,1954. For this festive occasion, *The Southeast Georgian* produced a 60th Anniversary Edition honoring the newspaper's continuous service to Kingsland and Camden citizens. Evening festivities featured a dance and a beauty contest, but program chairman Howard H. Davis and acting mayor Robert L. Edenfield welcomed a large crowd and numerous dignitaries at the 10:30 a.m. kick-off. Tables teeming with delicious barbeque awaited festival-goers as they queued up in lines for serving at this signal event. Hitting the political stump,

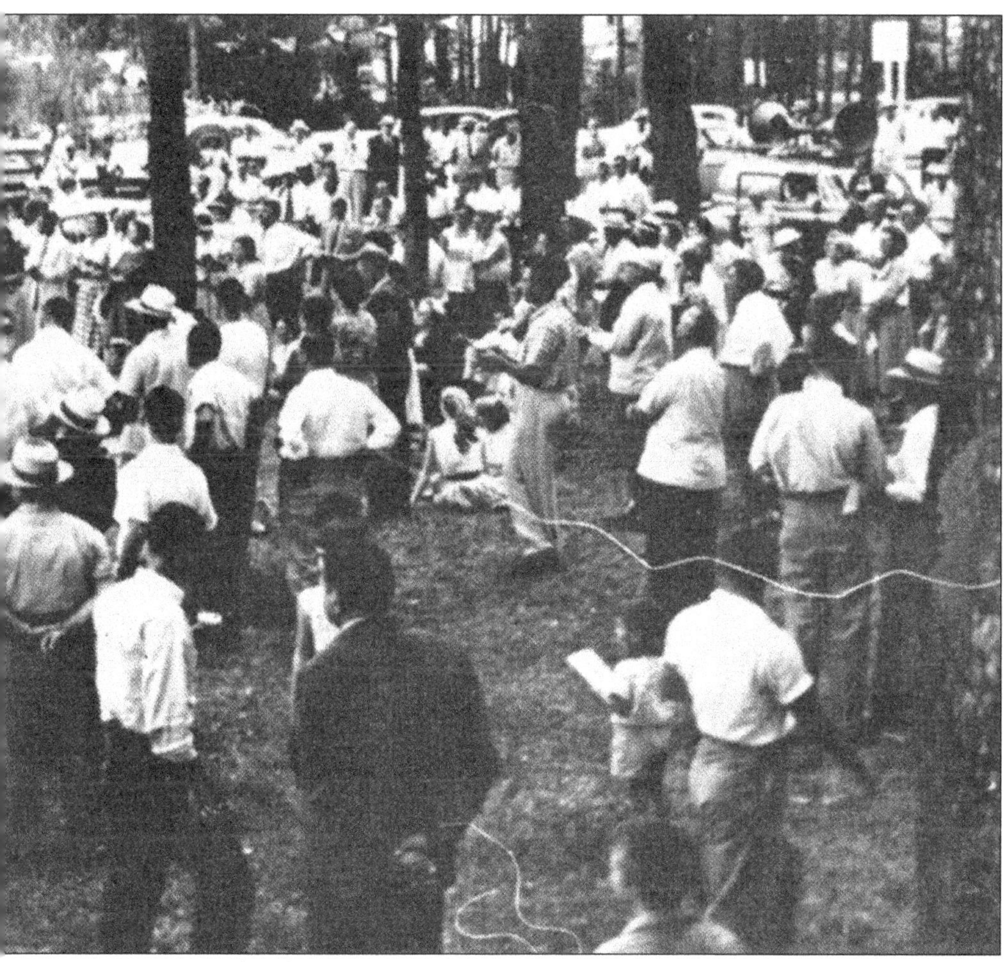

Gov. Herman Talmadge was a highlight of the speech-laden affair. Although unable to succeed himself due to Georgia law, Talmadge spoke at length and was accompanied by the four candidates for lieutenant governor and the six candidates for governor: Ben Garland; future governor Marvin Griffin (1955–1959); Charles "Charlie" Gowen of Atlanta/St. Simons Island; Fred Hand; Tom Linder; and M.E. Thompson. (Courtesy of Maxine Wells.)

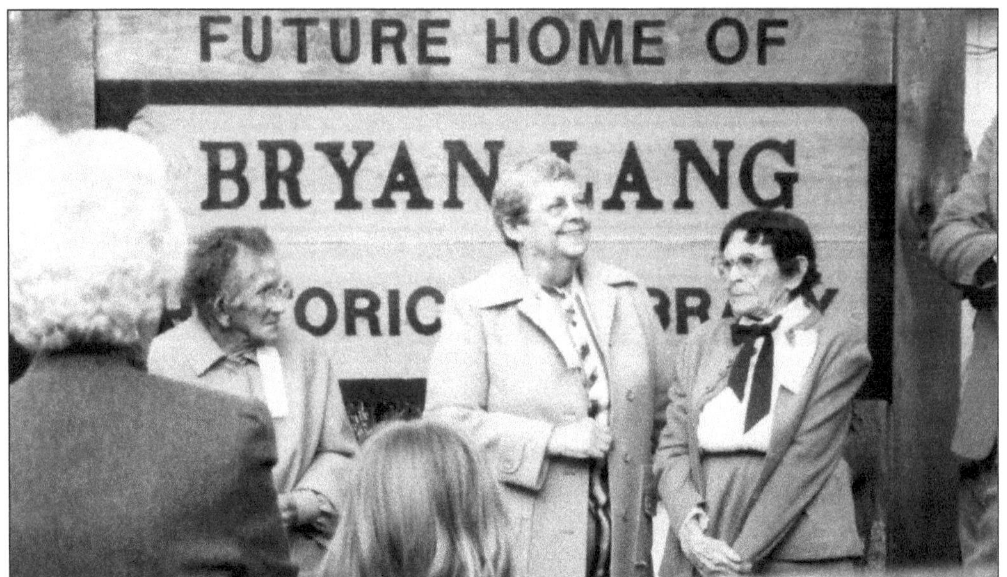

A weekend of events in Camden's three small cities commemorated a "Celebration of Freedom" with a full schedule: merchant programs, competition basketball, historic tours and marker dedication, dancing, music, food, parades, political speeches, and a Freedom Festival in St. Marys. A highlight of this three-day program was the groundbreaking ceremony for a regional repository, the Bryan-Lang Historical Library, sponsored by the Woodbine Citizens' Steering Committee and the City of Woodbine. Held at the Courthouse Complex on Sunday, February 3, 1985 the groundbreaking was attended by a stellar cast of local dignitaries, including the following seen here: 96-year old Mrs. Cobb Lang Readdick (left), the beloved novelist Eugenia "Genie" Price (center), and "Miss Bebe" Lang (right). The Bryan-Lang Historical Library was dedicated on November 8, 1987. (Courtesy of Bryan-Lang Historical Library.)

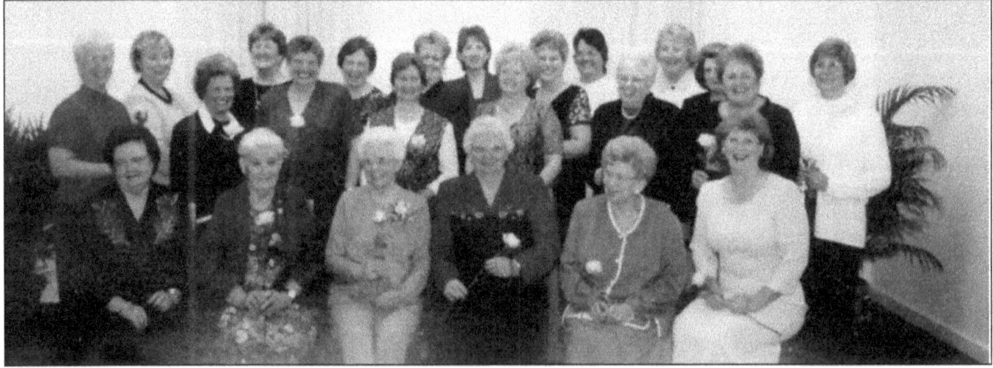

Celebrating 50 years of service, members of the Woodbine Woman's Club gathered for an anniversary celebration in February 2001. Over 20 participants assembled to remember their past accomplishments, such as the important reminiscences of Club women in the newly re-published 1969 book *Pen Portraits: Stories of Pioneer Camden Women and Their Families*, and to plan future achievements in service to their community. Pictured, from left to right, are (front row) Dixie Griffis, Katie Cooler, Virginia Proctor, Helen Keene, Bettie Lee Cottle, and Theresa Sawyer; (back row) Rhetta Sutton, Joan Derry, Bebe Williams, Marilyn Alexander, Jackie Walls, Leslie Swiacke, Janet Heath, two unidentified women, Bonnie Rogers, Barbara Thomson, ? Magoon, Delores Quattlebaum, Nancy Joiner, Lucy Proctor Gay, unidentified, and Margaret Williams. (Courtesy of Mrs. Henry E. Williams Sr.)

Six

EDUCATION

In the early 1800s, the Camden County Academy offered a curriculum to a few, and later, one-room schools catered to the needs of a dispersed, rural population prior to the consolidation of schools. Through the reminiscences of a Camden County lady, we glean an image of educational opportunities available to prominent families. Mamie S. Pickering's father wished a better life for his children and hired a tutor for $15 per month with room and board included. This educator also taught music; Mamie's brothers learned the banjo, guitar, and violin while she played the piano. Their circumstances were typical of affluent Camden families; many other families did without except for instruction in the domestic arts for young women. From an early age, boys hunted, fished, and farmed alongside their fathers or other elders; some apprenticed to a trade. Through the years a huge population growth has facilitated the enhancement of educational opportunities in public schooling.

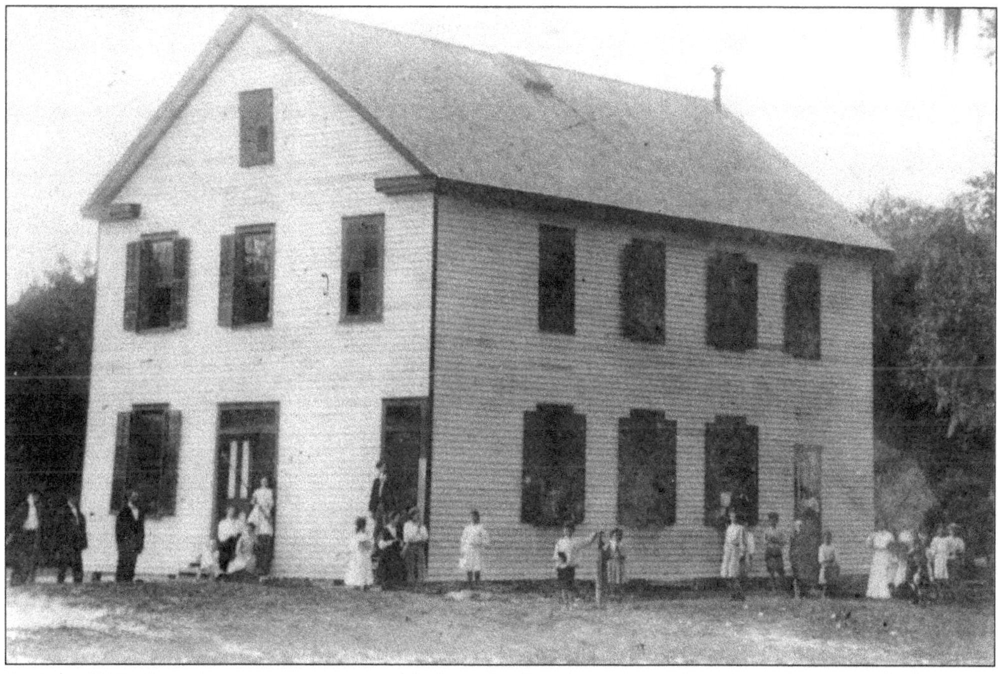

In July 1838 St. Marys citizens assembled at the Presbyterian Church and discussed the need for building an academy—a "commodious brick structure with four classrooms"—completed by 1840. Rev. Washington Baird served as superintendent, and the new academy attracted families who moved from outlying areas closer to town to take advantage of the opportunity. Later, the building was rented by private instructors, but was burned when the 9th Maine Infantry Regiment set fire to the town of St. Marys in 1862. Seen here is the two-story Camden County Academy, located at Osborne and Conyers Streets. In the 1870s other private instructors, such as Cecilia Vocelle, also taught classes. The Camden County Academy offered instruction in the basics and the fine arts, such as vocal and instrumental music, drawing, and oil painting. (Courtesy of Eloise Bailey Thompson.)

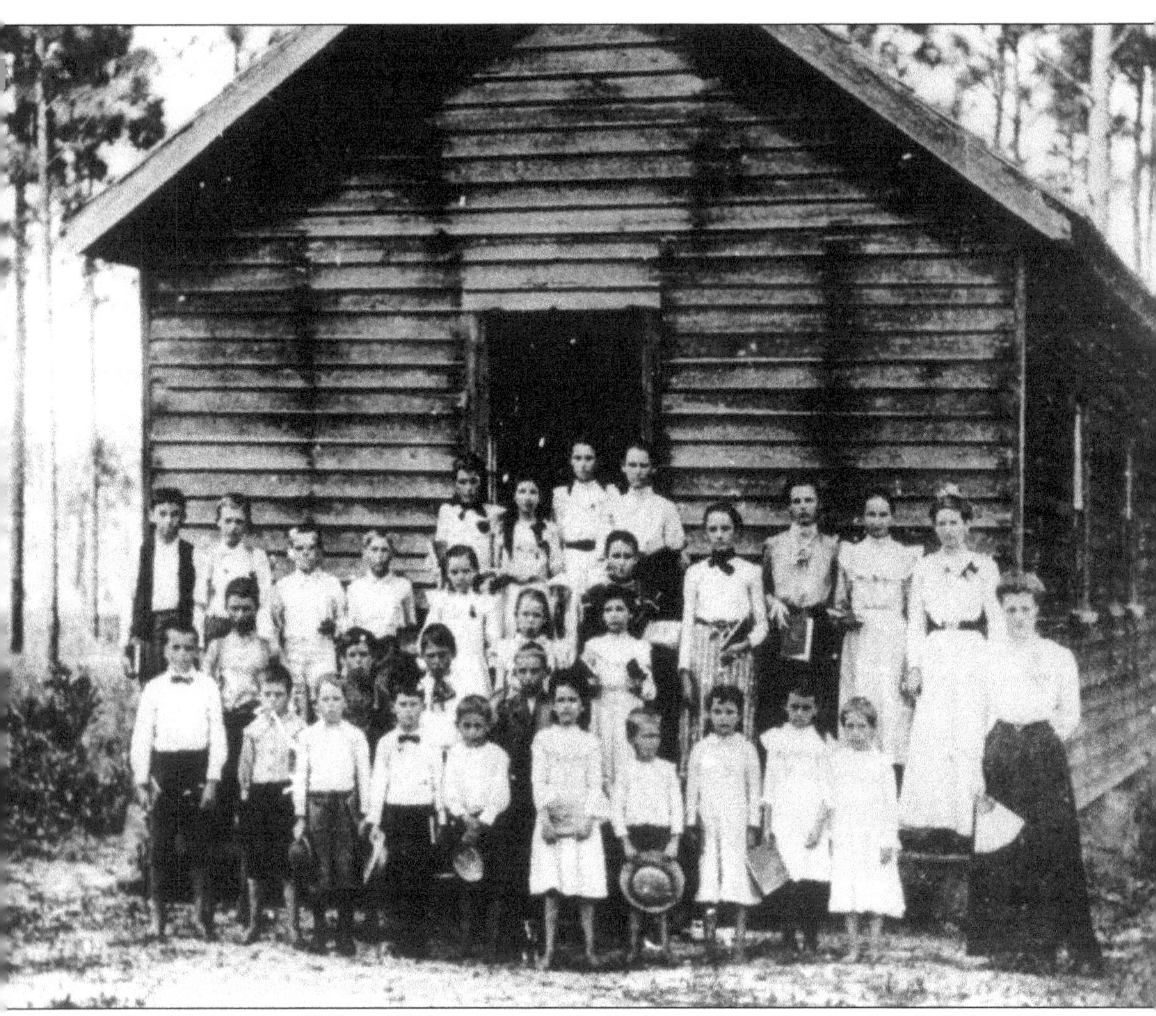

In 1901, at the old Harrell School located about one-quarter mile directly behind Bickley Chapel, a group of students and their teacher have gathered for the occasion of a class picture. This one-room schoolhouse was moved from the Stewart house site on Incachee Road to its Bartram Trail/State Highway 259 site, and its presence offered educational opportunities for rural children. Their surnames suggest those families who lived in the vicinity of Midriver, Burnt Fort, and the Old Post Road/Bartram Trail. From left to right are (front row) Leighton Anderson, Marion C. Joiner, ? Liles, Hamp Harrell, Nevill Drury, Annie Buie, Archie Buie, Nora Ribron, Hettie Harrell, and Pearl Drury; (second row) Allen Ribron, Sinclair Ribron, Horace Joiner, and Mills Drury; (third row) Oliver Drury, Cornelius Stewart, Leland Anderson, Gus Spradley, Ida Drury, Hattie Liles, Flora Buie, Agnes Harrell (standing behind Flora), Mamie Drury, Nettie Joiner, Edna Stewart, Mary Riley Buie, and teacher Maude Mitchell of Tennessee; (fourth row) Edna Drury, Kate Buie, Lucretia Ribron, and Mamie Harrell. The identification of students was provided by Kate Buie Harrell and Flora Buie Gray, wife of Capt. Charles E. Gray Sr. (1880–1969), a revered tugboat captain. (Courtesy of Shirley Joiner Thompson.)

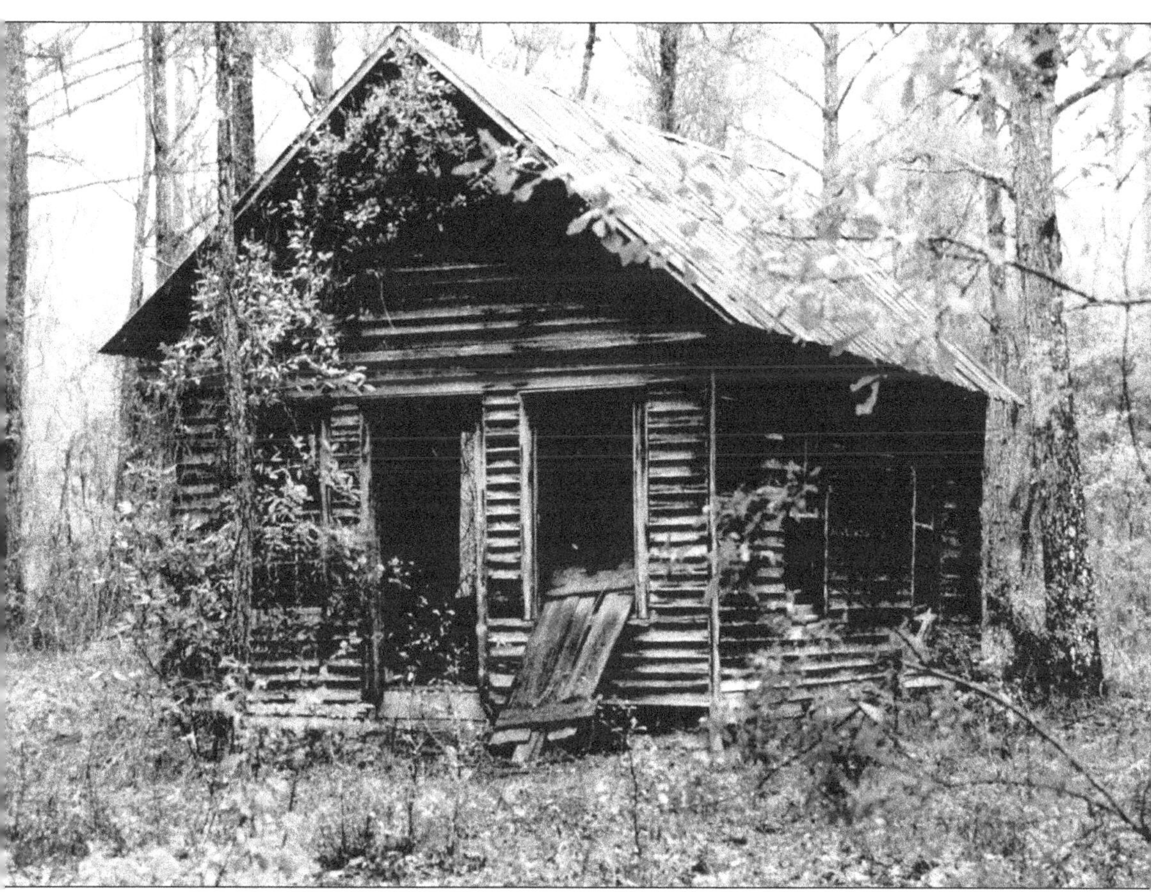

Through the work of a Burnt Fort School Restoration Committee, fundraising continues for the preservation of Camden's last remaining, one-room schoolhouse, shown here. Currently located just east of the rustic Burnt Fort Chapel and Cemetery, this historic building remains a high priority for those committed to needed repairs and moving the structure closer to the chapel. It was built about 1900 at the Midriver community, across Gelzer Branch and near the J.O. Dyal summer home. When Camden's schools consolidated, the old schoolhouse was moved to its present location. Supervised by Andrew B. Godley and John A. Wells, a team of oxen hauled the structure four miles in three days to arrive at its current location. In 1918, about 20 students attended the Burnt Fort School and their teachers included Mary Schmidt, the future Mrs. James Vocelle; Agnes Liles; Edna Moody; and Mary Lee Clark, later superintendent of Camden County schools and honored with the naming of a middle school. After consolidating with the White Oak School about 1922, the old structure at Burnt Fort served as a residence for the Harbin Liles family. (Courtesy of Rodney Sheffield.)

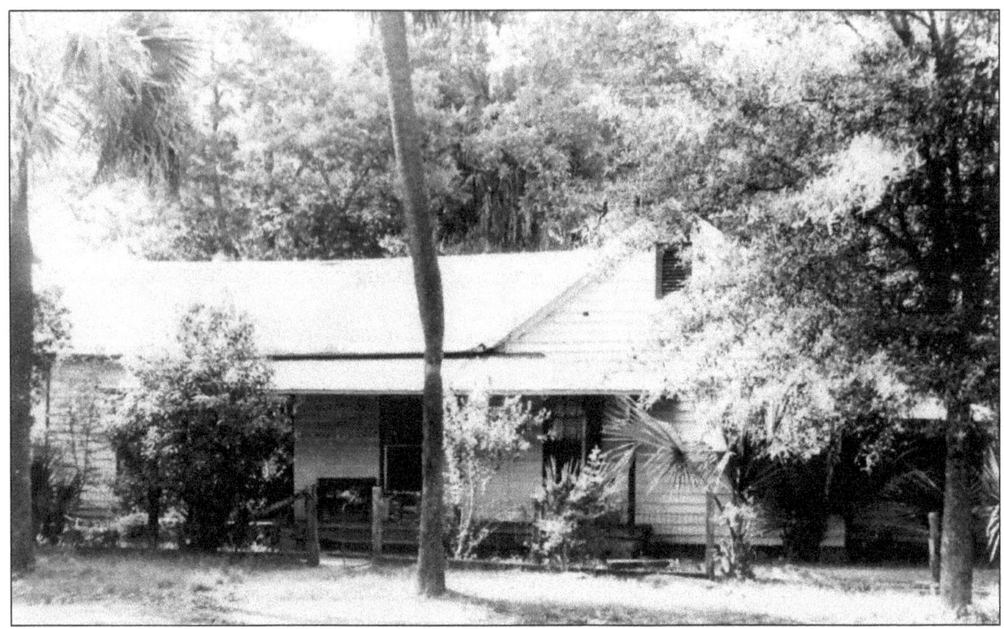

Located in the Caney Branch area northeast of Kingsland, a one-room schoolhouse served Kingsland area children prior to the coming of the railroad in the early 1890s. With the growth of the small city and the demand for educational opportunities, another one-room structure was erected on Lily Street. In response to increased enrollment, another larger school was built at Hilton and Satilla Streets, and "the first schoolhouse for Kingsland," shown here, became the private residence of E.M. Atkinson. The house no longer stands. (Courtesy of Eloise Bailey Thompson.)

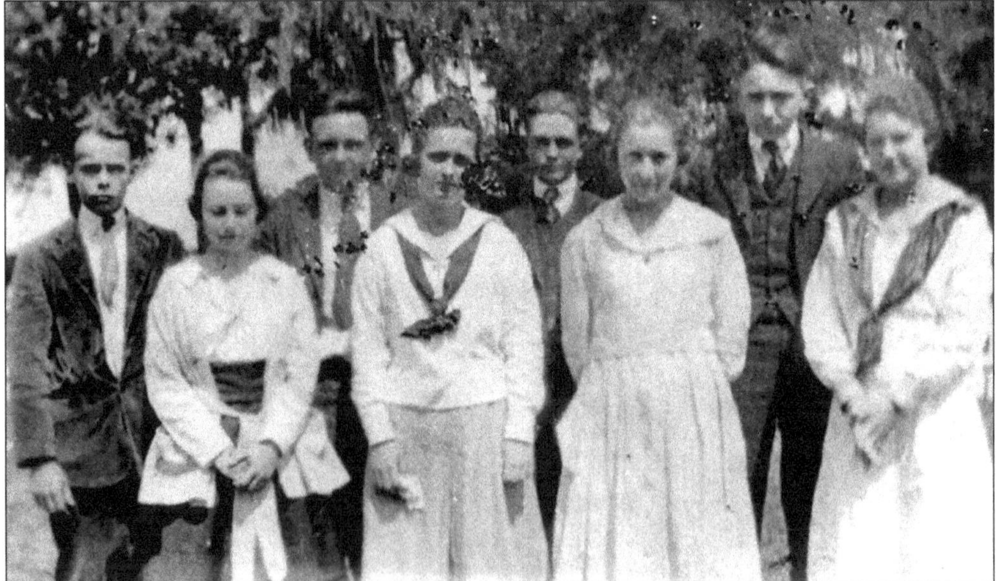

Eight graduating classmates of St. Mary's High School pose for the camera, *c.* 1921. They are, from left to right, John MacDonell, Hugh Thigpen, Jamie Hopper, Wilbur Smith, Clara Bell Higginbotham, Catherine Bealey, Agnes Carlton, and Estelle Frohock. (Courtesy of Eloise Bailey Thompson.)

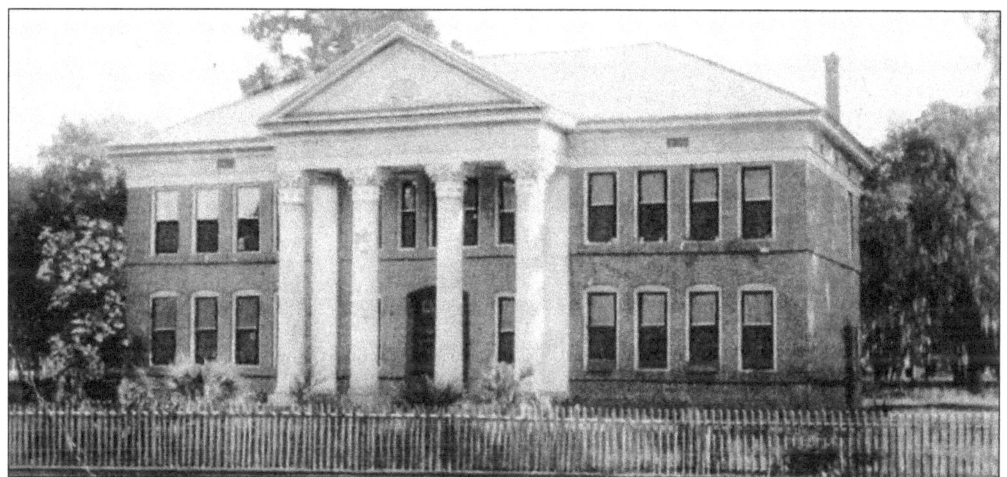

Captured by the cameraman in an E.C. Kropp postcard, the St. Marys Consolidated School reflects the popular Greek Revival architecture replete with Corinthian columns. Generations of students and their teachers walked these halls. In 1921–1922, Camden's consolidated school records listed the following teachers: Professor H.B. Gray, Mrs. Ruth Phillips, Mrs. S. Bealey, and Misses Berta Watt, Merle Daly, and Willie B. Wilson. (Courtesy of Eloise Bailey Thompson.)

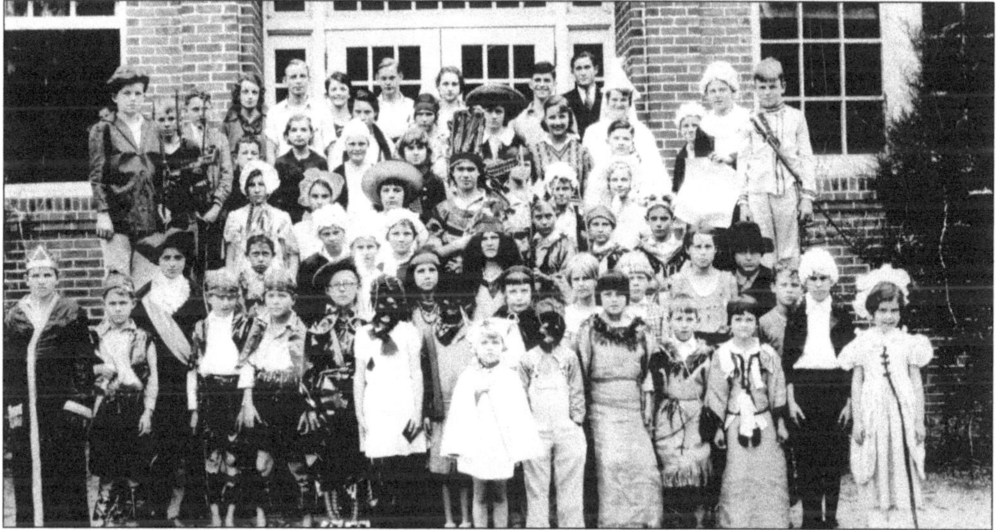

Through a grassroots effort a community landmark, the Woodbine Elementary School at the intersection of Second Street and Camden Avenue, was rescued from the wrecking ball and preserved for future generations as a Woodbine Community Center. Built in 1926, the one-story school features masonry construction, bands of ribbon windows, a projecting center gable with recessed main entrances, and trabeated main door. Opened in October 1926, the school was expanded in the 1930s with a one-story addition constructed by the Works Project Administration (WPA) to accommodate increased enrollment. Here, costumed students attending the Woodbine Consolidated School have gathered for a school picture in the early 1930s. Pictured are the following: (front row) ? McKinney holding a candle (left), Perry Tapley (sixth from left); Katie Miller (Cooler) (ninth from left), and Beatrice Lang Colson (Williams) (right); (second row) Susie "Florence Nightingale" Bedell; J.P. McKendree (top left) and Professor C.W. Miller (top right). (Courtesy of Bryan-Lang Historical Library.)

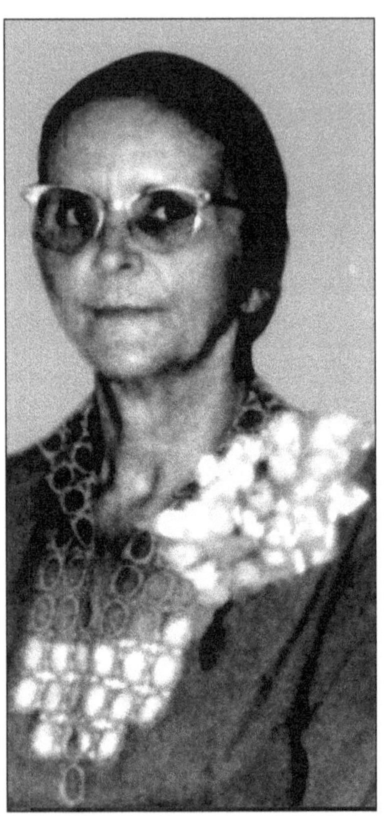

The daughter of Downey Sheffield (1881–1962), Floy S. Miley devoted over 44 years of her life to the education of Camden County children. Married to Shalor Miley who served as principal of Kingsland's Consolidated schools, she rests in the Sheffield Cemetery, located southwest of the old Coleraine–St. Marys Road and Highway 17. Across the years, this dedicated educator witnessed many changes in educational opportunities for Camden's youth. (Courtesy of Rodney Sheffield.)

In the 1932–1933 school year, Kingsland area children and educator Floy Sheffield Miley (far right) pose for their classroom picture. As seen in the following image, many of these students enjoyed two years continuity not only with their classmates but their dedicated teacher. From left to right are (front) E. Brown, L.D. Nelson, W. Brazell, C. Cooner, S. Gross, C. .Seals, C. Lewis, L. Gay, O. Brazell, O. Outlaw, and J. Simpson; (second row) R. Sutton, A. Allen, L. Peeples, H. Peeples, E. Harrison, M. Hill, V. Marr, V. Allen, J. Jarvis, C. Barlow, and K. Peeples; (third row) W. Marr, M. Fleming, G. Stalnaker, L. Bruce, and Mrs. Miley; (fourth row) A. Sheffield, U. Clark, W. Jarvis, and M. Carmichael; (fifth row) H. Marr, V. Peeples, V. Horne, and B. Kennison; (back row) S. Brown, B. Horne, and R. McCollough. (Courtesy of Rodney Sheffield.)

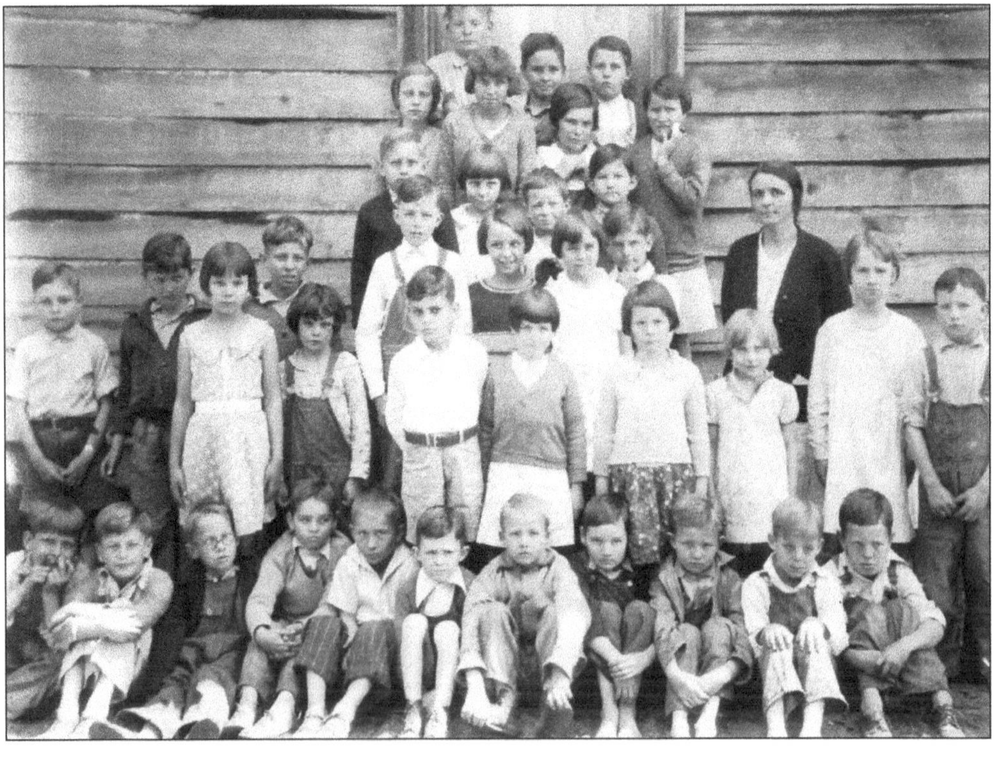

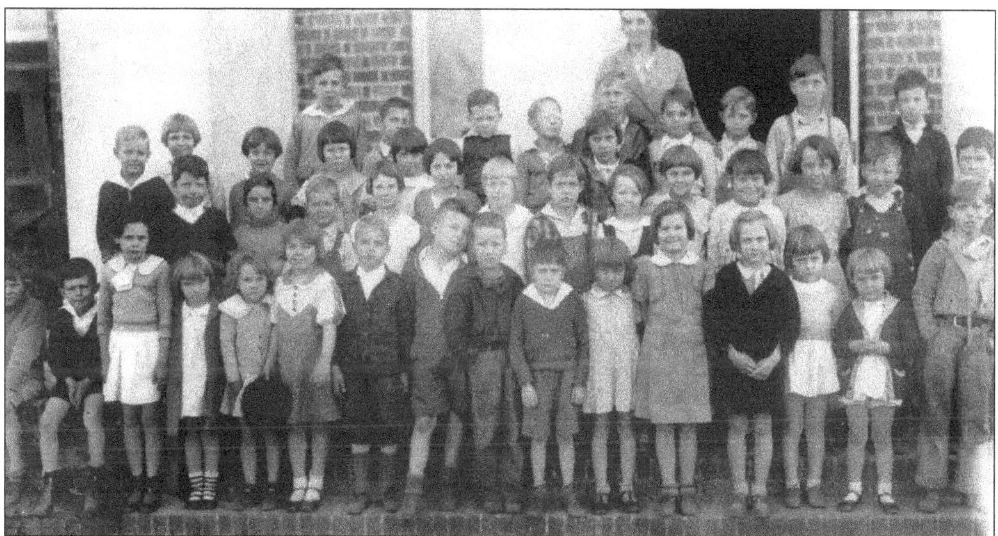

In the 1933–1934 school year, Kingsland area children, preschool visitors, and teacher Floy Sheffield Miley (1900–1999) pose for their classroom picture. From left to right are (front row) J. Atkinson, C. Seals, E.Harrison, W. Miley, G. Horne, R. Horne, J.S. Haddock, R. Powell, E. Wainwright, R. Bruce, unidentified, E. Peeples, unidentified, M. Wells, J. Sheffield, and O. Outlaw; (second row) R. Chauncey, E. Hill, A. Gay, M. Cottle, A. Cooner, B. Mills, E. Outlaw, V. Roddenberry, unidentified, G. Peeples, M. Fleming, F. Perdue, and L. Gay; (third row) Quincey Liles, Dorothy Liles, Lettie Allen, Verdie Allen, Viola Marr, and unidentified; (fourth row) H. Peeples, E. Brown, unidentified, W. Brazell, A. Sheffield, unidentified, O. Brazell, B. Horne, and K. Peeples. Later, M. Wells compiled an important 1980 publication *Remember When: A Pictorial Reminiscence of Kingsland, Georgia*, honoring her mother, Audrey Fiveash Wells, and her father, J. Nolan Wells, Kingsland mayor 1950–1952 and 1955–1963. (Courtesy of Rodney Sheffield.)

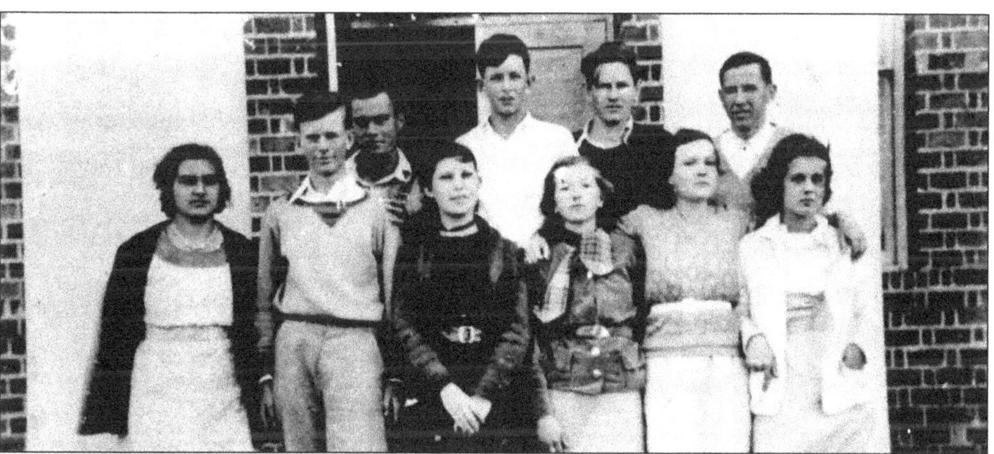

When the 11th grade meant completion of public schooling, ten Kingsland High School seniors gathered for their class picture. From left to right are (front row) Maureen Sheffield, class vice-president; Floyd McKendree; Julia Casey, class secretary; Caroline Casey; Rhoda Peeples, class treasurer; and Minnie Gross, class president and daughter of naval stores producer and timber baron J.H. Gross Sr. (1873–1948) and Ollie Sauls Gross (1883–1969); (second row) Gus Groover, James Kittrell, Rosser Godley, and Wilbur Bailey. (Courtesy of Eloise Bailey Thompson.)

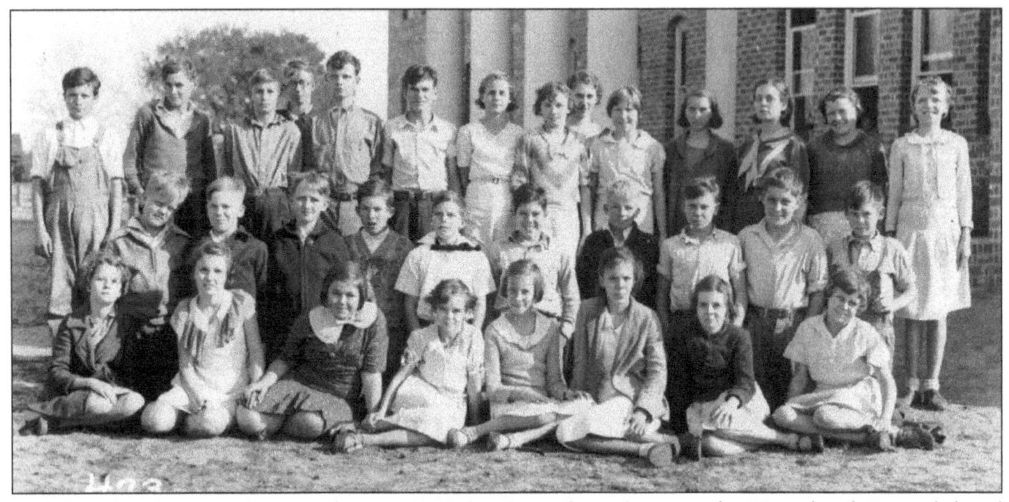

Middle school age students gather in 1935 for their class photo at the Kingsland Consolidated School. From left to right are (front row) Leslie Brazell, Annis Peeples, Elaine Morgan, Alice Waterman, Dorothy Lee Cooner, Morita Boyett, Earlene Peeples, and Louise Mills; (second row) Ray Simpson, W.G. Perdue, Wilbur Sheffield, Edison Peeples, Garrett Duncan, Robert Harrison, Willis Lewis, T.J. Boyett, Elmo Brown, and Connie Lee Hickox; (third row) Daniel Peeples, O.C. Peeples, Buster Royal, Wilbur Cooner, Earl Brazell, Aldine Bruce, Tassie Mae Allen, Aline Peeples, teacher R.L. Hart, Alice Clark, Edna Mae Horn, Kathleen Cooner, Mary Kennison, and Rita Chauncey. (Courtesy of Daniel Peeples.)

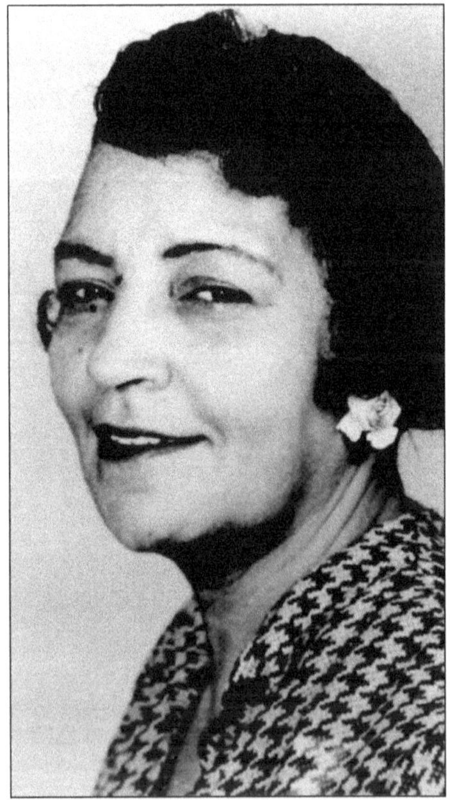

A North Carolinian by birth, Lillie Maude Slade Harris (1902–1985) married Camden County native and World War I veteran Tola Harris (1896–1963) in December 1925. He was the son of masonry contractor George Wright Harris (1840–1919) and educator Matilda Ann Thompkins Harris (1857–1931), who for 60 years sought educational opportunities for African Americans. She was honored with the naming of two schools, including the Matilda Harris Elementary School, a 1999 Georgia School of Excellence. Tola Harris served as principal of the Camden County Training School (1924–1936) as well as a county agent (1936–1957), while his talented wife contributed toward the education of county youth. Prior to her 1969 retirement, Lillie Harris spent over 40 years as an elementary and high school teacher, as well as principal of the Camden County Training Center. Her professional associations and volunteer commitments were numerous, and in 1964, Harris received a bronze 4-H club National Honorary Membership plaque making her the first black woman in Georgia to receive this honor. (Courtesy of Dr. Ann H. Stoddard.)

Lottie Orlena Harris (1882–1963) was the fourth child of nine born to G.W. Harris and educator Matilda Ann T. Harris. Following in her able mother's steps, Lottie Harris served as the second home demonstration agent, as well as the second Jeanes supervisor. Through the success of Harris's fundraising efforts, a 4-H building was constructed, providing opportunities in a segregated South for Camden County girls who used the dormitory as housing during winter while attending high school. At the turpentine community of Silco, the Harris Memorial School's naming honored this educator's life work and commitment to educational opportunities for African-American youth. (Courtesy of Dr. Ann H. Stoddard.)

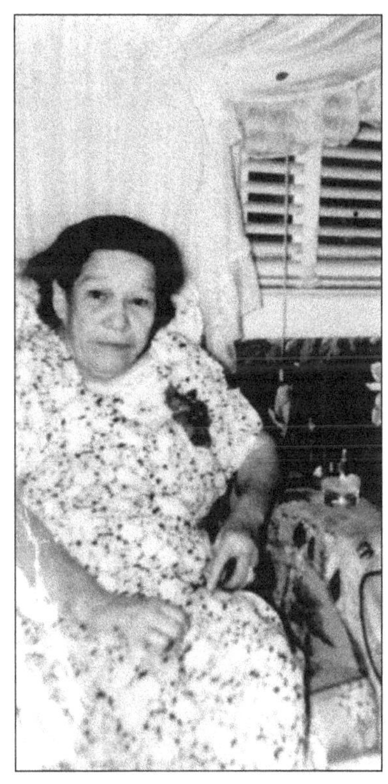

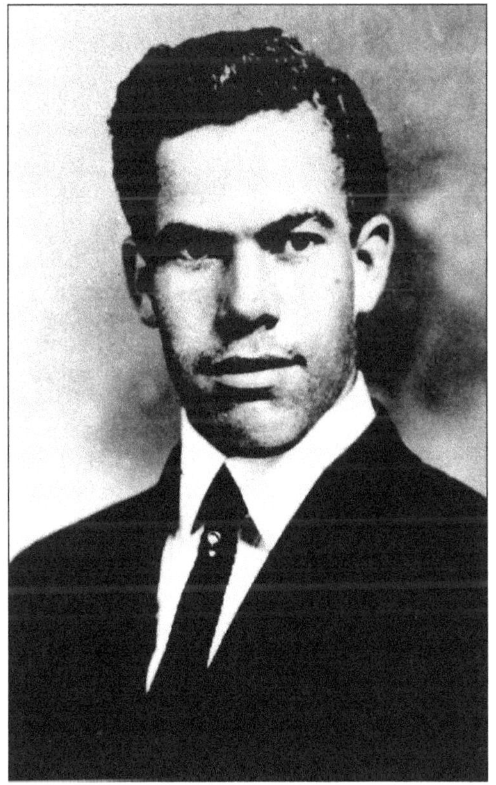

Born into a family of enterprising educators, Henry Vincent Harris (1893–1968), whose sister's image appears above, benefited from his mother's great devotion to education, and he racked up an impressive list of accomplishments. He continued his education at Savannah State College and later served as a principal in the Moultrie, Georgia school system. Harris was a co-founder of the GTEA, an early 20th-century, state-level professional organization for African-American teachers. St. Simons Island businessman Jasper Barnes (1913–1998) recalled how Harris influenced his life's choices. A member of the Class of 1933 at the old Colored Memorial School in Brunswick where Harris taught, Barnes achieved a high level of expertise under Vincent Harris's tutelage in vocational studies. Harris gave Barnes a $5 gold piece for ninth-grade achievements as best-all-around student in brick masonry and carpentry, and this motivating gift influenced Barnes's quest for success in the business world. (Courtesy of Dr. Ann H. Stoddard.)

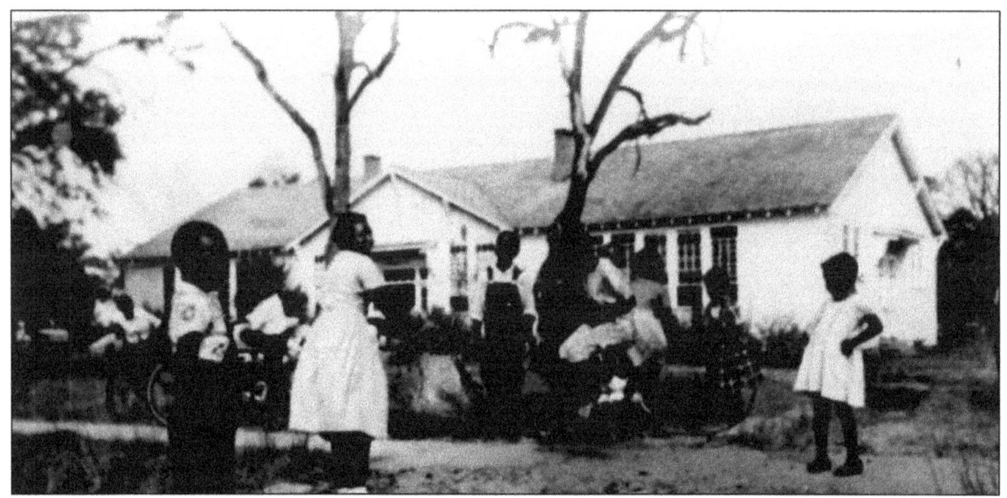

Children play in the schoolyard at Kinlaw School, located in the Kinlaw community northeast of Kingsland and built as one of several county-wide Rosenwald Schools. Endowed by Sears, Roebuck & Co. executive and philanthropist Julius Rosenwald (1862–1932), the Rosenwald Fund was created in 1917 for the "well-being of mankind" and stipulated that the principal plus interest on $30 million was to be spent within 25 years after his death. Rosenwald's humanitarian interests contributed toward building 4,500 schools for African Americans within the South, 339 of which were built in 1929. Prior to Matilda Harris's encouragement for educational opportunities resulting in one-teacher schools within the African-American community, church buildings were used. Consolidated schools were made possible when, in 1927, Rosenwald funds were matched by community funds through Harris's lobbying and hard work. Today, community supporters hold an annual tribute each March in recognition of the teachers and students who attended the Kinlaw-Rosenwald School, or the old school at Kinlaw. (Courtesy of St. Marys Woman's Club.)

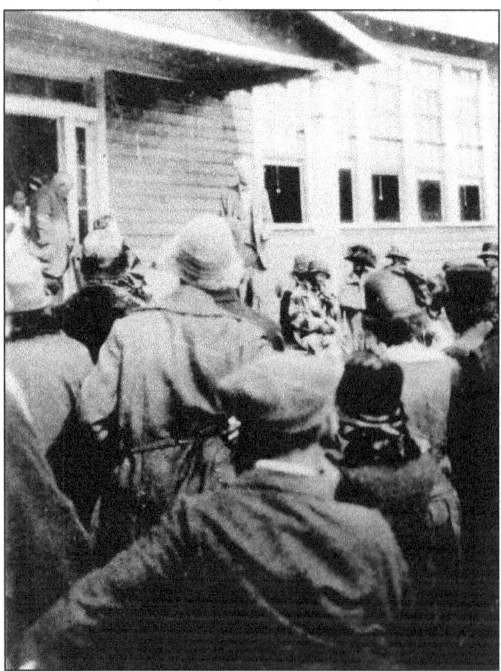

In this 1930s winter image, a group meeting of citizens is in progress at the Kinlaw School. A large crowd appears to be listening to the educator on the steps. During this challenging period, some Camden students moved to Glynn County, lived with extended family, attended the historic Colored Memorial School located on Albany Street in Brunswick, and returned to Camden County only on holidays and other special occasions. Other students, such as Cornelia Scott Collier, were sent to Liberty County where students lived dormitory-style and attended Dorchester Academy. (Courtesy of Dr. Ann H. Stoddard.)

Seven

SOCIAL, RELIGIOUS, AND CULTURAL AFFAIRS

Blessed with a balmy climate and prevailing sea breezes, St. Marys has benefited from its waterfront location. Attracting gifted men and women in search of an outdoor lifestyle, Camden's climate awaits the naturalist and is conducive to hunting, fishing, and crabbing year-round. Humanitarian pursuits and social occasions, parades and political suppers, competitive sports and a growing interest in dramatic arts characterize those events represented here. Although only a few of the numerous churches spread throughout Camden's landscape have been presented, a strong ministry within the faith community serves as a hallmark of this southeast Georgia county. Influenced by the presence of Naval Submarine Base, Kings Bay, a diverse group of patriotic, dedicated men and women contribute toward enriching our lives and the story of St. Marys and Camden County.

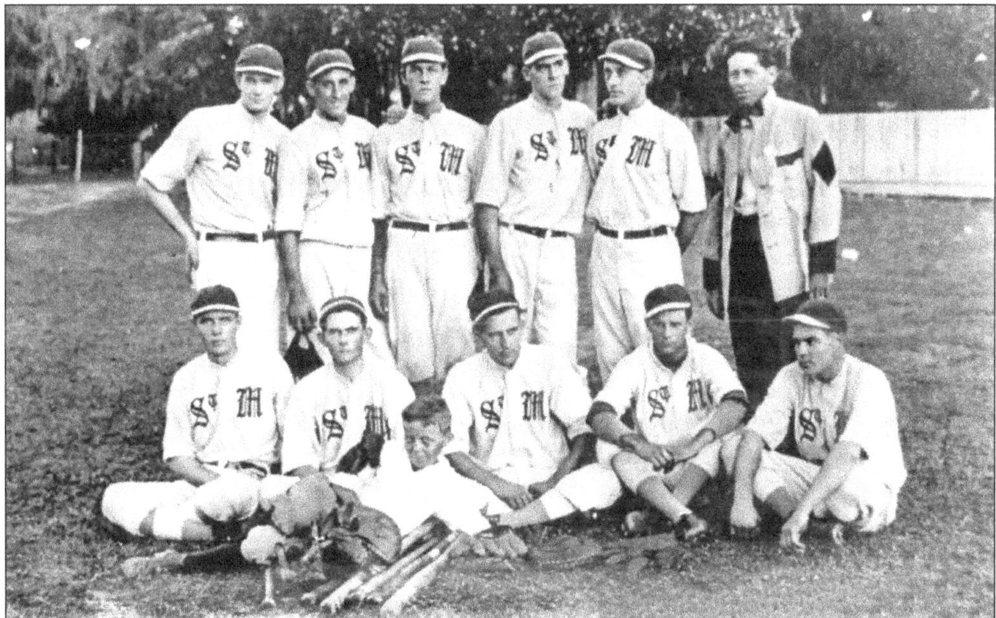

In the mid-1870s, a city ordinance in St. Marys designated grounds for two baseball clubs—the Star Laurel Leaf Club and the Eureka Baseball Club—and each club was assigned exclusive use of separate tracts located in the vicinity of the Presbyterian Church. By 1882 town records suggest an element of rowdiness because members were barred from playing near the church; subsequently, the ordinance was amended when players promised good behavior. Pictured, from left to right, are (front row) Ward Thigpen, Henry McCoy, Seward Smith, Edward Culpepper, George Johnson, and Johnson Hawkins; (second row) Rufe Bailey, Robert Hoff, Charlie Gillican, Pat Brandon, Howard Davis, and Manager M. McEvoy. Playing America's great pastime, a championship St. Marys Baseball Club was 9-1 in competition sports during the summer of 1914. (Courtesy of Eloise Bailey Thompson.)

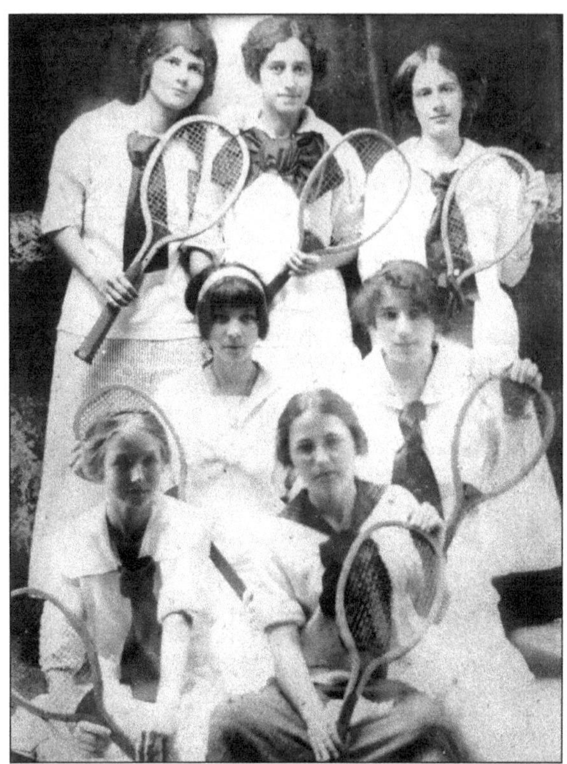

In keeping with an outdoor lifestyle, Camden's climate offered excellent opportunities for various recreational pursuits, including hunting and fishing, and, as seen in these images, all-American pastimes, such as tennis and baseball. Capturing a turn-of-the-20th-century group in their tennis outfits, the cameraman photographed a group of seven serious St. Marys tennis players, including, in the back row at left, Marie Banks, and, in the back row at center, Maude Register Bunkley (1886–1967). (Courtesy of Eloise Bailey Thompson.)

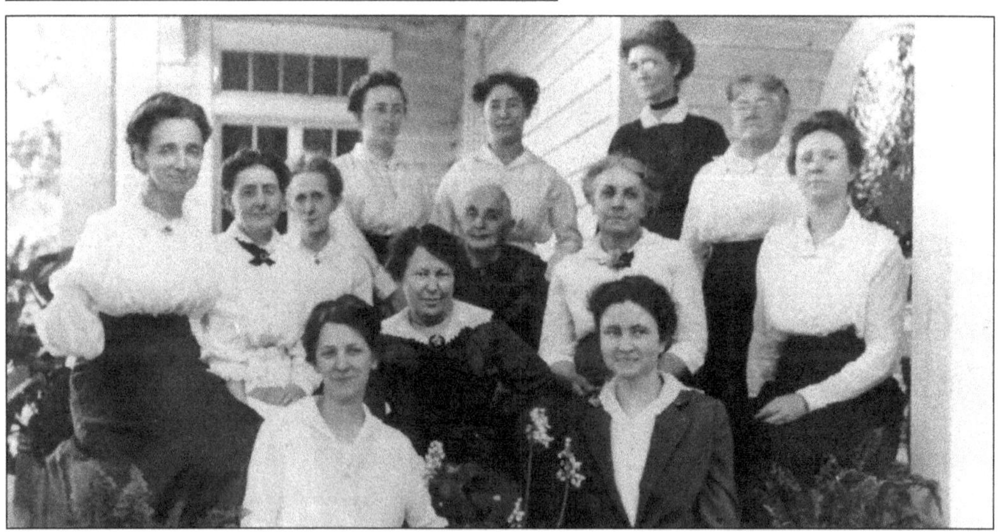

In a 1916 image, ladies of the Woman's Missionary Society of the St. Marys Methodist Church have gathered on Mrs. T.B. Kemp's porch. Born on Cumberland Island where her father, William R. Bunkley (1825–1879), developed a resort hotel at High Point, Madena Isabel Bunkley married Robert Tompkins, seen in an image on page 16. After his death, she married Rev. Thomas Bryan Kemp (1860–1957) of the St. Marys Methodist Church. Pictured here, from left to right, are (front row) Mrs. G.W. Brandon, Mrs. E.N. Stone, and Miss Semora Brandon; (second row) Mrs. W.R. Smith, Mrs. H.P. Trimble, Miss Mollie Long, Mrs. Isabelle Bunkley, Mrs. T.B. Kemp, and unidentified; (third row) Mrs. J.R. Webb, Mrs. Lizzie Williams, Mrs. J.H. Banks, and Mrs. L. Johnson. (Courtesy of Eloise Bailey Thompson.)

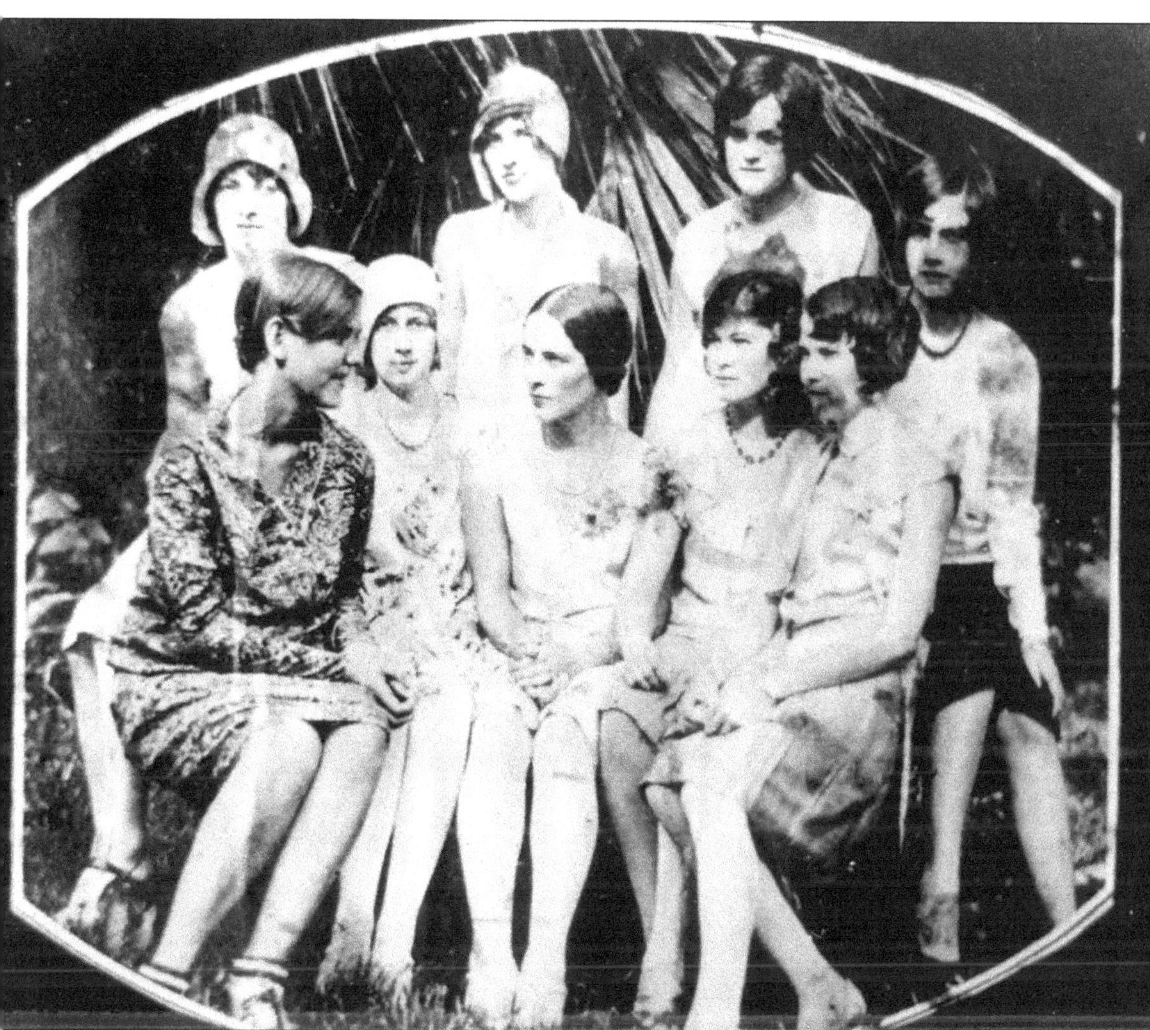

These lovely "Belles of St. Marys" appeared in an *Atlanta Journal* edition of 1932; the image was repeated in a feature story of the *Camden County Tribune* on August 5, 1955. With the exception of Brunswick's Alberta Weeks (front row, left), who was visiting in Camden County, all of these young women were residents of St. Marys. They are, from left to right, as follows: (front row) Weeks, Alice Smith, Lucille Townsend, Christine Hopper, and Aline Arnow; (second row) Susan Arnow, Elice Townsend, Eleanor Lang, and Susan Yates. Aline and "Susie" Arnow were the daughters of Isaac F. "Ike" Arnow (1869–1957) and his second wife, Annie E. Mungin (1881–1968). Arnow diligently studied Camden's history and was recognized as an authority on the subject, as well as a devotee of ornithological studies. Born in St. Marys, he operated a mercantile business there, farmed and raised cattle, served as deputy collector of customs for port of St. Marys form 1898 to 1899, and was politically active on the city and county level. He was appointed St. Marys postmaster in 1929 and served St. Marys citizens until 1943. This occupation placed Arnow in a singular position to interact with city residents. Through engaging conversations, he learned about the richness of Camden's past in much the same way that Glynn County's Margaret Davis Cate (1888–1961) cultivated her "sense of place" through her postal work and extensive historical writings. (Courtesy of Eloise Bailey Thompson.)

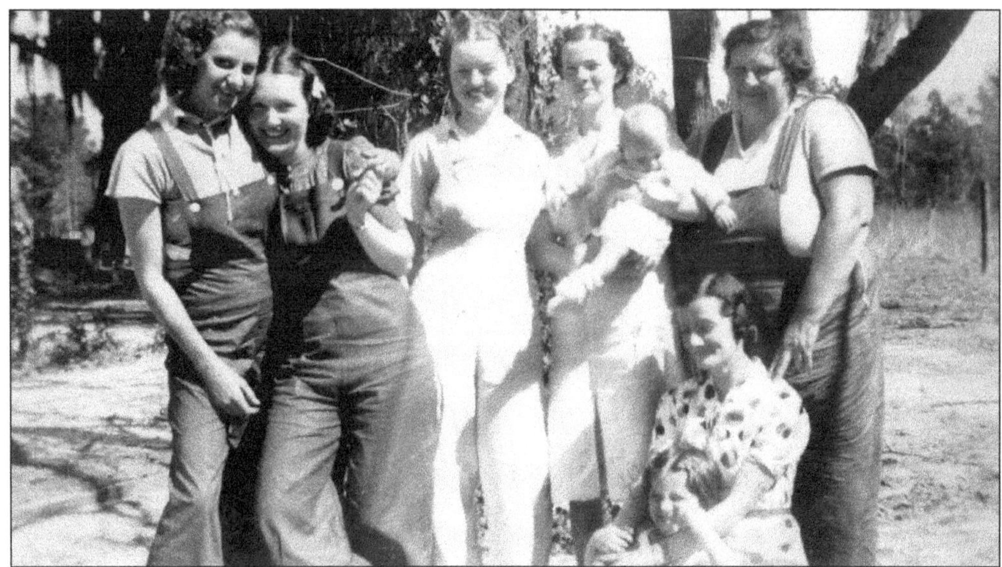

During the 1930s and 1940s, a group of ladies from the Midriver area of Camden met weekly to play an easy type of bridge known as "setback." Members dubbed their group "The Dirty Dozen," and they picnicked, fished, played cards, and shared news of family and friends in their beautiful, rural setting. These two images were taken at the Brown-Godley home where the group met. Later, this two-story frame home was called the Goodbread House after the marriage in 1832 of Janie D. Brown (1817–1861) to Sheriff Jacob L. Goodbread. A loss to historic preservationists, the Goodbread House was demolished in recent times. Shown from left to right are (front row) Cornelia "Neil" Buie (McClurd) and Maddie Brown (Clark); (back row) Katherine "Kitty" Godley, Sarah Buie, Mary S. Wright, Maggie Mae Godley holding a baby, and Annie Maude Godley. (Courtesy of Neil Buie McClurd.)

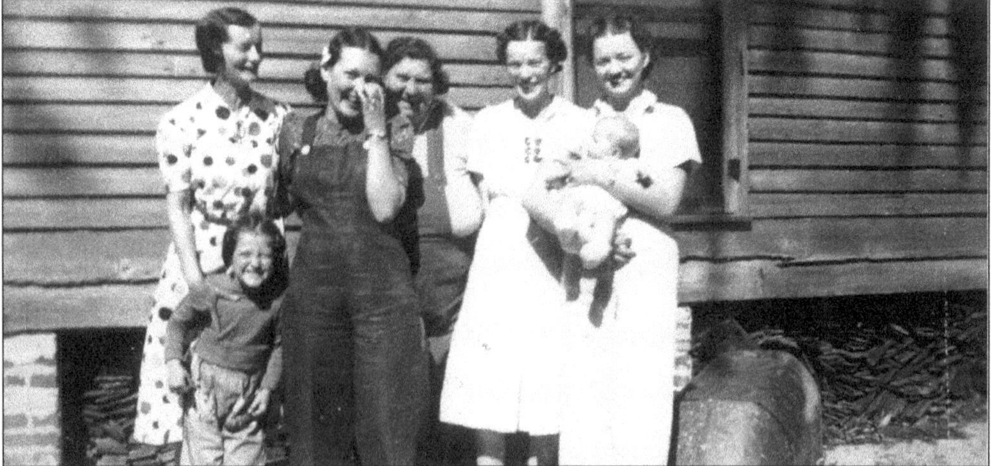

Shown here, from left to right, are mascot Corneila "Neil" Buie clowning beside her mother, Sarah Buie, Maddie Brown (Clark), Annie Maude Godley, Maggie Mae Godley, and Mary Wright holding a baby. In *Pen Portraits*, Maddie Brown Clark wrote about living at Midriver where her parents, Phillip Cato Brown (1866–1934) and Allie Agnes Reddick Brown (1873–1962) reared their children. Phillip Brown purchased a large store from L.T. McKinnon, and the Brown family ran the store and operated a post office there; he raised cattle, farmed, and cut timber to support his large family in this rural setting. (Courtesy of Neil Buie McClurd.)

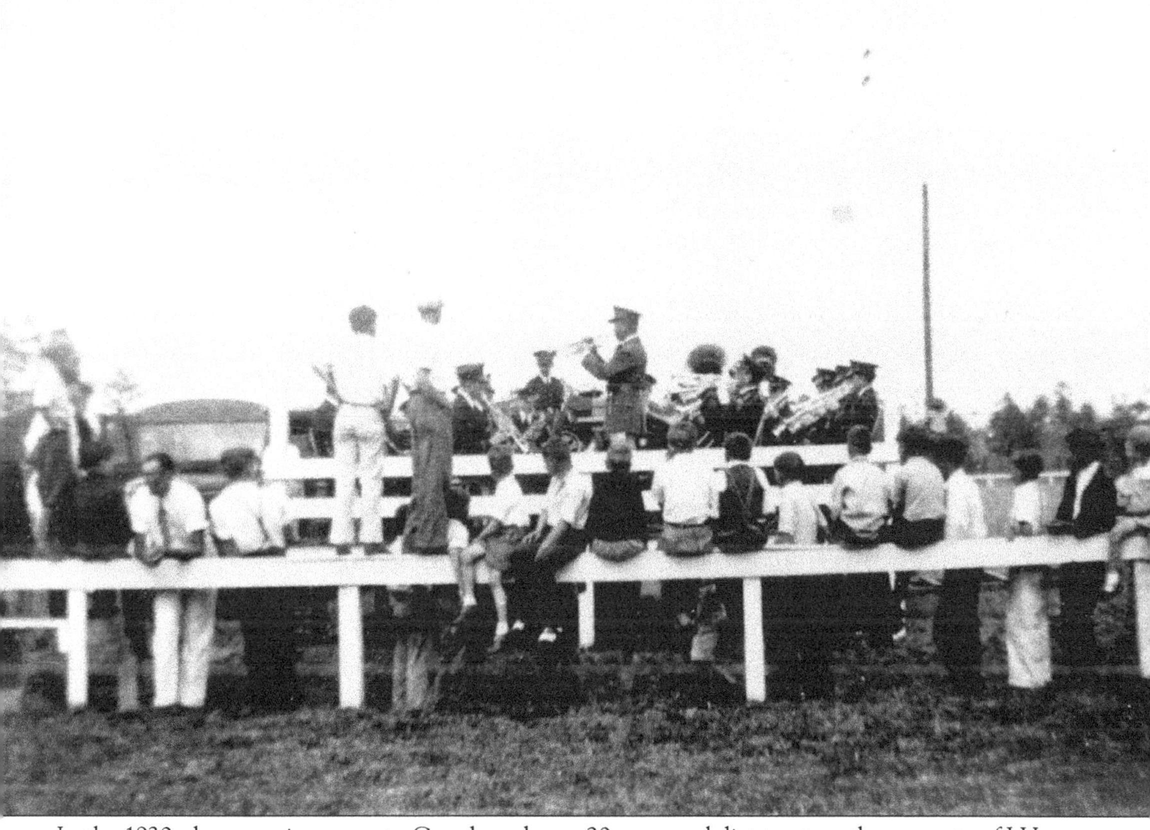

In the 1930s, horse racing came to Camden when a 20-acre oval dirt tract on the property of J.H. Gross was enclosed with board fencing. Later, Will Carnegie donated the funds for building a stadium or "stands" from strong cypress timbers, suitable for seating 275 race enthusiasts; Walter Lang of St. Marys cut the cypress poles and timber for the hurdles used in the steeplechase. Originating through the camaraderie of quail-hunting partners, J.H. Gross, his son Edmund, and Robert W. "Bob" Ferguson of Cumberland Island, the legendary Camden horse races began in 1931 on a half-mile-long dirt track in St. Marys. These friends initially raced Cumberland's marsh tackies and Gross's "plug horses," and from this beginning two annual races were held, in the fall and spring at the Camden Park Race Track; no admission was charged. Opening with great fanfare in December 1934 with a crowd of 3,153 present, the opportunity was ripe for political stumping, and state-level politicians, including Gov. Eugene "Gene" Talmadge, attended. As word spread, larger crowds came, and eventually races were held on fixed tracks in Jesup/Wayne County and in Glenville/Tattnall County. Race enthusiasts anticipated 5 to 7 "runs" each day pitting the prowess of Shetland ponies, Woods ponies, Cow ponies, Saddle ponies, and Lightweight pony races in which Camden's jockey Joe Dan Proctor took the prize! (Courtesy of Maxine Wells.)

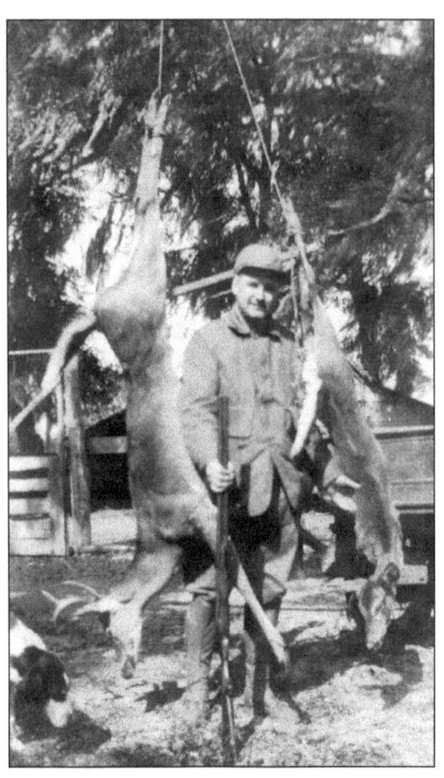

In the following two images are typical scenes of outdoor recreation pursuits, occasions on which Camden Countians and their friends share time with one another fishing and hunting. One of the earliest clubs was re-organized on October 13, 1832 as the Camden Hunting Club when members met and dined at Fairfield Plantation and elected Charles Rinaldo Floyd (1797–1845) as president. In this exclusive male-only club, members represented the Hopkins, Dilworth, Hardee, Gowen, Berrie, Nightingale, Holland, Holzendorf, Sadler, and Floyd families. In this 20th-century image taken on Sheffield's Island, Ida West S. Deal and her pharmacist husband, Homer Deal, were visiting from Clayton, Georgia with Camden County family. Deal bagged two young white tail deer using a 12-gauge double-barrel shotgun. (Courtesy of Rodney Sheffield.)

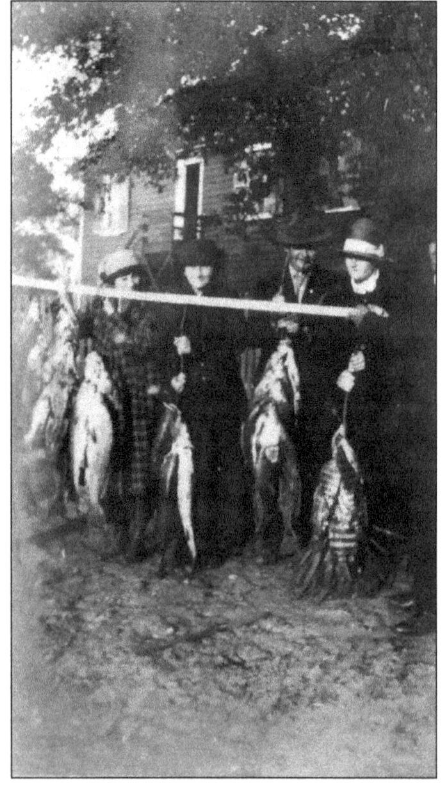

In the background of this 1920s image taken at Sheffield's Store in Kingsland five members of the Sheffield family hold a pole displaying a large fish catch. From left to right are Shirley P. Sheffield, Frances Brown Sheffield, Sherard C. Sheffield, Mary Elizabeth Randall Sheffield "Mamie" Carlton, and ? Carlton. They caught a double-string of sheepshead, large trout, and spot-tail bass fished for on oyster bed creeks. Creating stories for generations to come, this family gathering could boast of abundance and plenty in the inshore waters of Camden. Today, wildlife and fisheries must be conserved for future generations. (Courtesy of Rodney Sheffield.)

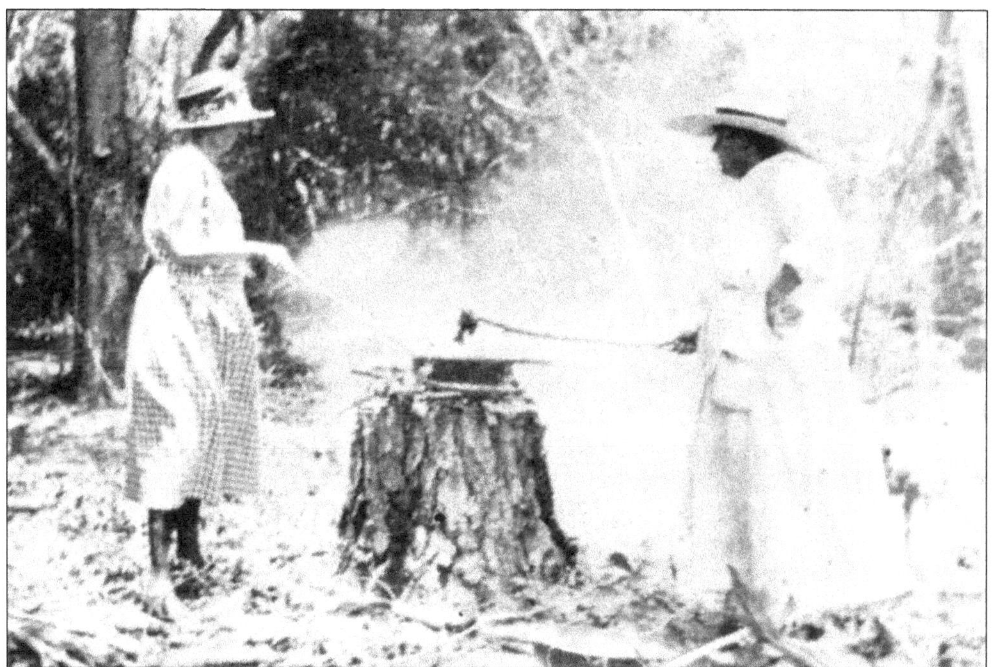

Shown in a 1920s image, sisters-in-law Shirley P. Sheffield and Frances Brown Sheffield fry fish at Sheffield's Island in a "make-do" circumstance. They made a fire in the stump of a large pine tree that was filled with flammable, resinous gum. Beforehand, Isham "Icey" Peeples (1866–1943) had cut timber on the island using a cross-cut saw and hauled out the logs, leaving stumps put to an ingenious culinary use by the Sheffield ladies. (Courtesy of Maxine Wells and Rodney Sheffield.)

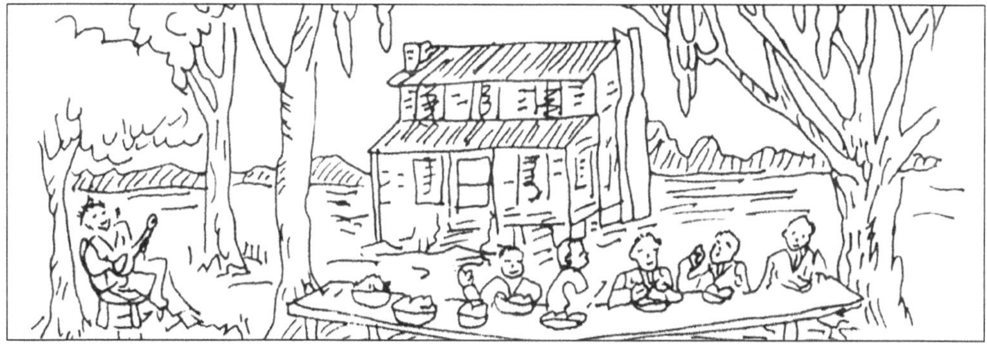

An all-time stellar event in old Camden featured a chitterling supper hosted by Capt. John Franklin Atkinson (1882–1949) at the ancestral home of the Atkinson family, Black Hammock. While the plantation was re-christened the "Chitlin' Switch" in jest by Atkinson friends and cohorts, these outdoorsmen and politicians of similar interest gathered for conviviality. Held throughout the 1930s and 1940s, this annual affair took place under the spreading great live oaks and magnolias. Col. James D. Gould Jr. (1896–1975) and the legendary Judge Eustace C. Butts (1875–1946) were two of the popular orators in attendance, and other coastal luminaries included members of the Aiken, Abbott, Buie, Brown, Clark, Dean, Dial, Fendig, Ferguson, Godley, Harper, Jones, Kaufman, Leotis, Liles, McCarthy, McCaskill, McCrary, Miller, Nightingale, Nolan, Parker, Quarterman, Royal, Scarlett, Simmons, Sutlive, Taylor, Thompson, Torras, Wainwright, Way, Winchester, Wood, and Wright families. (Courtesy of the Russell family.)

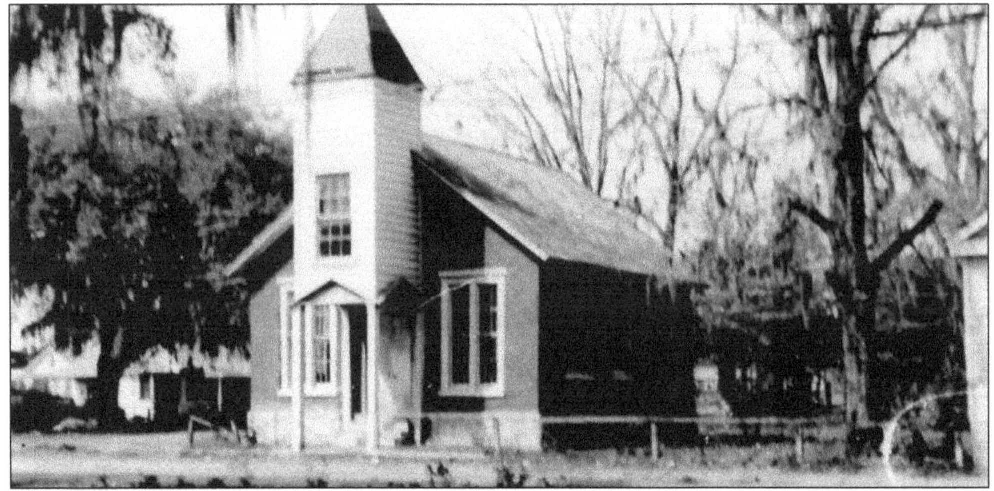

Shown in this 1940s image, Our Lady Star of the Sea Catholic Church still had its belfry intact, and the Vocelle residence can be seen on the left. Acceding to requests, the city in 1826 deeded a portion of Public Square 89 to the parish but financial constraints prevented the congregation from constructing a church for its Catholic worshippers. Subsequently, befriended by Marie Ponce DuFour (1793–1851) who in 1847 purchased a failed Bank of St. Marys, the small Catholic group gathered for worship in the former bank building, located on the northwest corner of Osborne and Bryant Streets. When the 9th Maine Infantry assaulted St. Marys during the American Civil War, the little brick church was damaged, repaired, and remained in use until a newer one was built on the corner of Ready and Dillingham Streets in 1952. (Courtesy of Eloise Bailey Thompson.)

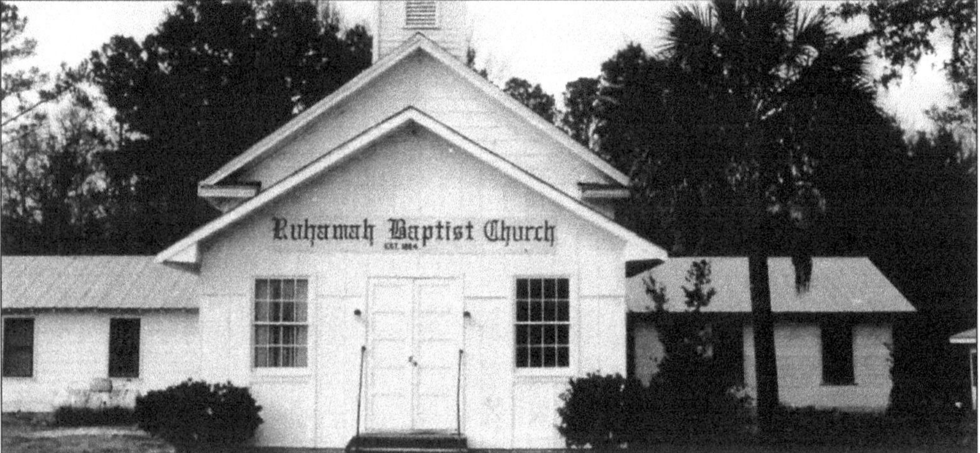

Organized on August 25, 1870 as the first Baptist Church in Camden County, Hebron Missionary Baptist Church received 14 members into the fold: Joseph Mills Sr. and Eliza Mills; A.B. Brown and Mariah Brown; Deacon W.J. Caldwell and Julia A. Caldwell; Marguerite Marr and Elizabeth Marr, Deacon Stephen Williams; Eliot Roberts; James Cooner; Sarah Ellis; Jane A. Allen; and Sarah A. Manning. Rev. Gideon A. Mallette donated the land upon which the church was erected, but by April 1878, 23 members requested letters of dismission for the purpose of forming Providence Church at Griffin Bluff. Fourteen years after its founding, on October 23, 1884 the Church dissolved and its membership received letters of dismission. On December 3, 1884 the former members of Hebron gathered and organized the Ruhamah Church, located on Highway 40 West. (Courtesy of Rodney Sheffield.)

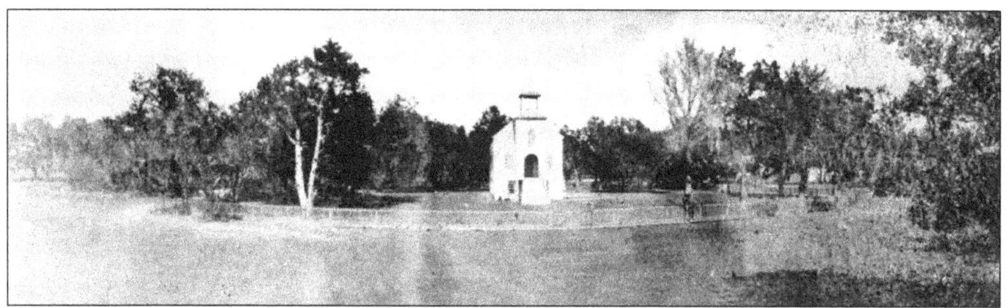

Shown in a panoramic view, the First Presbyterian Church of St. Marys was surrounded by a picket fence; in the background is a small cemetery on the left where Rev. Horace Pratt's first wife, Jane Wood Pratt, and her Loyalist parents, John Wood (1752–1829) and Laleah Johnston Wood (1760–1836), rest. St. Marys native James S. Silva (1832–1918) wrote for *The Southeast Georgian* between 1914 and 1915 about the 1840s period. He reminisced about how the entrance to this old building faced the east side and featured a covered portico reached by steps on both sides. Dating from 1808 and built with public funds by skilled craftsmen dedicated to their labor, this historic structure holds the distinction of being one of Georgia's earliest buildings used for worship. It served as a Union Church until 1822 when the Presbyterian Church organized; in 1828, the First Presbyterian Church of St. Marys incorporated. (Courtesy of Eloise Bailey Thompson.)

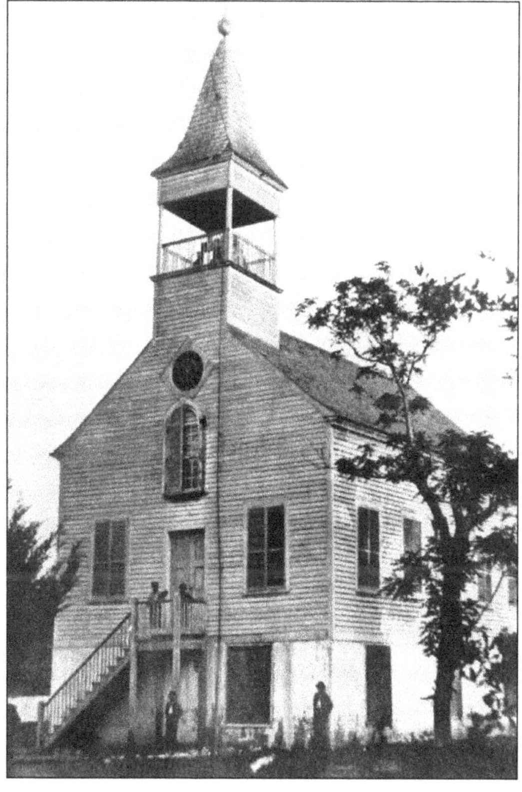

Through the years, the First Presbyterian Church has survived disasters, such as a 1956 fire that destroyed the bell tower as well as the havoc and destruction in St. Marys during the American Civil War. Citizen Maggie Ross told of the sturdy church being saved from fire by a miraculous rainstorm. Seen here, a segregated entranceway on the north end of the Church leads to a gallery for those African Americans who chose to attend worship services. Notice the steeple and an open belfry where a weather vane once topped the spire. While Rev. Horace Southworth Pratt (1794–1840) ministered to his congregation's spirituality for 19 years, he garnered a devout following between 1822 and 1839 and increased church membership. The Pratt's "Orange Hall" home was just a few steps away from his church; this magnificent structure serves as a showcase today and hosts social and cultural events, as well as serving the city of St. Marys as a Welcome Center. (Courtesy of Eloise Bailey Thompson.)

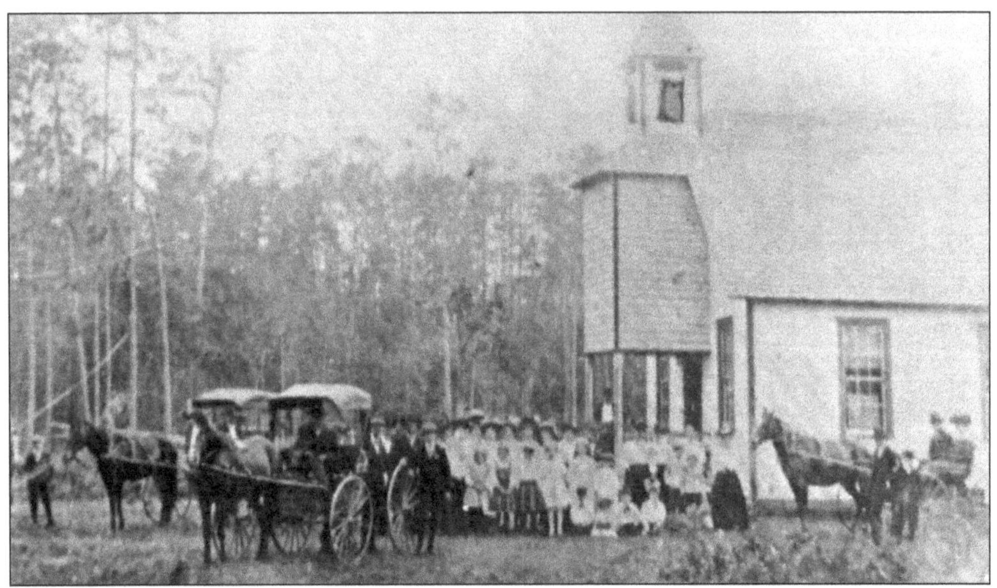

Pictured here are congregants of Kingsland Baptist Church in 1910. Former Ruhamah Church members met in private homes for worship, and on October 10, 1897 formally organized as the Kingsland Missionary Baptist Church, later joining the St. Marys River Association. A presbytery was formed consisting of Rev. N.S. Wainwright, Rev. J.A. Thompson, and W.F. Allen; W.H. Peeples was elected permanent clerk. During its formative years, worship continued in various homes, but in 1902 the first sanctuary was built on the southwest corner of William and Arizona Streets. (Courtesy of Maxine Wells.)

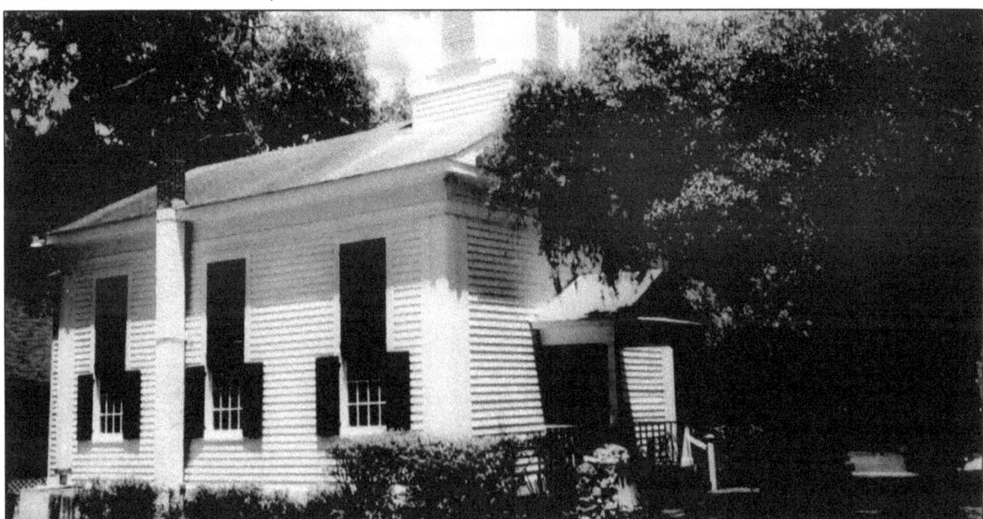

Shown in this image, the chapel of historic St. Marys United Methodist Church stands as a reminder of the long tradition of Methodism in port of St. Marys. Celebrating its bicentennial in 1999, the church constructed its original building upon land deeded by the city council in 1812, and church rolls document congregants in 1839 with names such as Arnow, Bachlott, Bessent, Clubb, Downs, Johnson, Lang, and Seals. A new bicentennial book chronicles the contributions of so many, including the work of Bishop Arthur James Moore. Honored by the naming of the Methodist Conference Center at Epworth-by-the Sea on St. Simons Island, Bishop Moore began his ministry in St. Marys. (Courtesy of Forrest "Frosty" Barefoot.)

As the population shifted from the mill villages toward the Florida Central and Peninsular Railroad at Woodbine, former parishioners of the old St. Clements Church at Satilla Bluff were sorely in need of a house of worship. In 1898 J.K. Bedell deeded one-half acre of land for the construction of the St. Mark's Episcopal Church, which was completed in 1900 and located on Bedell Avenue and Highway 17. Built from timbers milled at Satilla Bluff, this one-story church features a four-sided spire, square tower with louvered lanterns, and Gothic-style windows. In 1953, the Georgia DOT successfully completed a challenging move several feet from the church's original location for road widening. Included in the Woodbine Historic District with its National Register listing on May 12, 1999, St. Mark's Episcopal Church represents one of the few surviving 20th-century examples of an enduring coastal concrete, or tabby, construction in coastal Georgia. (Courtesy of Bryan-Lang Historical Library.)

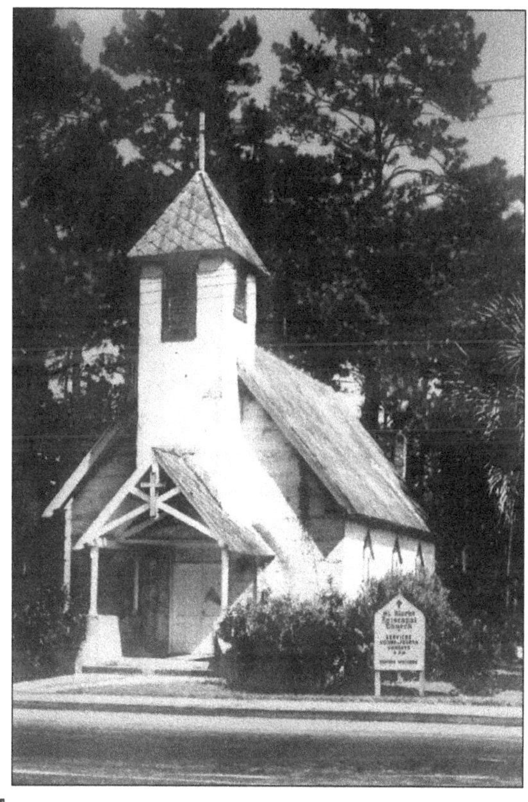

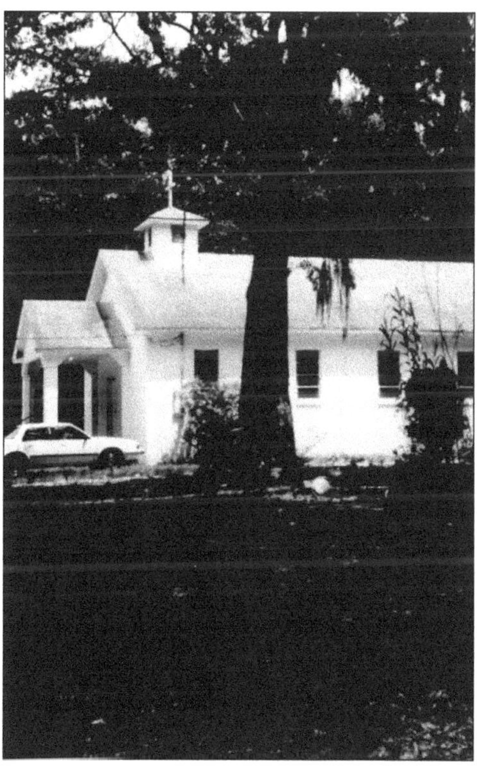

Located at Spring Bluff in north Camden, the Rising Daughter Church originated in the 1870s through the work of area residents, such as the Cohen, Massey, Scarlett, Robinson, Frazier, Harris, and Scott families. With the loss of records, much of the church's history was passed on through oral traditions, and the new Rising Daughter Church was organized in July 1947. After the structure fell into disrepair, the old building was demolished, and while the new Rising Daughter church was built, the congregation worshipped at the nearby Mt. Orum Baptist Church that had formed in July 1907 when the congregation split. Another church, Mt. Sinai Baptist Church at Honey Creek, was dedicated on the third Sunday in February 1950 by Rev. O.C. Hunt, and A.H. Denegal served as its pastor. Through the years, various repairs and additions have been made to accommodate the congregation's needs. The small church graveyard serves as the resting spot for some of Camden's oldest African-American families. (Courtesy of the Author.)

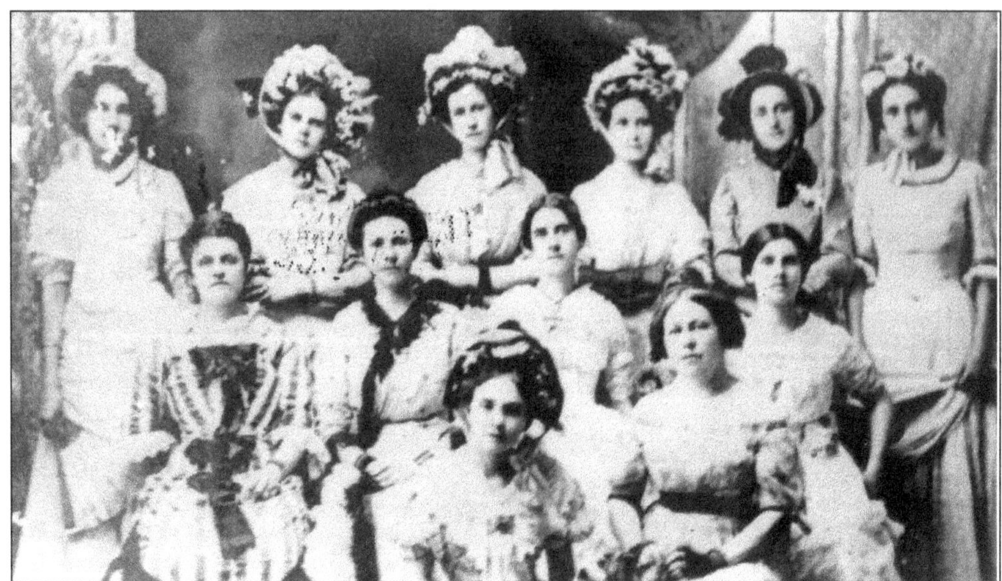

In the 21st century a community theatre group, the Camden Area Players, Inc., puts on four productions each year and moves forward with ambitious plans to renovate a waterfront building adjacent to the new Howard Gilman Memorial Park. Another service organization, Arts Camden, advocates the visual and performing arts and holds monthly meetings at St. Marys City Hall. Local thespians opened the St. Marys theater season in fall 1910 and performed "A Night of Old Songs." From left to right are (front row) Gertrude Bunkley and Ella Stone; (second row) Addie Bailey Goodbread, Signora Brandon Bachlott, Essie Bessent Mahoney, and Sara Tilton; (third row) Catherine Phillips, Lutie Banks Rose, Ethel Brandon, Ria Bachlott Rudulph, Beulah Register Hill, and Ruth Register Russell. (Courtesy of Eloise Bailey Thompson.)

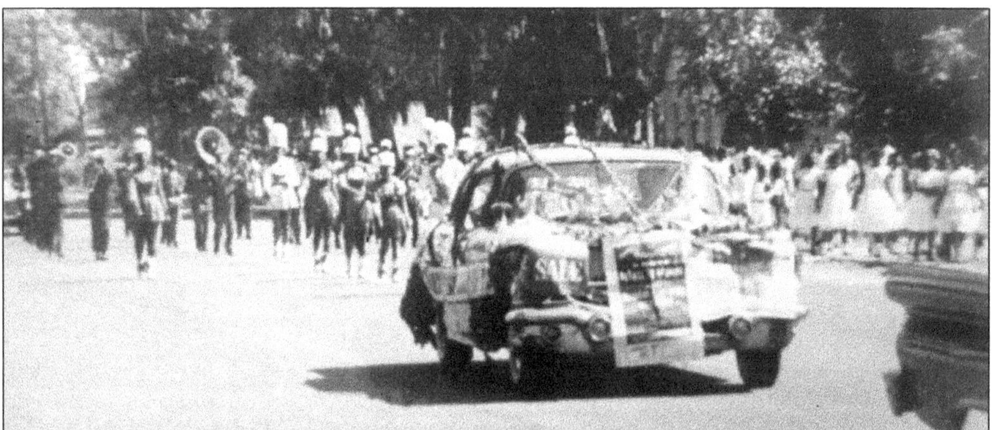

In this 1960s image, a marching band and students from Matilda Harris Elementary School celebrate at a May Day Parade in St. Marys. Posters and period automobiles decorated with bunting attract the eyes of children clothed in Sunday school dress standing on the sidelines. Today, Camden Countians can participate in a variety of special events, such as the February Mardi Gras Festival sponsored by the St. Marys Downtown Merchants Association (SMDMA), or Woodbine's annual Crawfish Festival, which has proven a lucrative, crowd-attracting weekend program through the organization and oversight of the Woodbine Citizens Steering Committee. (Courtesy of Eloise Bailey Thompson.)

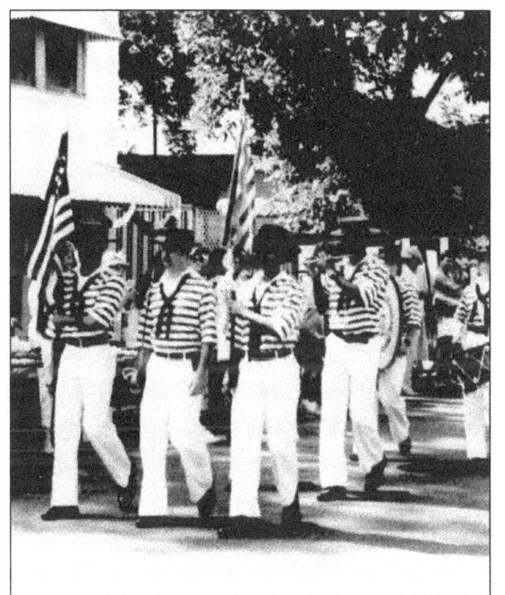

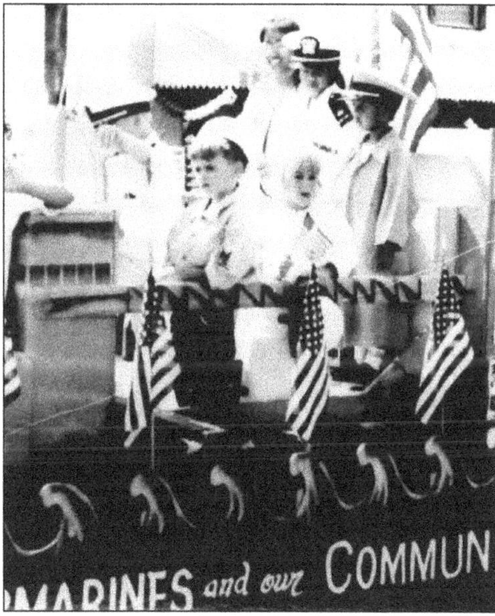

Kingsland hosts a Labor Day Catfish Festival; St. Marys offers a Rock Shrimp Festival in October, and emphasizes traditional holiday festivities, such as a longstanding Fourth of July Festival. Because of local interest in Camden's participation, a War of 1812 unit carrying flag colors marched to fife and drum at the July 4, 1987 parade, pictured here. In the second image, young children aboard a water-themed float honor their parents and our country in patriotic recognition of the Naval Submarine Base, Kings Bay. (Courtesy of Eloise Bailey Thompson.)

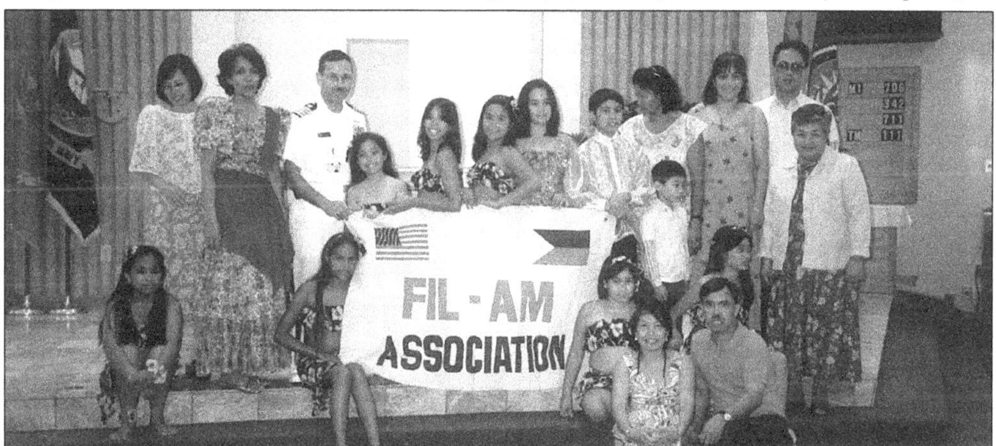

Established about 1979, the non-profit Filipino-American Association perpetuates the Filipino culture and their rich traditions. Members of a growing cadre of devoted volunteers participate in a special emphasis program held each May honoring Asian/Pacific-American Heritage Month. Activities were held at Naval Submarine Base, Kings Bay where members of the group prepared delicious foods and performed a challenging Filipino dance, the Tinikling clappers. Pictured here, from left to right, are (front row) Rosa Tamisin and Gaudencio "Ding" Tamisin, the father of the Filipino-American Association; (second row) Nicole Cabanes; Jansen Balisi; Murphy Newton; and Azie Gaza; (third row) Magie Gaza; Carol Ramos; Capt. Edwin Victoriano, Trident Refit Facility supply officer; Carsline Ramos; Gene Valdez; Laurence Valdez; Cristina Newton; Harold Ramos; Nita Newton; Offie Garrido; Joel Garrido; and Mrs. Anne. (Courtesy of Filipino-American Association of Camden, St. Marys.)

BIBLIOGRAPHY

Bailey, Eloise and Virginia Proctor (eds.). *Camden's Challenge: A History of Camden County Georgia*, compiled by Marguerite Reddick. Jacksonville, FL: Paramount Press, 1978; updated and revised by Peggy Aronson, Alpharetta, GA: W.H. Wolfe Associates, 1994.

Bailey, Eloise. *Orange Hall.* St. Marys, GA: Camden Printing Company, Inc., 1983.

Barefoot, Patricia. *Falling for Coastal Magic: Stories of Southeast Georgia.* The Saltmarsh Press, Inc. of St. Simons Island, GA. Kearney, NE: Morris Publishing and Printer, 1998.

Bullard, Mary R. *Robert Stafford of Cumberland Island: Growth of a Planter.* DeLeon Springs, FL: E.O. Painter Printing Company, 1986.

Christian, John H. *Founders of St. Marys.* Nd.

Huxford, Folks. *Camden County Georgia.* Homerville, GA: Huxford Genealogical Society, Inc., Nd.

Miller, Mary E. *Cumberland Island, The Unsung Northend.* Darien, GA: The Darien News Press, 1990.

Rockefeller, Nancy Carnegie. *The Carnegies and Cumberland Island.* Nd.

Silva, James S. (Coll.). *Early Reminiscence of Camden County, Georgia, By An Old St. Marys Boy In His 82nd Year 1914–1915.* Kingsland, GA: *The Southeast Georgian*, Inc., Nd.

Stegeman, John F. and Janet A. Stegeman. *Caty: A Biography of Catharine Littlefield Greene.* Athens, GA: The University of Georgia Press, 1977.

Thompson, Eloise Bailey. *St. Marys United Methodist Church, 1799–1999.* St. Marys: Camden Printing Company, 1999.

Thompson, Shirley Joiner. *Legacy: The Lives and Times of Marion Clayborne Joiner, Sr. and Elmira Virginia Drury Joiner.* Brunswick, GA: Neeld Printing House, Inc., 1994.

Vanstory, Burnette. *Georgia's Land of the Golden Isles.* Athens, GA: The University of Georgia Press, 1981.

Vocelle, James T. *History of Camden County Georgia (1914).* Reprint. St. Marys: Camden Printing Company, 1989.

Wells, Maxine. *Remember When: A Pictorial Reminiscence of Kingsland Georgia.* Convention Press, Inc., 1980.

Woodbine Woman's Club. *Pen Portraits: Stories of Pioneer Camden Women and Their Families Also Other Autobiographies, Articles and Interesting Pictures (1969).* Revised. St. Marys: Camden Printing Company, 2000.

www.ingramcontent.com/pod-product-compliance
Lightning Source LLC
LaVergne TN
LVHW060626110826
845147LV00015B/949

* 9 7 8 0 7 3 8 5 1 3 8 5 0 *